Preface

This book explores the rich heritage of the English language – the deriving of words from the names of people. The idea for the book originally arose several years ago, after an evening meal with my mother. We quite simply tried to list as many objects named after people as we could. We quickly exhausted the very familiar **mackintosh**, **wellington**, **sandwich**; the scientific **ampere**, **watt**, **volt**, and so on. The idea of listing such words lay fairly dormant with the passage of time, until it was suggested to me that I might write a book dealing with such words. Naturally, I began to tackle the task enthusiastically, since the subject was close to my heart.

Eponyms are people who give their names to words. Most eponymous words derive from a person's surname: **boycott**, from the Irish landlord Captain Charles Cunningham Boycott, **dahlia**, from the Swedish botanist Anders Dahl, the **sousaphone**, from the American bandmaster John Philip Sousa, and **volt**, from the Italian physicist Count Alessandro Volta. Some eponymous words come from literary, biblical or mythological sources: **malapropism**, from Mrs Malaprop in Sheridan's *The Rivals*, **Dickensian** – as in *a real old-fashioned Dickensian Christmas* – from the English writer Charles Dickens, **as old as Methuselah**, from the age of the Old Testament patriarch, and **aphrodisiac**, from the Greek goddess of love and beauty Aphrodite. In this book, I have concentrated on the better-known eponymous words in general use and have sought to give background detail on interesting aspects of an individual's life.

The entries are listed according to the name of the thing referred to, not the name the thing derives from. So there is an entry **spoonerism**, but not one for Rev William Archibald Spooner. Note that when the name of the thing is itself a person's name, this is listed in alphabetical order: eg an **Aunt Sally** is listed at **Aunt**.

For this new edition, over a hundred new entries have been added. I would like to thank Alice Grandison for her work in researching and compiling this new material, and Inna Frampton for checking the text.

A Thematic Index has also been added. This lists all the eponymous words associated with 17 common subjects, eg *Caesar salad* is listed under **Food and Drink**; *Dolby* is listed under **Music**; and *Hubble Space Telescope* is listed under **Science**. Whenever an entry has an accompanying image, you can go to the Index to see all of the other eponyms relating to the same subject.

Martin Manser

A

Aaron's beard

Aaron's beard is another name for rose of Sharon (also called St John's wort) – a creeping shrub, *Hypericum calycinum*, which has large yellow flowers. The term derives from the Bible: 'It is like the precious ointment upon the head, that ran down the beard, even Aaron's beard: that went down to the skirts of his garments' (Psalm 133:2). **Aaron** was the brother of Moses.

Aaron has also given his name to **Aaron's rod**, which is a mullein, *Verbascum thapsus*, a plant that has tall spikes of yellow flowers and broad hairy leaves. The name Aaron's rod comes from one of the rods that were placed in the tabernacle. Aaron's rod had the next day budded, blossomed and produced almonds (Numbers 17:1–13).

Abernethy biscuit

The ancient town of Abernethy in Perthshire, Scotland, surprisingly, is not the origin of the name of **Abernethy biscuits**. These hard unleavened biscuits, which originally contained caraway seeds, were baked to a recipe invented by **Dr John Abernethy** (1764–1831), an English anatomist, physiologist and surgeon, who was interested in dietary reform.

abigail

Abigail is an archaic word for a lady's maid. The name comes originally from Nabal's wife, **Abigail**, in the Bible (1 Samuel 25). Abigail apologized for her husband's meanness in refusing to give food to David's followers. She herself provided food for them, waylaying David even as he planned to attack Nabal and his people. In the space of 17 verses of the Bible text, Abigail refers to herself as 'thine handmaid' six times. Later, after Nabal's death, Abigail became David's wife.

The name and occupation came into more general use from the 'waiting gentlewoman' in the play *The Scornful Lady* by Sir Francis Beaumont and John Fletcher, first performed in 1610.

Swift, Fielding and other novelists of the period used the name further and it became popularized by the notoriety of **Abigail Hill**, lady-in-waiting to Queen Anne, 1704–1714, who used her friendship with the queen to try to secure personal favours.

> **Abigail Hill is said to have had a remarkably red nose, making her the butt of many contemporary jokes.**

Abraham's bosom

 Abraham's bosom refers to the sleeping-place of the blessed in death. It is well known from Shakespeare's *Richard III*: 'The sons of Edward sleep in Abraham's bosom' (Act 4, Scene 3), but originally it was a figure of speech used by Jesus in the parable of Lazarus and the rich man (Luke 16:19–31): 'The beggar [Lazarus] died, and was carried by the angels into Abraham's bosom' (verse 22).

In the Old Testament, **Abraham** is revered as the father of the Hebrew people. In the language of the Talmud to sit in Abraham's bosom meant to enter paradise.

academy

Nowadays an **academy** is a school that gives a particular training – for example, a military academy, or, as in Scotland, a secondary school. An academy is also an association of learned people organized to promote literature, art or science: the Royal Academy, the French Academy, etc.

The word academy comes from the Academeia, a pleasure garden in the suburbs of Athens where the philosopher Plato taught in the late fourth century BC. The garden itself was named after the Greek mythological hero **Academos**.

according to Cocker

The phrase **according to Cocker** means in a manner that is correct, accurate or reliable. The expression honours the English arithmetician **Edward Cocker** (1631–1675). He is the reputed author of a popular book on mathematics titled *Arithmetick*, which went into more than a hundred editions.

The expression was popularized when introduced into the play *The Apprentice* (1756) by the actor and playwright Arthur Murphy (1727–1805).

according to Hoyle

The American equivalent of 'according to Cocker' (qv) is **according to Hoyle**. This expression honours the British clubman and expert on games **Sir Edmund Hoyle** (1672–1769). At that time the game of whist was very popular and Hoyle was the first person to prepare an authoritative guide to its rules, *A Short Treatise on the Game of Whist*, published in 1742. He also compiled *Hoyle's Standard Games*, the authoritative book of rules of card games. The expert reputation of

> **Hoyle is known as 'The Father of Whist'.**

Hoyle meant that the expression 'according to Hoyle' was applied not only to a method of play in accordance with the rules but also more generally to correct or honourable behaviour.

Achilles' heel

To mention an **Achilles' heel** is to refer to a weakness, fault or vulnerable spot in a person or thing that is otherwise strong: 'The party knows that its group of political extremists might well be its Achilles' heel.'

The expression derives from Greek mythology. Thetis, the mother of **Achilles**, is said to have dipped him into the River Styx to make him invulnerable. His one weak spot was the heel by which Thetis held him during the dipping and which therefore was not touched by the water. It was during the siege of Troy that Achilles was mortally wounded by a poisoned arrow that was shot into his heel.

The fibrous cord connecting the heel-bone to the muscles of the calf is known as the **Achilles tendon**.

Ada

Ada is a high-level computer-programming language developed by the US Department of Defense and designed chiefly for dealing with real-time computerized control systems, such as those used in aircraft navigation. It was named in honour of the English mathematician **Augusta Ada King, Countess of Lovelace** (1816–1852) in 1979, and first became commercially available in the late 1980s.

> Ada was a daughter of Lord Byron, the poet.

Ada, Lady Lovelace worked as assistant to the English computing pioneer Charles Babbage (1792–1871) and collaborated with him on his mechanical computer. It was she who suggested that Babbage write a plan for the calculation of Bernoulli numbers by the machine – this plan was, in effect, the first 'computer program'.

Adam's apple

The visible projection at the front of the neck formed by the thyroid cartilage is called the **Adam's apple**. It is traditionally thought that this name derives from the story of **Adam** in the Bible (Genesis 2–3). There is a belief that, when Adam ate from the forbidden tree, a piece of apple stuck in his throat. It is however interesting to note that the Bible nowhere mentions that the fruit was in fact an apple.

Adam's name is also used in various other phrases. **Adam's ale** is water: the first human would have had nothing else to drink. The **old Adam** refers to the sinful nature of all human beings. If you **don't know someone from Adam**, you don't recognize him or her – you have no idea who he or she is: 'I think you'd better explain to Mr Chadwick who I am – he won't know me from Adam.' The expression derives from the fact that Adam, as the first man, is someone whom one could not know.

Adams–Stokes syndrome

See **Stokes–Adams syndrome**.

Addison's disease

 Addison's disease is caused by underactivity of the adrenal glands, resulting in extreme weakness, weight loss, low blood pressure and bronzing of the skin. It was named after **Thomas Addison** (1793–1860), an English physician specializing in endocrinology, who identified it in 1849.

Addison also identified pernicious anaemia, a severe form of anaemia associated with inadequate absorption of vitamin B_{12}, which is also known as **addisonian anaemia**.

adonis

Adonis, 'a handsome young man', was a youth in Greek mythology who was renowned for his great beauty. Loved by Aphrodite, he was killed by a boar while hunting but resurrected by Persephone. He was celebrated in many festivals as a vegetation god, his death and restoration to life symbolizing the seasonal decay and rebirth of nature.

Aladdin's cave

'With everything from children's games to computer software, the shop's a real **Aladdin's cave** for bargain hunters!' The expression, referring to a source or place of great riches, comes originally from the oriental story *Aladdin, or the Wonderful Lamp*. **Aladdin**, the poor son of a Chinese tailor, is used by a Moorish magician to fetch from an underground cave a lamp with magical powers.

albert

 An **albert** is a kind of watch chain usually attached to a waistcoat. The name comes from **Prince Albert** (1819–1861), Prince Consort of Queen Victoria. When he visited Birmingham in 1849, the jewellers of that city presented him with such a chain. Very satisfied with their gift, he wore it from that time onwards and created a fashion.

See also **Prince Albert**.

Aldis lamp

Aldis lamp

 Aldis lamp is a trademark used to describe a portable lamp with a movable device, used for transmitting Morse code. This lamp was named after its British inventor, **A C W Aldis** (1878–1953). The Aldis lamp has been used by the Royal Navy since World War I, but has now been abandoned in favour of more secure communications systems.

Alexander technique

 The **Alexander technique** is an alternative therapy for the treatment of back and neck pain by correcting poor posture and movement. It was devised by **Frederick Matthias Alexander** (1869–1955), an Australian actor who suffered from chronic laryngitis. He discovered that muscular tension was at the root of his problem and developed a technique

> John Cleese, Dame Judi Dench and Sir Paul McCartney have all studied the Alexander Technique.

for releasing undue tension and so restoring balance, coordination and ease of movement.

alexandrine

 An **alexandrine** is a verse metre made up of a line of twelve syllables, usually with major stresses on the sixth and final syllables. The name comes from twelfth-century French poems about **Alexander the Great** (356–323 BC), king of Macedonia. The alexandrine has been the dominant metre of French poetry since the sixteenth century, and was much used by Racine and Corneille.

algorithm

 An **algorithm** is a step-by-step method of solving mathematical problems. The word algorithm is an alteration of the Middle English *algorisme* and comes from Old French and Medieval Latin. Ultimately it comes from the name of the ninth-century Arab mathematician **Mohammed ibn Musa al-Khuwarizmi**. He introduced the Indian decimal system and the use of zero into Arabic mathematics.

Alice band

An **Alice band** is a hairband, usually made of flexible plastic covered with a decorative material, which is worn by girls or women and, more recently, by some footballers to keep the hair back off the face. It is named after the ribbon worn by the character of **Alice** in the illustrations to Lewis Carroll's children's story *Through the Looking Glass* (1871) by the English cartoonist and illustrator Sir John Tenniel (1820–1914).

Through the Looking Glass was a sequel to *Alice's Adventures in Wonderland*, published in 1865. This earlier book is the origin of the expression **Alice-in-Wonderland** used to describe a strange, fantastic world in which the normal laws of logic and reason have been suspended. The story was in fact originally titled 'Alice's Adventures Under Ground'.

The character of Alice was modelled on Alice Liddell, daughter of Dean Henry George Liddell, co-author of the standard Greek–English Dictionary, *Liddell & Scott's Greek Lexicon*.

Alzheimer's disease

Alzheimer's disease is a common type of dementia with no known cure, which produces rapid mental deterioration. In 1907, **Alois Alzheimer** (1864–1915), a renowned German neurologist who specialized in neurohistology, published a description of presenile dementia. Because Alzheimer described the mental deterioration of middle-aged patients, Alzheimer's Disease originally was applied only to presenile cases, but it is now also used of patients of advanced years.

Amati

An **Amati** is a violin, cello or viola made by a member of the Amati family of Cremona, Italy, who, during the sixteenth and seventeenth centuries, developed the basic proportions of these instruments. **Andrea Amati** (1525–1611), the founder of the great Cremona school of violin-making, made many instruments for Charles IX of France, for use at the Court of Versailles. His sons **Antonio Amati** (1560–1649) and

Hieronymus Amati (1562–1630), who worked both together and separately, also made instruments for the French Court. Hieronymus' son **Niccolo Amati** (1596–1684) is considered the greatest instrument-maker of all the Amatis.

See also **Stradivarius**.

Ames test

 The **Ames test** is a screening test for the carcinogenic effect of a substance, based on its ability to cause mutations in specific salmonella bacteria. Chemicals that induce mutations in bacterial DNA are likely to induce mutations in mammalian cells too, and the Ames test produces results in two days, making it faster and less expensive than tests on animals. This test was devised in 1976 by the American biochemist and molecular geneticist **Bruce Ames** (born 1928), professor of biochemistry and molecular biology and director of the National Institute of Environmental Health Sciences Center at the University of California.

Amish

 The **Amish** are a Protestant group which split off from the Mennonites in Switzerland in 1690 under the leadership of **Jakob Amman** (c. 1644–1730), a Mennonite bishop who favoured excommunication, or 'shunning', as a form of discipline. In the eighteenth century, in order to escape persecution in Europe, the Amish emigrated to North America, many settling in Pennsylvania. The Amish tend to live in agricultural communities, separate from the rest of society. They reject modern technology, including cars and television, and wear very plain traditional clothes, the men having beards.

ammonia

 Ammonia is a colourless, poisonous, highly soluble gas that is used in making fertilizers, explosives, etc. The word comes from Latin *sal ammoniacus* – 'sal ammoniac'. Ammoniac is a salt or gum resin thought to have been obtained from a district in Libya near the temple of the Egyptian god **Ammon**.

ampere

 Ampere – often shortened to amp – is a common domestic word: we are familiar with 13-amp plugs, a 5-amp fuse, etc. The ampere is the basic metric unit of electric current. The word comes from the name of the French physicist **André Marie Ampère** (1775–1836), noted for his discoveries about the nature of electricity and magnetism.

Although Ampère enjoyed a brilliant career, his private life was tragically unhappy. When he was only 18, he saw his father guillotined during the Reign of Terror; he was so shocked that he was unable to speak for over a year. He married at 24, but his wife died a year later. These personal tragedies led him to immerse himself in his work.

Anderson shelter

 An **Anderson shelter** was a partly prefabricated air-raid shelter. It was named after **John Anderson**, 1st Viscount Waverley (1882–1958), a civil servant who entered parliament. As home secretary and minister of home security (1939–1940) he was faced with the urgent need to supply air-raid shelters to protect the civilian population. Designed by the engineer William, later Sir William, Paterson, the Anderson shelter could easily be erected by a non-specialist. About three million Anderson shelters were distributed. Anderson later became chancellor of the exchequer (1943–1945).

See also **Morrison shelter**.

Andromeda strain

 The Andromeda Strain (published in 1969) is a science-fiction novel by American author Michael Crichton (born 1942) about a deadly virus that has come to Earth from outer space and threatens to wipe out the human race. The term **Andromeda strain** has since come to mean any virus or bacterium that can change form and is extremely resistant to destruction.

In Greek mythology, **Andromeda** was a princess who was saved by Perseus from being devoured by a sea monster.

ångström

 An **ångström** is a unit of length formerly in technical use to measure the wavelengths of electromagnetic radiations. It is named after the Swedish physicist and astronomer **Anders Jonas Ångström** (1814–1874). He was a student and later professor at the University of Uppsala; he founded the science of spectroscopy, his studies of the sun's spectra resulting in the discovery, in 1862, of hydrogen in the sun.

Annie Oakley

 In American (especially theatrical) slang, an **Annie Oakley** is a free ticket. The name is the shortened name of the American markswoman **Phoebe Anne Oakley Mozee** (1860–1926). She was the star rifle-shooter of Buffalo Bill's Wild West Show.

> **Annie Oakley's life was fictionalized in the 1946 musical *Annie Get Your Gun*.**

The complimentary tickets have a hole punched in them to ensure that they are not exchanged for cash at the box office. The tickets are probably so called because of Annie's most famous trick: tossing a playing-card – especially the five of hearts – into the air and shooting holes through all the card's pips.

Anthony Eden

 An **Anthony Eden** is a type of black felt hat worn by fashionable men in the 1930s. It was named after the then British Conservative foreign secretary **Robert Anthony Eden** (1897–1977), later the 1st Earl of Avon. Prime minister from 1955 till 1957, Anthony Eden was forced to resign after the Suez Crisis in 1956, in which he ordered military action, in league with Israel and France, against Egypt.

Apgar score

 The **Apgar score** is a method of assessing a newborn baby's physical condition by allotting a score of 0, 1 or 2 for each of the following: skin colour, pulse, reflex irritability, muscle tone and respiration. This test is applied at one minute, five minutes and ten minutes after birth. A low

Apgar score indicates the need for emergency medical attention. The Apgar score was developed in 1952 by **Virginia Apgar** (1909–1974), an American paediatrician. Early in her career, when Dr Apgar was an anaesthetist working in a hospital delivery room, she became concerned about the lack of medical attention afforded newborn babies, which led her to devise this simple test to signal the need for early intervention, thus saving the lives of many newborn babies.

aphrodisiac

An **aphrodisiac** is a substance that stimulates sexual desire. The word comes from the name of **Aphrodite**, the goddess of love and beauty in Greek mythology. According to one of the earliest of Greek poets, Hesiod, she was born from the foam (*aphros*) of the sea. According to Homer, she was the daughter of Dione and Zeus.

Appleton layer

The **Appleton layer** is the former name of the F-layer of the earth's atmosphere – the layer in the ionosphere about 150–1000 km above the earth. Of all the three different layers in the ionosphere, the F-layer contains the highest proportion of free electrons and is the most useful for long-range radio transmission.

The Appleton layer was so called because it was discovered by the British physicist **Sir Edward Appleton** (1892–1963).

See also **Heaviside layer**.

arachnid

An **arachnid** is an invertebrate insect-like animal with eight legs that belongs to the order Arachnida, which includes spiders, scorpions, ticks and mites. The word arachnid comes ultimately from **Arachne**, in Greek mythology a girl from Lydia who presumptuously challenged the goddess Athena to a weaving contest. Jealous, Athena tore Arachne's attractive tapestry to pieces, whereupon Arachne tried to hang herself. Not content with this outcome, Athena changed Arachne into a spider (in Greek, *arachne*).

Archimedes' principle

The Greek mathematician and scientist **Archimedes** (c. 287–c. 212 BC) is noted for his work in geometry, mechanics and hydrostatics. He is well known for his discovery that when a body is immersed in a liquid its apparent loss of weight equals the weight of the water that is displaced (**Archimedes' principle**). It is

> **Archimedes is said to have been killed by a Roman soldier because he was so engrossed in a mathematical problem that he refused to accompany him into custody when the Romans invaded Syracuse.**

alleged that he discovered this while taking a bath; on noticing that his body displaced the water in his bath, he is said to have exclaimed, '*Eureka!*' ('I have found it!'). His discovery enabled him to give a response to King Hiero II. The king had asked Archimedes to find out the amount of gold in a crown that had been made for him, since he suspected that it was not made of pure gold. Archimedes' discovery led him to realize that since gold was heavier than silver, a floating vessel holding a pure-gold crown would displace more water than one holding a crown made of mixed metals. His tests proved that the king had in fact been supplied with a crown made of gold and base metal.

Archimedes is also remembered for a device for raising water (**Archimedes' screw**). He reputedly invented it, but it was probably already known to the Egyptians.

Asperger's syndrome

Asperger's syndrome is a developmental disorder, related to but generally less severe than autism. The main characteristics of Asperger's syndrome are poor social skills, communication difficulties, preoccupation with a particular subject and insistence on repetitive routines. Asperger's syndrome was first described in 1944 by the Austrian psychiatrist **Hans Asperger** (1906–1980).

Atkins diet

The popular but unorthodox **Atkins diet**, devised by the American **Dr Robert C Atkins** (1930–2003), was first introduced in the book *Dr Atkins' Diet Revolution* in 1972. Atkins' weight-loss plan advocates a high-protein low-carbohydrate diet, combined with vitamin and mineral supplements and exercise. This was a controversial approach at a time when a healthy diet was was generally considered to be one that was low in fat and high in carbohydrates. Nevertheless, the book and its successor *Dr Atkins' New Diet Revolution* have sold in their millions. The endorsement of several glamorous – and slender – celebrities has undoubtedly contributed to the diet's popularity.

atlas

In Greek mythology **Atlas** was one of the Titans who, as a punishment for his part in the attempt to overthrow Zeus, was condemned to hold up the heavens on his shoulders for the rest of his life. **Atlas** came to be used to refer to a book of maps after a drawing of Atlas was included on the title-page of a collection of maps by the mapmaker Mercator, published in the late sixteenth century.

See also **Mercator projection**; **Peters projection**.

aubrietia

The trailing perennial plant bearing small purple flowers that is widely grown in rock gardens is known as **aubrietia** or **aubretia**. It was named in 1763 by the French naturalist Michel Adamson after the French painter of flowers and animals **Claude Aubriet** (1665–1742).

Augean

It is difficult to think of a worse mess than stables for 3000 oxen would be in if they had not been cleaned out for 30 years. The stables of **King Augeas** in Greek mythology were, however, in this condition. The cleansing of these stables was one of the twelve labours of Hercules: he caused the River Alpheus to flow through them, cleansing them in a day.

(Incidentally, when Hercules had successfully completed the task, Augeas meanly refused him a reward.) The phrase '**to clean the Augean stables**' has come to refer to the task of removing the accumulation of different sorts of corruption.

August

The first Roman emperor, Octavian (63 BC–AD 14), was the great-nephew and adopted son of Julius Caesar. After Caesar's assassination in 44 BC, Octavian ruled Rome jointly with Mark Antony and Lepidus. Octavian defeated Mark Antony at Actium in 31 BC to become, two years later, the first emperor, the Senate later awarding him the title **Augustus** ('venerable') for his distinguished service to the state.

> **August originally had 30 days, but Augustus did not want Julius Caesar's month to have more days than his own, and so he moved a day from February to August to give both August and July 31 days.**

Julius Caesar had chosen to rename the month of July (qv) after himself. Not wishing to be outdone, Augustus wanted to have a month named after himself as well. His birth month was September, but he chose the eighth month (hitherto called Sextilis), as this had been the month in which he had achieved his greatest civil and military triumphs. Thus Sextilis became **August**.

Aunt Sally

Originally, an **Aunt Sally** was an effigy of an old woman at which one threw objects at a fair. This sense has broadened and the expression is now applied to any easy target for insults or criticism: 'In times of peace, a large part of a dictator's role would be as a sort of national Aunt Sally, a symbol on which citizens could vent their frustration.' (*Punch*).

The explanation of this expression is not certain: the elderly fairground figure resembles an aunt, but it has not been satisfactorily explained why the name **Sally** was chosen to stand for the unfortunate target.

Avogadro's constant

In physics, **Avogadro's constant** is the number of atoms or molecules in one mole of any substance. This is named after **Amedeo Avogadro**, Conte di Quaregna e Ceretto (1776–1856). Born in Turin, Italy, Avogadro trained as a lawyer before turning to chemistry and physics. He was professor of higher physics at the University of Turin (1820–1856).

> Avogadro also served as a public official, and introduced the decimal system into Piedmont.

His name is also attached to **Avogadro's law**, which he first proposed in 1811, stating that equal volumes of gas at equal temperature and pressure contain an equal number of gas molecules. This law was not generally accepted until after 1858, when the Italian chemist Stanislao Cannizzaro (1826–1910) formulated a system of atomic weights based on it.

axel

An **axel** is a standard jump in figure skating, in which the skater takes off from the forward outside edge of one skate and lands on the rear outside edge of the other. A single axel involves one and a half turns in the air, a double axel two and a half turns and a triple axel three and a half turns. The axel is named after the Norwegian skater **Axel Paulsen** (1855–1938), who first executed the single axel in 1882 in Vienna, Austria.

B

Babbitt

Babbitt is a derogatory term applied to a narrow-minded unimaginative self-important middle-class businessman who has no interest in art or intellectual pursuits. The original Babbitt was **George F Babbitt**, the central character in the satirical novel *Babbitt* (1922) by the American novelist Sinclair Lewis (1885–1951). George Babbitt is a Midwestern estate agent with conformist, even philistine, attitudes who, feeling vaguely dissatisfied with his life at the age of 46, tries to adopt a more bohemian way of life. Ultimately, his need for social acceptance sees him returning to his old conservative environment.

> In 1930, Sinclair Lewis became the first American writer to be awarded the Nobel prize for literature.

Babinski effect

The **Babinski effect** is a reflex movement in which the toes curl upwards, rather than downwards, when the sole of the foot is stroked. Although this reflex is normal in children under the age of two, in an older person it is an indication of a lesion in the brain or spinal cord. An abnormal Babinski effect can be either temporary or permanent. The Babinski effect is named after **Joseph-Francois-Félix Babinski** (1857–1932), the leading French neurologist who first discovered its diagnostic significance. Babinski was the son of a Polish engineer who, with his wife, fled Warsaw for Paris in 1848.

bacchanalia

Bacchanalia is used to refer to a drunken orgy. It derives from *Bacchanalia*, ancient mysteries or orgies in honour of **Bacchus** (the Roman name of the Greek god Dionysus), the god of wine. Coming from southern Italy, the cult reached Rome in the second century BC. The Roman festival of Bacchus, celebrated with dancing, song and revelry, was marked by drunkenness, debauchery and sexual immorality. A decree from the Senate in 186 BC prohibited Bacchanalia in Rome.

Bach flower remedy

 Bach flower remedies are a group of 38 natural remedies extracted from wild flowers and used to alleviate a variety of mental and emotional problems. This system was developed in the 1930s by the English physician and homeopath **Dr Edward Bach** (1887–1936). During World War I, Dr Bach observed how stress and trauma adversely affected the recovery of his patients; he became dissatisfied with the approach of orthodox medicine, which focuses on the disease rather than the patient. Dr Bach developed his system of homeopathic remedies to achieve health, both physical and mental, by treating the negative emotions that he believed cause a breakdown in health and hinder recovery.

Baedeker

 A **Baedeker** at one time referred only to a travel guidebook published by the German **Karl Baedeker** (1801–1859), but it is now sometimes used to refer to any authoritative travel guide. Baedeker's publishing firm was established in 1827. The fame of Baedeker's guides developed during the first three editions of J A Klein's *Rhineland Journey* (1833, second edition 1835, third edition 1839). By 1872, the firm had published guides to the whole of Europe, the guides being published in German, English and French. These guides were well known for being authoritative and comprehensive – even Chekhov was to write from Venice, 'Here I am alone with my thoughts and my Baedeker.'

During World War II, German air raids (1941–1942) on English sites of cultural or historical importance, such as Canterbury and York, were known as **Baedeker raids**, because the German Luftwaffe used the Baedeker to determine the targets.

Bahai

 Bahai is a religious faith based on the teachings of Mirza Husain Ali (1817–1892), later known as **Baha-Ullah**, which means 'the glory of

God' in Arabic. Baha-Ullah, born in Persia, was a follower of Mirza Ali Mohammed, known as Bab-ed-Din or the Bab, who founded the Persian sect, Babism. In 1863, Baha-Ullah claimed to be the divine manifestation that the Bab had prophesied 19 years earlier. Bahai emphasizes spiritual unity and world peace.

Bailey bridge

A **Bailey bridge** is a kind of temporary military bridge. Named after its inventor, the English engineer **Sir Donald Bailey** (1901–1985), the Bailey bridge played a crucial role in the Allied victory in World War II. As Field Marshal Montgomery put it, 'Without the Bailey bridge we should not have won the war.' Bailey bridges were quickly assembled from prefabricated lattice-steel welded panels linked by pinned joints; they were capable of supporting heavy vehicles such as tanks and trains. Bailey bridges are still used in flood and disaster areas throughout the world.

Baily's beads

Baily's beads are a group of brilliant points of light, resembling a string of beads, that appear around the moon immediately before and after a total eclipse. They were first detected on 15 May 1836 by the English astronomer **Francis Baily** (1774–1844).

> **Baily made a fortune as a stockbroker before devoting himself to astronomy in his retirement.**

Baily was instrumental in the foundation of the Royal Astronomical Society in 1820, receiving its Gold Medal in 1827 for his work in preparing the Society's catalogue of 2881 stars.

bain-marie

A **bain-marie** is a vessel that is filled with hot water, into which another vessel is placed in order to cook slowly, or keep warm, a sauce or other food. *Bain-marie* is French for 'bath of Mary', which may refer to **Mary**, the mother of Jesus Christ. Others believe this to be an inaccurate translation from the original Greek, which is believed to refer to **Miriam**, the sister of Moses and Aaron in the Old Testament, who is said to have written a book on alchemy.

Bakelite

 Bakelite is the trademark for a kind of synthetic thermosetting resin and plastic used to make electrical insulating material and plastic fittings. Bakelite is named after the Belgian-born American chemist **Leo Hendrik Baekeland** (1863–1944). He discovered that the sticky resin formed by heating phenols and aldehydes under pressure had a number of useful properties: it was hard and strong, yet light; it could be moulded and coloured. In 1909 he announced the invention of Bakelite and, as president of the Bakelite Corporation (1910–1939), he saw his product find many applications throughout the world.

Baker day

In 1987, **Kenneth Wilfred Baker** (born 1934), later Lord Baker of Dorking, the Conservative British secretary of state for education (1986–1989), introduced in-service training days for teachers, which, in effect, give pupils a number of extra days off in every school year. These days came to be known as **Baker days**.

balboa

 The **balboa** is the basic monetary unit of Panama, which is divided into 100 centésimos. This is named after the Spanish explorer **Vasco Nuñez de Balboa** (c. 1475–1519). Balboa sailed to the northern coast of South America in 1500, and then spent some time farming in the Dominican Republic, before joining the expedition led by Rodrigo de Bastidas that established a colony in Darién, Panama, in 1510. In 1513, Balboa attained the western coast of the isthmus of Darién, where he became the first European to view the Pacific Ocean, allegedly from the mountain, Cerro Pirre.

banksia

 Banksia is a genus of approximately 75 species of shrubs and small trees native to Australia, with narrow leathery evergreen leaves and cylindrical flower heads that grow in dense clusters. This genus was named after the English botanist and explorer **Sir Joseph Banks** (1743–1820), who travelled round the world on the *Endeavour* with Captain Cook in 1768–1771, landing in Australia in 1770. Banks and another botanist from the *Endeavour*, Daniel Solander, collected many new species in Australia, including those which were later included in the new genus, *Banksia*. Sir Joseph Banks played a great part in establishing botany as a science.

banting

Banting is a method of slimming by eating high amounts of protein and avoiding sugar, starch and fat. It is named after a London undertaker **William Banting** (1797–1878). Grossly overweight himself, Banting tried various slimming methods with no success, so he resorted to a strict diet. He lost 46

Banting's diet undoubtedly helped him: he was in his sixties when he started slimming and he lived to be 81.

pounds (21 kg), reducing his waist measurement by 12 inches (32 cm). His efforts attracted some publicity, and he wrote a book about his experience, *Letter on Corpulence* (1863), outlining his methods of slimming.

baroque

The highly ornate style of architecture and art that flourished in Europe from the late sixteenth to the early eighteenth centuries is known as **baroque**. There are different theories as to the word's origin: it may have come via French from the Portuguese *barroco*, 'irregular pearl'. Alternatively, the word may perhaps derive via French from the name **Federigo Barocci** (c. 1535–1612), an Italian artist who painted in this style.

Barr body

The **Barr body**, also known as the 'sex chromatin', is a small dark mass of condensed inactive X-chromosome in the cell nuclei of females, which is used to test genetic femaleness, for example of a fetus or of an athlete. X inactivation occurs around the sixteenth day of the development of an embryo.

The Barr body was named in honour of the Canadian anatomist and geneticist **Murray Llewellyn Barr** (1908–1995), who, in late 1948, made the discovery that enabled determination of the genetic sex of an individual.

Bartholin's glands

The **Bartholin's glands** are two small oval glands, one on each side of the lower vagina, that secrete a lubricating mucus

Bartholin's interest in anatomy should have come as no surprise: his grandfather, father and brother were all medical professors at the University of Copenhagen.

during sexual stimulation. They were first described by the Danish anatomist **Caspar Thomeson Bartholin** (1655–1738).

Bartlett pear

A **Bartlett pear** (also known as a Williams pear) is a kind of pear tree with a large juicy yellow sweet fruit. It is named after **Enoch Bartlett** (1779–1860), a merchant in Massachusetts, USA, but Bartlett was not the first to develop the fruit. It was a Captain Thomas Brewer who imported the trees from England; Bartlett, who bought up Brewer's farm, distributed the pears using his own name in the early 1800s.

Baskerville

The style of type known as **Baskerville** derives its name from its designer, the English printer **John**

The Baskerville typeface:
ABCDEFGHIJKLMNOPQRSTUVWXYZ
abcdefghijklmnopqrstuvwxyz

Baskerville (1706–1775). At first a writing-master in Birmingham, Baskerville had by 1754 established a printing office and type-foundry in that city. His first work, an edition of the Latin poems of Virgil, was printed in 1757. As printer to Cambridge University, he later produced editions of the Book of Common Prayer and the Bible. His books are notable for their high quality of presswork and type, and he was the first to use original high-gloss paper. The typeface that is named after him, Baskerville, is of a traditional style, with exaggerated serifs and open curves.

Batesian mimicry

 In zoology, **Batesian mimicry** is a form of protective mimicry in which a harmless species closely resembles another, more distasteful or noxious, species in appearance, so that it is avoided by predators. This phenomenon was first described by the English naturalist **Henry W Bates** (1825–1892).

See also **Müllerian mimicry**.

Bath Oliver

 The **Bath Oliver** is a kind of unsweetened biscuit often eaten with cheese. It was invented by **William Oliver** (1695–1764), an English physician. Born in Penzance, Cornwall, Dr Oliver's first practice was in Plymouth, where he introduced the smallpox inoculation in 1724, before moving to Bath in 1728. On his death, Dr Oliver is said to have left his biscuit recipe to his coachman, Atkins, along with a sack of flour and some money. This enabled Atkins to start a business baking Bath Oliver biscuits, which made him a rich man.

batiste

 Batiste is a fine, soft, sheer fabric of plain weave, used especially in shirts, lingerie, dresses and handkerchiefs. The word derives from French *toile de baptiste*, baptist cloth, and probably comes ultimately from the thirteenth-century French weaver, **Baptiste of Cambrai**, as he is reputed to have been its first manufacturer.

The town of Cambrai in north-east France was known from the sixteenth century for its cambric linen cloth; it seems that the English merchants, wanting a different name for the new Cambrai fabric, called it after the French weaver, but misspelt his name in the process.

Batten's disease

 Batten's disease is an inherited degenerative disorder of the nervous system that affects children, causing mental impairment, seizures and loss of sight and motor skills, and culminating in death, usually in the late teens or early twenties. This disorder is not contagious and is quite rare, but there is currently neither a known cure nor an effective treatment. Batten's disease is named after the British paediatrician **F E Batten** (1865–1918), who first described it in 1903.

baud

 A **baud** is a unit of measuring the speed of electronic data transmission, one baud equalling one unit of information per second. It is named after the French inventor and pioneer of telegraphic communication **Jean M E Baudot** (1845–1903).

> **When Baudot was commemorated with a series of French stamps in 1949, his year of birth was wrongly printed as 1848.**

A baud was originally equivalent to twice the number of Morse code (qv) dots transmitted continuously per second. With the development of electronics, the term has been used to describe any of several different units.

BCG

 This abbreviation is well known amongst schoolchildren who are having their **BCG** vaccine. The initials stand for *bacille* (or bacillus) Calmette–Guérin, after the French bacteriologists who developed the vaccine – **Albert Léon Charles Calmette** (1863–1933) and **Camille Guérin** (1872–1961). The vaccine stimulates the body's defence system against tuberculosis.

Beaufort scale

The **Beaufort scale** is a measure of wind speed. The scale was devised in 1805 by the surveyor **Sir Francis Beaufort** (1774–1857), who later became a rear-admiral and official hydrographer to the Royal Navy. The scale is based on easily observable features such as the movement of trees and smoke. It has the numbers 0 to 12, 0 being 'calm' and 12 'hurricane', or as Beaufort described it, 'that which no canvas could withstand'.

béchamel sauce

A **béchamel sauce** is a white sauce made from flour, butter and milk and flavoured with vegetables and seasonings. It comes from the French sauce *béchamel* and is named after the French financier **Marquis Louis de Béchamel** (died 1703), the steward of Louis XIV of France, who is reputed to have invented it. It seems that the original béchamel sauce was a more elaborate mixture; it included in its ingredients old hens and old partridges.

becquerel

A **becquerel** is the basic metric unit of radiation activity, equal to one disintegration per second. It is named after the discoverer of radioactivity, the French physicist **Antoine-Henri Becquerel** (1852–1908).

The becquerel has now displaced the curie (qv) as a measurement of radiation activity.

begonia

Begonia is a genus of succulent herbaceous plants, originally found in the tropics. The genus contains about 1000 species, grown as pot or bedding plants and having showy, often brightly coloured, flowers with asymmetrical leaves.

Begonias are named after the French patron of science **Michel Bégon** (1638–1710). While working as Royal Commissioner in Santo Domingo, his enthusiastic amateur interest in botany led him to direct a study of the island's plant life. Among the plants found was the one that is now named after him. He later took species of the plant back to France, introducing them to his fellow European botanists. Species of the plant were brought to England in 1777 – 67 years after Bégon's death – and it was here that the genus of plant was named *Begonia* in his memory.

Belisha beacon

The **Belisha beacon**, a flashing light in an amber ball that is mounted on a post to mark a pedestrian crossing, is named after the British politician, 1st Baron (Isaac) **Leslie Hore-Belisha** (1893–1957). Hore-Belisha was National Liberal minister of transport from 1934 to 1937, and later secretary of state for war (1937–1940). His introduction of Belisha beacons as a road-safety measure to reduce the number of accidents was successful.

> **Belisha also introduced the driving test and the Highway Code.**

Bellini

A **Bellini** is a pink cocktail made with chilled champagne, chilled peach nectar or peach schnapps, a dash of grenadine and a dash of lemon juice. It was invented in 1948 by Giuseppe Cipriani at Harry's Bar in Venice, a favourite haunt of Ernest Hemingway and Orson Welles, among others. The Bellini was named in honour of **Giovanni Bellini** (c. 1430–1516), the Venetian Renaissance artist, allegedly because Cipriani was inspired by the pink glow in one of his paintings.

Bell's palsy

Bell's palsy is a paralysis of the face, resulting from a lesion of the facial nerve and causing a lopsided appearance. In most cases, the paralysis disappears spontaneously. This condition was first described in 1821 by **Sir Charles Bell** (1774–1842), an eminent British surgeon and anatomist, whose published works include *Idea of a New Anatomy* (published in 1811) and *The Nervous System of the Human Body* (published in 1839).

Benedictine

The name of a wine or spirit is often taken from the region where it was developed. Examples include champagne from Champagne, the former province in north-east France, and cognac from Cognac, the town in south-west France. The brandy-based liqueur known as **Benedictine** is, however, named after a person, **St Benedict** (c. 480–c. 547). St Benedict does not seem to have considered establishing a monastic order himself although the rule of St Benedict (c. 540) became the basis of the rule of Western Christian monastic orders.

It was in a Benedictine monastery at Fécamp, northern France, in about 1510 that a monk, Don Bernando Vincelli, first made the liqueur. His fellow monks declared it 'refreshing and recuperative'. During the French Revolution the monastery was destroyed. The secret formula for making the liqueur was kept safe, however, and some 50 years later Benedictine was manufactured by a Frenchman, Le Grand, his distillery standing on the site of the former abbey.

Bernoulli effect

In hydrodynamics, the **Bernoulli effect** is the principle that the pressure of a fluid varies in inverse proportion to the speed of flow. This principle was expounded by the Swiss mathematician and physicist **Daniel Bernoulli** (1700–1782), a member of the Bernoulli family of distinguished mathematicians. Daniel Bernoulli's best-known work, *Hydrodynamica*, which examined the mechanical properties of fluids, was published in 1738.

Bessemer process

The **Bessemer process** is a method for converting pig iron into steel, invented in 1856 by the British engineer **Sir Henry Bessemer** (1813–1898). Molten pig iron is loaded into a refractory-lined furnace (**Bessemer converter**) at about 1250°C. In the original version, air was blown into the furnace and the impurities removed. The result was that the quality of steel was improved and the costs of production were reduced. The modern version of the process has oxygen and steam blown into the furnace instead of air.

An identical process was developed at almost the same time by the American inventor William Kelly (1811–1888), and a long legal battle followed over which company, Kelly's or the one using the Bessemer process, should produce the steel in the USA. The dispute was finally resolved when the rival companies merged.

Betty Martin

The idiomatic expression '**all my eye and Betty Martin**' is used as a response to state that something is untrue or utter nonsense. The expression is often shortened to 'all my eye' or 'my eye'. The expression is traditionally seen as a garbled version of the Latin prayer: *O mihi, beate Martini* (O grant me, blessed Martin), but since there is no fixed prayer resembling this, the explanation seems unlikely.

Eric Partridge (*A Dictionary of Catch Phrases*) suggests an alternative theory of the origin of the expression: in the late eighteenth century, 'an abandoned woman ... named Grace ... induced a Mr Martin to marry her. She became notorious as **Betty Martin**: and favourite expressions of hers were "my eye!" and "all my eye!".'

Bevin boy

In the UK during World War II, a **Bevin boy** was a young man who was selected by ballot to work as a miner instead of doing National Service. The first Bevin boy was Frank Murphy from Manchester, who received a letter on his eighteenth birthday, in 1943, telling him to report for training. Bevin boys were named after **Ernest Bevin** (1881–1951), the Minister of Labour and National Service, who originated this scheme. Bevin was also one of the founders of the Transport and General Workers' Union and one of the organizers of the General Strike in 1926.

> On hearing a political rival described as being 'his own worst enemy', Bevin is said to have replied, 'Not while I'm alive, he's not!'

Bewick's swan

The **Bewick's swan** is a small white swan (*Cygnus bewickii*) with a black and yellow bill that is native to northern Asia and north-eastern Europe and that winters in northern or western Europe or central Asia. It takes its name from **Thomas Bewick** (1753–1828), the English illustrator and wood engraver noted especially for his woodcuts of birds and animals. Bewick famously illustrated *A History of British Birds* (1797 and 1804) and *A History of Quadrupeds* (1790).

Bic

Bic, like Biro, is a trademark used to describe a kind of ballpoint pen. Its name is a shortened version of the surname of **Marcel Bich** (1914–1994), the French co-founder, along with Edouard Buffard, of the Bic Corporation, which started off making parts for fountain pens and mechanical pencils. In 1949 Bich introduced the ballpoint pen.

> The Bic Corporation now produces many other consumer products, including cigarette lighters and shavers.

See also **Biro**.

Biedermeier

Biedermeier is used as a noun or an adjective to describe a style of German decoration and furniture of the mid-nineteenth century. The style, marked by simple, solid and conventional features, is named after the unimaginative and bourgeois author **Gottlieb Biedermeier**, an imaginary writer of poems actually penned by Ludwig Eichrodt, the pseudonym of Rudolf Rodt (1827–1892).

Big Ben

Big Ben is the great bell in the clock tower in the Houses of Parliament in London. The bell, which weighs 13.5 tons, chimes out the hours, half-hours and quarter-hours. It is generally held to be named after **Sir Benjamin Hall**, Baron Llanover, who was the Chief Commissioner of

Works in 1856, when the bell was cast, although some people believe it was named after **Benjamin Caunt**, a boxer whose nickname was Big Ben.

Big Bertha

 Big Bertha was the name given to one of the three large German guns (with a range of some 75 miles) that were used to bombard Paris in the last months of World War I. The name is a translation of the German *dicke Bertha*, 'fat Bertha', the uncomplimentary reference being to **Bertha Krupp von Bohlen und Halbach** (1886–1957), whose husband owned the Krupp armaments factory at Essen. The Germans originally used the name *die dicke Bertha* to refer to their 42-cm howitzer, it being wrongly believed that it was made at the Krupp factory. The name was later used to refer to the gun of a larger range.

bignonia

 Bignonia – not to be confused with begonia (qv) – is a tropical American flowering shrub, grown for its trumpet-shaped yellow or red flowers. (It is sometimes called cross vine.) The species is named after **Abbé Jean-Paul Bignon** (1662–1743), who was court librarian to Louis XIV, the name being given about 1700 by the French botanist Joseph Pitton de Tournefort (1656–1708) to honour the abbé.

Billings method

 The **Billings method** is a method of determining the time of ovulation by examining the colour and viscosity of the discharge from a woman's cervix. This can be used as a natural method of birth control by the avoidance of sexual intercourse at this time. Conversely, a couple who want to achieve a pregnancy can use the Billings method to determine the most likely time to conceive. The Billings method was named after **Drs John and Evelyn Billings**, the Australian physicians who devised it in the 1950s.

billycock

A **billycock** is the original name for a bowler hat. There are two theories as to the origin of this word. On the one hand billycock could be derived from bullycocked hat, a hat tilted at an aggressive angle. On the other hand, billycock could come from the name **William** (Billy) **Coke**, an English sportsman. In about 1850 the London hatters Lock's of St James's made a hat for Billy Coke. It is said that he wanted a hat that was more practical than a traditional 'topper', as the tall topper kept being knocked off by branches when Coke rode to the hounds.

Biro

Biro is a trademark used to describe a kind of ballpoint pen. It is named after its Hungarian-born inventor **László Jozsef Biró** (1900–1985). Biró patented his ballpoint pen, containing quick-drying ink, in Hungary in 1938. The rise of Nazism meant that Biró left Hungary and settled in Argentina.

> Biró developed his pen in collaboration with his brother, Georg, who was a trained chemist.

Biró's pen soon proved popular: for instance, Royal Air Force navigators found that it wrote better at high altitudes than a conventional fountain pen. Towards the end of World War II, Biró found an English company who backed his product, but the company was soon taken over by the French firm Bic. So it is that the ballpoint pen is known in France as a bic and in the UK as a biro.

Black Maria

A **Black Maria** is a police van for transporting prisoners and suspects. It is traditionally thought that the expression originally referred to **Maria Lee**, a strong, powerfully built African-American woman who, in about 1800, kept a boarding-house for sailors in Boston. She was also known for the help she gave to the police: the expression, 'send for the Black Maria', it is supposed, became common when there was trouble and the drunk and disorderly needed to be removed. When the first police horse vans were introduced in Britain in 1938 they may well have been named in honour of this awesome lady.

Blairism

Blairism is the term used to describe the movement of the Labour Party away from its traditional socialist roots and towards the political centre under the leadership of **Tony Blair** (born 1953). Blair coined the term 'New Labour' and steered the Party towards support for free enterprise, anti-inflationary policies and decentralization of government.

Tony Blair studied law at Oxford University, and was elected MP for Sedgefield in 1983. In 1994 he was elected leader of the Labour Party after the sudden death of John Smith. When Labour achieved a landslide win in the 1997 general election, he became the third-youngest British prime minister ever, after Pitt the Younger and Lord Liverpool.

blimp

A **blimp** (or **Colonel Blimp**) is a pompous, reactionary person with extremely conservative views. The origin of the word is the cartoon character **Colonel Blimp** invented by the New-Zealand-born political cartoonist Sir David Low (1891–1963) in daily papers, particularly the *London Evening Standard*, of the 1930s and 1940s. Blimp was depicted as an elderly, unimaginative, unprogressive character. The adjective blimpish, derived from blimp, means 'reactionary or very conservative'.

The word blimp probably gained greater currency because it also referred to a small, non-rigid airship used in World War I.

Bloody Mary

A **Bloody Mary** is a cocktail drink that consists mainly of vodka and tomato juice. The expression was originally the nickname of **Queen Mary I of England** (1516–1558). As queen (1553–1558), Mary's aim was to restore Roman Catholicism to England: earlier Protestant legislation was repealed and heresy laws were reintroduced. Nearly 300 men and women were burnt at the stake, including the bishops Hugh Latimer and Nicholas Ridley, and the Archbishop of Canterbury, Thomas Cranmer. It was as Latimer was burnt at the stake with Ridley that he encouraged his fellow sufferer with the famous words, 'Be of good comfort, Master Ridley, and play the man. We shall this day light such a candle by God's grace in England as I trust shall never be put out.'

Mary's cruel actions earned her the nickname 'Bloody Mary' and so it is that she has been remembered by the red of the cocktail.

bloomers

 The word **bloomers** nowadays refers to the women's undergarment that has full, loose legs gathered at the knee. The word owes its origin to the American feminist **Amelia Jenks Bloomer** (1818–1894), but the garment Bloomer introduced into American society was not the garment known as bloomers today. The original garment was an entire costume consisting of a loose-fitting tunic, a short knee-length skirt and billowing Turkish-style trousers gathered by elastic at the ankle. The costume, made originally from a design by Elizabeth Smith Miller, was worn by Mrs Bloomer and introduced at a ball in Lowell, Massachusetts, in July 1851. The outfit aroused considerable controversy at the time, largely because it was thought that trousers were a garment to be worn only by men.

Later, bloomers came to refer to just the trousers in the outfit, then, towards the end of the nineteenth century, to knee-length knickerbockers worn by cyclists, and today, in somewhat informal and wry usage, to the variety of women's underwear.

See also **knickerbockers**.

bluchers

 Bluchers were a new style of half-boots introduced by Prussian general **Field Marshal Gebhard Leberecht von Blücher** (1742–1819) for his troops to wear during the Napoleonic Wars. Von Blücher played a significant role in the defeat of Napoleon at the Battle of Waterloo (18 June 1815). In 1814 he was created Prince of Wahlstadt.

See also **Wellington boot**.

bluebeard

 Bluebeard, referring to a man who marries and then kills one wife after another, was originally a character in European folklore. The earliest literary form of the fairytale is that of Charles Perrault (1628–1703), published in 1697, in which six wives are the victims of the seductive yet evil desires of the husband and the seventh is rescued by the opportune arrival of her brothers, who then kill the murderer.

The original **Bluebeard** is thought by some to have been Gilles de Retz, Marquis de Laval, who lived in Brittany and who was accused of murdering six of his seven wives; in 1440 he was burnt at the stake for his crimes. Other sources, however, assign the original Bluebeard to an earlier date.

blurb

A **blurb** is a short publicity notice on the jacket or cover of a book. The word was coined in 1907 by the American humorist and illustrator Gelett Burgess (1866–1951) to promote his book *Are you a Bromide?*

In the early years of the twentieth century, American novels commonly had a picture of an attractive young woman on the cover. In an effort to parody this practice, Burgess produced a picture of a sickly sweet girl, **Miss Belinda Blurb** – for the purpose, he hoped, of 'blurbing a blurb to end all blurbs'. The outstanding success of this example meant that the word became associated with all such publicity copy.

bobbitt

If a woman **bobbitts** her husband or partner, she cuts off his penis, usually as an act of vengeance for his infidelity or abusive treatment. In 1993 in the USA, **Lorena Bobbitt** cut off the penis of her husband, **John Wayne Bobbitt**, with a kitchen knife while he was in a drunken sleep after raping her.

> John Wayne Bobbitt later had a career in pornography, starring in the adult films *John Wayne Bobbitt Uncut* and *Frankenpenis*.

She was charged with malicious wounding and found not guilty by reason of insanity. The fact that Mrs Bobbitt threw the offending organ from her car as she drove off enabled it to be sewn back on.

bobby

The name for a policeman in British informal usage is a **bobby**. Bobby is the familiar form of Robert, coming from, as is well known, the British statesman **Sir Robert Peel** (1788–1850). In 1812 Peel was appointed chief secretary for Ireland; in 1814 he founded the Irish Constabulary, members of which were nicknamed peelers. As home secretary, Peel passed the Metropolitan Police Act, which founded the Metropolitan Police (1829). The word bobby was then used to describe the new London police force, later passing into general use to refer to all British policemen.

Bob's your uncle

'**Bob's your uncle**' is a slang expression meaning everything is or will be fine; there'll be no difficulties. The phrase became current in the 1880s, but its origin is uncertain. A possible explanation is the allusion to the appointments of Arthur Balfour (1848–1930) to various posts such as secretary for Ireland, first lord of the treasury and leader of the House of Commons. The appointments were made by Balfour's uncle, the prime minister **Robert** (hence Bob) **Gascoyne Cecil**, 3rd Marquess of Salisbury (1830–1903). The apparently nepotistic choice meant that with Prime Minister Bob as his uncle, Arthur Balfour had no problem obtaining whatever he wanted.

Bodoni

Bodoni is a style of typeface named after the Italian printer, **Giambattista Bodoni** (1740–1813), who designed it. Bodoni managed the Stamperia Reale for the Duke of Parma from 1768 and produced typographically beautiful editions of Homer, Virgil and Horace.

The Bodoni typeface:
ABCDEFGHIJKLMNOPQRSTUVWXYZ
abcdefghijklmnopqrstuvwxyz

bogus

There are a number of different theories as to the origin of the word

bogus meaning 'counterfeit; sham'. Some sources suggest that the word is an alteration of the name **Borghese**, an Italian man who in the 1830s supplied counterfeit banknotes to the American West. The Boston *Courier* reported that in about 1837 the people shortened Borghese's name to bogus, his banknotes being called bogus currency.

Other sources suggest that the word bogus referred originally to a device used for making counterfeit coins. The first citation of the word used in this way is in 1827, some ten years earlier than the usage described above. Still others suggest that bogus is derived from the French *bagasse*, 'rubbish'. The origin of bogus remains unproven; it may well be that all the sources mentioned have exercised an influence on the word's acceptance.

bohrium

 The artificially produced radioactive transuranic element known as **bohrium** (formerly called unnilseptium and nielsbohrium) is named in honour of the Danish physicist and pioneer in quantum physics, **Niels Henrik David Bohr** (1885–1962).

Bohr's theory of atomic structure was published between 1913 and 1915 and earned him the Nobel prize (qv) for physics in 1922. His atomic model, using quantum theory and Planck's constant, is the basis for current quantum–mechanical models. As professor of physics at the University of Copenhagen, Bohr made several major contributions to theoretical physics. During World War II, Bohr escaped from occupied Denmark to Sweden, and from there to Britain and then the USA, where he worked on the development of the first atomic bomb.

bolivar

 The **bolivar** is the standard monetary unit of Venezuela, consisting of 100 centimos. Both the bolivar and the South American country **Bolivia** owe their names to the soldier and statesman **Simón Bolívar** (1783–1830), known as the Liberator for his unremitting struggle to free Venezuela, Colombia, Ecuador and Peru from Spanish rule. He succeeded in liberating these countries, but failed to join them in one united republican confederation. In 1825 Upper Peru became a separate state, taking the name Bolivia in honour of Bolívar, who later became its president. He is one of the very few men in history who not only has had a country named after him but also drew up that country's constitution.

Booker Prize

The **Booker Prize**, formerly known as the Booker McConnell Prize, now more properly called the Man Booker Prize for Fiction, is one of the most prestigious literary prizes in the world. It is a financial prize awarded annually, formerly by **Booker McConnell**, an international conglomerate, and now sponsored by investment bankers the Man Group, for the best English-language novel by an author from the UK, the Republic of Ireland or the Commonwealth. The prize was set up in 1968 by Booker Brothers and is administered by Book Trust in the UK.

Boolean algebra

George Boole (1815–1864) was a British mathematician who applied the methods of algebra to logic, in the same way that conventional algebra is used to express relationships in mathematics. In **Boolean algebra**, variables express not numbers but logical statements and the relationships between them. Boole's work was developed further by such philosopher-mathematicians as Frege, Russell and Whitehead and is important in the logic of computers.

> **Boole was appointed professor of mathematics at Cork University at the age of 34 despite being self-taught and never receiving a degree.**

Bosman ruling

The **Bosman ruling** was a decision of the European Court of Justice in December 1995 that allowed a footballer whose contract had expired to join a new club within the European Union without any transfer fee changing hands. Thus it has become customary for European football clubs to talk of signing an uncontracted player 'on a Bosman'.

Jean-Marc Bosman (born 1964) was a footballer with the Belgian club RFC Liege. When his contract expired, he faced the prospect of a 60% cut in pay, and so he attempted to move to the French club Dunkerque. However, RFC Liege demanded a higher transfer fee than Dunkerque were prepared to play. Bosman challenged the system that allowed a club to retain a player against his will in this way. Although he eventually won his case, Bosman paid a high price: having no financial resources, he had to live in a lock-up garage until the case was settled; his marriage fell apart; he became an alcoholic; and he never played professional football again.

boson

Bosons are subatomic particles, such as photons or pions, that have either zero or integral spin and obey the rules of **Bose–Einstein statistics**, in that they form totally symmetrical composite quantum states. The boson is named after **Satyendra Nath Bose** (1894–1974), an Indian physicist who specialized in mathematical physics. The concept of Bose–Einstein statistics was developed for photons by Bose in 1920, and was generalized to atoms by Einstein in 1924. Bose also worked with Marie Curie in Paris in the 1920s.

See also **einsteinium**.

botch

To **botch** a job means to do it badly or clumsily. The origin of this word is uncertain, but some people associate it with **Sir Thomas Bouch** (1822–1890), the Scottish engineer who designed the original Tay Railway Bridge, which was opened in 1878 and collapsed under a moving train on 28 December 1879. Sir Thomas Bouch was blamed for the Tay Bridge Disaster and dismissed from working on the Forth Bridge. The existing Tay Railway Bridge was opened in 1887.

bougainvillaea

Bougainvillaea is the name given to a genus of tropical South American woody climbing shrub bearing bright purple or red bracts that cover the flowers. The genus is named after the French navigator **Louis**

Antoine de Bougainville (1729–1811). On an expedition round the world under his leadership (1766–1769), the Solomon Islands were sighted. **Bougainville**, the largest island in the Solomon Islands archipelago is named after him, and is part of Papua New Guinea. Naturalists on Bougainville's expedition named the shrub in his honour.

bowdlerize

If a book has been **bowdlerized**, it means that all the words or passages considered indecent have been removed. The word is traditionally thought to have come from the name of the British doctor **Thomas Bowdler** (1734–1825). Having retired from medicine, Bowdler published his *Family Shakespeare* in 1818; it excluded or modified words and expressions and even characters and plots that he found objectionable. The title page explains that, 'Nothing is added to the text; but those expressions are omitted which cannot with propriety be read aloud in a family.' Inspired by his success in this venture, Bowdler then published his expurgated version of Gibbon's *History of the Decline and Fall of the Roman Empire* in 1823.

Some recent research has, however, suggested that it was not Thomas Bowdler but his sister, Henrietta Maria, known as Harriet, who edited the original *Family Shakespeare*, first published in 1807. This, it seems, was followed by the revised and second edition of 1818, with Thomas Bowdler as editor.

bowie knife

A **bowie knife** is a stout hunting knife, with a long, one-edged blade curving to a point. It is named after the American soldier and adventurer **James Bowie** (1799–1836). It was James Bowie who popularized the knife, but he did not invent it. It seems it was originally designed by his father or by his older brother **Rezin Pleasant Bowie** (1793–1841).

Bowie's exploits made him something of an American folk hero. He is said to have used the knife to kill six men and wound 15 others in the course of a duel at Natchez, Mississippi, in about 1827. James later became a colonel in the Texan army in the war of independence against

Mexico. In 1836, fewer than 200 Texans, including James Bowie and the legendary Davy Crockett, held out against some 4000 Mexicans for 13 days at the Alamo, but the Texans were eventually all slaughtered, James Bowie being slain on his sickbed.

bowler

 There are various theories as to the origin of the word **bowler**, the stiff felt hat that has a rounded crown and a narrow brim. The word may well be derived from the name **Bowler**, a family of nineteenth-century London hatters. Some sources suggest that the name of the hatmaker was Beaulieu; others suppose that the hat is so named because of its shape – it resembles a bowl or basin, and since it is round and stiff, it could be bowled along.

See also **billycock**.

Box and Cox

The expression **Box and Cox** means alternating or in turn. The origin of the expression lies in the farce *Box and Cox* by the English dramatist J M Morton (1811–1891), published in 1847. In the farce, two men, one named **Box** and the other **Cox** lived in the same room, the one occupying the room by day and the other by night and neither knowing of the other's existence. In 1867 the play was adapted as a comic opera with music by Sir Arthur Sullivan and text by Sir Francis Cowley Burnand.

boycott

Boycott is one of the most well-known eponyms in the English language. To boycott a person, organization, etc, means to refuse to deal with them, as an expression of

> Boycott's name has passed into other European languages, as in the German verb *boykottieren*.

disapproval and often as a means of trying to force them to accept certain conditions. The word comes from the name of the Irish landlord **Captain Charles Cunningham Boycott** (1832–1897).

After retiring from the British army, Boycott was hired to look after the Earl of Erne's estates in County Mayo, Ireland. In 1880 the Irish Land League, wanting land reform, proposed a reduction in rents, stating that landlords who refused to accept such rents should be ostracized. Boycott refused and was promptly ostracized. His workers were forced to leave him, tradesmen refused to supply him, and his wife was threatened – indeed he was persecuted to such a degree that he and his wife were forced to flee to England, in so doing making the first boycott a success.

Boyle's law

 Boyle's law states that at a constant temperature, the pressure of a gas is inversely proportionate to its volume. This law is named after the Irish-born British physicist and chemist **Robert Boyle** (1627–1691). In fact, Boyle's law is only roughly true for real gases; a gas that obeys Boyle's law completely (which would exist only in hypothetical instances) is called an ideal gas or a perfect gas.

See also **Mariotte's law**.

boysenberry

 The **boysenberry** was developed in the 1920s or 1930s as a hybrid of the loganberry (qv), blackberry and raspberry by **Rudolph Boysen** (died 1950), an American botanist and horticulturist.

Bradshaw

 Bradshaw was the informal name for the British railway passenger timetable *Bradshaw's Railway Guide*. First issued in 1839, it is named after its original publisher **George Bradshaw** (1801–1853). It was discontinued in 1961.

braggadocio

The word **braggadocio**, meaning 'empty boasting' comes from the character **Braggadocchio** in the poem *The Faerie Queene* by the English poet Edmund Spenser (c. 1552–1599). The character personified boasting and the poem records his adventures and ultimate exposure. Spenser probably coined the name from the English word braggart and the Italian suffix *-occhio* meaning 'great'. He may have had in mind the Duke d'Alençon, one of the many suitors of Queen Elizabeth I.

Braille

The name of the system of raised dots by which blind people can read comes from the Frenchman **Louis Braille** (1809–1852). Blinded at the age of three by an accident with an awl in his father's workshop, Braille went, at the age of ten, to study at the National Institute for the Blind in Paris. The Institute then possessed only three books, each in 20 parts and weighing 400 pounds (180 kg). The cumbersome text was written in large embossed letters to be felt by hand, yet Braille learned to read using this means.

At that same time an artillery captain, Charles Barbier, invented a primitive method of 'night writing'. Combinations of raised dots and dashes were used to communicate messages that could be understood by touch – that is, without the need for illumination. Barbier demonstrated his invention at the institute and Braille was inspired to refine it for use by the blind.

At the age of 20, Braille published his first book in his new system, soon applying his skill as a musician – he enjoyed organ playing – to adapt his system for use in music. He remained a teacher at the institute until his death in 1852.

Bramley

The word referring to the variety of cooking apple known as a **Bramley** probably comes from the name **Matthew Bramley**, an English butcher who is said to have first grown it around 1850. Bramley lived in Southwell, Nottinghamshire, and it is thought that the first Bramley was the result of a bud mutation: a variation in which only part of the tree was affected.

Bright's disease

Bright's disease is an inflammatory disease of the kidneys, characterized by albumin in the urine. Now more usually known as nephritis, or glomerulonephritis, this disease was named after **Richard Bright** (1789–1858), the English physician who first diagnosed it in 1827.

> **Bright served as physician extraordinary to Queen Victoria.**

Broca's area

Broca's area is the region of the brain concerned with the production of speech. It is located in the cortex of the dominant frontal lobe, ie in the left frontal lobe in most right-handed people. Broca's area is named after **Pierre-Paul Broca** (1824–1880), the French surgeon, neurosurgeon and anthropologist who discovered it and identified it as the brain's speech centre in 1861.

Broca found that damage to this area of the brain results in a condition now known as **Broca's aphasia**, in which the patient can say only a few simple words and is unable to write.

brougham

The name of the light, closed, four-wheeled, horse-drawn carriage with an open seat in front for the driver, honours the Scottish lawyer and statesman **Henry Peter Brougham**, Baron Brougham and Vaux (1778–1868). Brougham (both the name and the carriage are pronounced 'broom' or 'broo-erm') designed the carriage in about 1850, originally describing it as a 'garden chair on wheels'. The **brougham** remained a popular form of public transport until it was surpassed by the hansom cab (qv).

> **Brougham once enraged King William IV by making off with the Great Seal and using it as the centrepiece of a party game.**

Brougham's achievements include his advocacy, along with William Wilberforce, of the abolition of slavery; his defence in the House of Lords of Caroline of Brunswick against the charges of adultery brought by her husband, the Regent and later King George IV; and, as lord chancellor, his speech in the House of Lords that contributed to the passing of the Reform Bill of 1832.

Brownian movement

Brownian movement or **motion** is the name given to random movements made by small bodies suspended in a fluid due to collisions by surrounding molecules. This phenomenon was observed by the Scottish botanist **Robert Brown** (1773–1858) in 1827. Brown's observations paved the way for the kinetic theory of gases.

Browning automatic rifle

The **Browning automatic rifle** (often abbreviated to BAR), a portable gas-operated, air-cooled rifle, is named after its designer, the American **John Moses Browning** (1834–1926). Capable of firing 200–350 rounds a minute, the BAR was used widely in World War II and was the standard automatic weapon in the US army until about 1950. A prolific firearm designer, Browning also designed machine-guns, pistols and shotguns.

brucellosis

Brucellosis is an infectious disease of cattle, dogs and pigs, which can be transmitted to human beings in the form of undulant fever. Symptoms include fever, chills and miscarriage. Brucellosis is caused by bacteria of the genus *Brucella*, which was discovered in 1887 by the British bacteriologist and physician **Sir David Bruce** (1855–1931).

Bruce was born in Melbourne, Australia, of Scottish immigrant parents, but returned to Scotland when he was five years old. It was while in Malta as a military physician that he discovered the organism that causes brucellosis and demonstrated that this disease can be transmitted to human beings by the drinking of contaminated milk.

Buckley's chance

Buckley's chance is an Australian expression that means a very remote chance. Two chances, Buckley's and none, amounts in reality to next to no chance at all. The expression may derive from **William Buckley** (died 1856), who against all odds survived in the Australian outback with Aborigines for 30 years; perhaps a more likely suggestion is that the phrase is linked with a Melbourne store named **Buckley and Nunn**.

buckminsterfullerene

Buckminsterfullerene is the name given to carbon in the form of large molecules, each consisting of 60 carbon atoms linked in hexagons and pentagons to form a stable near-spherical structure. Because of its shape, it is sometimes colloquially referred to as **buckyballs**.

The name comes from the American engineer **Buckminster Fuller** (1895–1983). Fuller was influenced by aircraft design and aimed to create spaces for efficient, trouble-free living. From 1945 he designed geodesic domes, which were large dome-shaped enclosures built up from regular geometric shapes. His most famous dome was designed for the American Pavilion at the Montreal Expo of 1967.

Buddhism

The founder of **Buddhism** was the Hindu Prince Gautama Siddharta (c. 563–c. 483 BC). At the age of 16 he married his cousin, the Princess Yasodharma, who later bore him a son, Rahula. In his late twenties, he became dissatisfied with their life of luxury, so he left his family in order to try to find answers to the problems of human suffering and existence. Six years of asceticism followed, but these convinced him that self-mortification did not provide the solutions he was searching for. So, keeping himself from the extremes of self-mortification and indulgence, he turned to enlightenment alone, meditating within himself. He is traditionally said to have reached enlightenment while sitting under a fig tree in what is now called Buddh Gaya, a village in Bihar, in northeast India. He then took the title **Buddha**, meaning in Sanskrit 'the Awakened One'. The next 45 years of his life were devoted to teaching the principles of enlightenment.

buddleia

Buddleia is a genus of trees and shrubs that have showy clusters of yellow or mauve flowers. Native to tropical or warmer regions in Asia and America, the first specimens were collected in the early eighteenth century by the Scottish-born botanist William Houstoun (c. 1695–1733). He wished to name the plant after the Essex rector and botanist **Adam Buddle** (c. 1660–1715). This desire was later honoured by Linnaeus in his plant classification.

One particular species of buddleia, *Buddleia davidii*, was introduced into Britain from China in the late nineteenth century. This species is also known as the butterfly bush because its flowers are very attractive to butterflies. The word *davidii* is also eponymous – it comes from the French missionary and explorer Père Armand David, after whom Père David's deer (qv) is named.

Bunbury

Bunbury is the name of an invented friend used as an excuse to avoid fulfilling a social engagement or other obligation, and a **Bunburyist** is someone who uses this ploy. In Oscar Wilde's famous play *The Importance of Being Earnest* (1895), Algernon tells Jack that he has invented 'an invaluable permanent invalid called **Bunbury** in order that I may be able to go down into the country whenever I choose'. He accuses Jack of being a Bunburyist too because Jack pretends to have a younger brother called Ernest as an excuse for frequent trips up to town on the pretext of visiting him.

Bunsen burner

The **Bunsen burner**, the gas burner with an adjustable air valve used widely in chemistry laboratories, is named after the German chemist **Robert Wilhelm Bunsen** (1811–1899). Bunsen is generally credited with the invention of the Bunsen burner, although some authorities point out that similar designs had been developed earlier by such scientists as Michael Faraday. Even if this is true, it was certainly Bunsen who popularized the use of the burner.

> In cricketing parlance, 'Bunsen burner' is rhyming slang for a 'turner' – a pitch that offers assistance to spin bowlers.

Bunsen is also famous for his discovery, with the German physicist Gustav Robert Kirchoff (1824–1887), of the two chemical elements caesium and rubidium in 1860.

Buridan's ass

Buridan's ass is an illustration of a philosophical position. In the example, a hungry ass stands an equal distance between two identical bales of hay. He starves to death, however, because there is no reason why he should choose to eat one bale rather than the other. The dilemma is said to show the indecisiveness of the will when faced with two equal alternatives. The philosophical example is associated with the French philosopher **Jean Buridan** (c. 1295–1356), although it was first found in the philosophy of Aristotle.

burke

 To **burke** means to murder someone in such a way that no marks are left on the body. The word comes from the name of the notorious murderer **William Burke** (1792–1829). Originally an Irish labourer, Burke moved to Scotland in about 1818, renting a room in Edinburgh from a fellow countryman William Hare. When one of Hare's lodgers died owing him money, Hare and Burke took the body to an Edinburgh anatomist, Dr Robert Knox, who gave them seven pounds and ten shillings for it. Quickly realizing what profit there was to be made, Hare and Burke disposed of between 15 and 30 other unfortunates in a similar way. They were careful to suffocate their victims, leaving no marks of violence, so that it would appear that the bodies had been taken from graves. Burke and Hare were eventually caught with the body of a missing woman. Hare turned king's evidence, testifying against his accomplice and was set free, but Burke was hanged in January 1829. On the way to the gallows the crowd shouted, 'Burke him! Burke him!' wanting him to suffer the same fate as his victims. With all the publicity, Burke's name came to stand for the murderous act, and figuratively to mean 'hush up' or 'stifle'.

(qv).# burpee

A **burpee** is a gymnastic exercise that consists of a squat thrust made from and ending in a standing position. This dates from the 1930s and was named after its inventor, **Royal H Burpee**, an American psychologist. A **burpee test**, consisting of a series of burpees executed in rapid succession, was formerly used to measure agility.

busby

A **busby** is the name for the tall bearskin fur hat worn by soldiers, especially hussars and members of certain British army regiments. In the eighteenth century a busby was a large, bushy wig.

The word is traditionally thought to come from the name of the disciplinarian headmaster **Dr Richard Busby** (1606–1695). Headmaster of Westminster School, Busby had among his pupils Dryden, Locke and Christopher Wren. It is not certain, however, that Busby himself wore a bushy wig. It may be that his hair naturally stood on end, thus suggesting the wig that became fashionable.

51

Byronic

The adjective **Byronic** is sometimes used to mean wildly romantic yet melancholy and despairing. The word alludes to characteristics of the life and writings of George Gordon, **Lord Byron** (1788–1824). A significant romantic poet, whose writings included *Childe Harold's Pilgrimage* (1812–1818) and *Don Juan* (1819–1824), Byron is noted for his physical lameness, his attractive appearance, his many romantic liaisons and his journeyings on the European continent. Towards the end of his life, Byron became involved in the Greek struggle for independence. He died of malaria at Missolonghi in western Greece in 1824.

C

cabal

A **cabal** is a small group of people who meet secretly or unofficially, especially for the purpose of political intrigue. The word derives ultimately from Hebrew *qabbalah* (what is received or tradition). It is popularly believed, however, that the word cabal originated with the initials of the names of King Charles II's ministers from 1667 to 1673: Sir Thomas **Clifford** (1630–1673), Lord **Ashley** (later 1st Earl of Shaftesbury) (1621–1673), the 2nd Duke of **Buckingham** (1628– 1687), the 1st Earl of **Arlington** (1618–1685) and the Duke of **Lauderdale** (1616–1682). The political group's powerful scheming and intriguing met with great unpopularity. It was noticed that the ministers' initials made up the word cabal and it seems certain that the existence of this faction made the use of the word more current, adding to it pejorative connotations of reproach.

Cadmean victory

In Greek mythology, **Prince Cadmus** killed a dragon and planted its teeth, from which a race of armed warriors sprang up. Cadmus set the warriors fighting by throwing a stone among them, and only five escaped death. A **Cadmean victory** thus refers to a victory that is secured at an almost ruinous cost, the allusion being to the victory of the five survivors in the conflict with the multitude of other warriors.

It is interesting to note that this story also gave rise to the expression 'sow the dragon's teeth'. One can take a course of action that is intended to be peaceful, such as disposing of the dragon's teeth by burying them, but in reality the course of action leads to dissension or warfare.

See also **Pyrrhic victory**.

Caesarean section

A **Caesarean section** is a surgical incision through the walls of the abdomen and womb in order to deliver a baby. The expression is commonly thought to allude to the popular belief that **Julius Caesar** was born in this manner.

> **Various ancient sources report that Caesar was prone to epileptic fits.**

An alternative theory is that Caesarean comes from the Latin *caesus*, the past participle of the verb *caedere* 'to cut'.

See also **Caesar's wife**; **July**.

Caesar salad

The **Caesar salad** is an extremely popular tossed salad of lettuce, grated Parmesan cheese, croutons, garlic, olive oil and lemon juice. It was originally created in 1924 by **Caesar Cardini**, an Italian chef-restaurateur in Tijuana, Mexico. Realizing that supplies were running low on a particularly busy evening in the restaurant, he concocted his now-famous salad from staple ingredients from his kitchen, right in the middle of the restaurant, to the delight of the diners, many of whom were Hollywood celebrities.

Caesar's wife

The expression '**Caesar's wife must be above suspicion**' referred originally to **Julius Caesar**'s second wife Pompeia. According to rumours circulating in about 62 BC, it seems that her name was linked with Publius Clodius, a notorious dissolute man of the time. Caesar said that he did not believe such rumours but felt obliged to divorce her in any case because even the suggestion of wrongdoing was intolerable. The expression '**like Caesar's wife**' also comes from this account, to refer to someone who is pure and honest in morals.

Cain

See **raise Cain**.

calamine

Calamine, the pink powder of zinc oxide and ferric oxide that is used in soothing lotions for the skin, is an alteration of the Latin *cadmia*. This

Latin word derives ultimately from the Greek name **Cadmus**, the
legendary founder of Thebes, *kadmeia* meaning (Theban) earth.

See also **Cadmean victory**.

Callanetics

 Callanetics is a trademark for a system of non-impact exercises that
tone up the body by the frequent repetition of small precise movements
working on isolated muscle groups. This system was devised by the
American **Callan Pinckney** (born 1939), initially to alleviate her own
back and knee pain.

Calvinism

 The name of the theological system known as **Calvinism** comes from
the French theologian **John Calvin** (1509–1564), whose original name
was Jean Cauvin (sometimes also spelt Chauvin). Converted in about
1532, Calvin's most famous work is his *Institutes*, first published in
Latin (*Christianae Religionis Institutio*) in 1536.

Calvin has generally been held in low esteem. He himself wrote in 1559
that 'never was a man more assailed, stung, and torn by calumny' than
he was. He is known chiefly for his teaching on predestination, yet this
was taught earlier by Augustine and is found in the Bible. Calvin himself
was careful to keep this teaching in a healthy tension with other biblical
doctrines and it is some of his followers who have upset Calvin's
balance.

Calvin also sought to reform the behaviour of people in the city of
Geneva, to make the whole of Genevan society a model community
where every citizen came under a strict religious discipline. A wide range
of laws regulated the people's dress and morals. It is this rigorous and
austere aspect of Calvin's work that is recalled in the present-day
connotation of the word **Calvinist**, seen for example in the phrase 'a
strict Calvinist upbringing'.

calypso

A **calypso** is a kind of West Indian folk song, often improvised, with topical, usually satirical lyrics and a lively rhythm, which originated among the slaves in Trinidadian plantations.

> **Calypso's island is identified with modern-day Gavdos, the most southerly landmass in Europe.**

In Greek mythology, **Calypso** was a sea nymph who lived alone on the island of Ogygia until the arrival of Odysseus. Calypso fell in love with Odysseus and offered to make him immortal if he stayed with her forever. Odysseus refused because he did not want to be isolated from the world of mortals. Calypso kept him on the island for several years until Hermes intervened with an order from Zeus that Odysseus be released.

camellia

Camellia refers to a genus of ornamental shrubs, of which perhaps the best known is *Camellia japonica*. This has shiny evergreen leaves and showy, rose-like flowers. The word camellia comes from the name of the Moravian Jesuit missionary **George Josef Kamel** (1661–1706), also known by the Latinized form of his name, Camellus. Kamel lived in Manila in the Philippine Islands and there he ran a pharmacy, which was supplied by his herb garden. He published reports on the plants he grew in the *Philosophical Transactions of the Royal Society*. He was certainly the first to describe the shrub and some sources suggest that he may also have been the first to send specimens of it to Europe. In any event, it was the Swedish botanist Linnaeus who read of Kamel's accounts in *Philosophical Transactions* and later named the plant in his honour.

cant

The word **cant**, meaning 'insincere or hypocritical talk; repeated or specialized language', comes from the verb to cant, to talk whiningly like a beggar, and ultimately from the Latin *cantare*, to sing or chant. It is quite possible, however, that the meaning of the word and the frequency of its usage were influenced by the name of a Scottish minister **Andrew Cant** (1590–1663). Cant was a Presbyterian minister in Aberdeen; it was said of him that he talked 'in the pulpit in such a dialect that … he was understood by none but his own Congregation, and not by all of them', though how true this was is uncertain since many churches have said the same of their preachers! Andrew Cant and his brother Alexander were zealous leaders of the Covenanters – the Scottish Presbyterians who bound themselves on oath to defend their church. Some authorities describe the bigotry and hypocrisy of the Cant brothers, persecuting their religious opponents, yet also praying for them. So while the ultimate derivation of cant certainly is Latin *cantare*, it appears that the actions of the Cant brothers may well have supported the meaning of the word.

cardigan

The **cardigan**, the knitted jacket or sweater fastened with buttons, is named after the British cavalry officer James Thomas Brudenell, 7th **Earl of Cardigan** (1797–1868). The garment was first worn by British soldiers in the intense cold of the Crimean winter.

It was the Earl of Cardigan who led the Charge of the Light Brigade in the most famous battle of the Crimean War, near the village of Balaclava, on 25 October 1854. (Interestingly, the word for the woollen hood-like head-covering takes its name from this village.)

See also **raglan**.

Carnot engine

The **Carnot engine** is a hypothetical perfect engine in which all available energy is utilized. It was named after **Nicolas Léonard Sadi Carnot** (1796–1832), a French physicist and military engineer who first described this concept in 1824.

> Carnot's father was a prominent figure in the French revolution.

Carnot's work on the **Carnot cycle**, a series of changes in the physical condition of a gas in a reversible heat engine, became the basis for the second law of thermodynamics.

carpaccio

 Carpaccio is an Italian hors d'oeuvre consisting of thin slices of raw meat or fish, often served with a sauce. It takes its name from **Vittore Carpaccio** (c. 1455–1522), an Italian painter noted for his paintings of Venice and his use of vivid red colours, which are perhaps reminiscent of raw meat.

Casanova

A **Casanova** is a man noted for his, often unscrupulous, amorous adventures. The word comes from the name of the Italian adventurer **Giovanni Jacopo Casanova** (1725–1798). Born in Venice, the son of an actor, Casanova was expelled at the age of 16 from a seminary for monks for his immoral behaviour. He went on to live in many European cities, working at different times as, amongst other things, a preacher, a philosopher, a diplomat, a gambler and a violinist. He mixed with the wealthy aristocracy, engaging in many romantic liaisons, making and losing riches and friends wherever he went. He finally settled down as librarian to the Count von Waldstein in Bohemia, and it was here that he wrote his memoirs – about one and a half million words in twelve volumes – which were published posthumously between 1826 and 1838.

Cassandra

A **Cassandra** is a person whose prophecies of misfortune are ignored. The original **Cassandra** was a daughter of Priam, king of Troy in Greek legend. She was endowed with the gift of prophecy, but after she rejected the advances of Apollo, she suffered the punishment of her prophecies being eternally disbelieved.

> The pseudonym Cassandra was used by the English journalist William Connor (1909–1967).

Cassandra prophesied the sacking of Troy. When Troy was captured, she fell by lot to Agamemnon, who took her back to Greece and to whom she prophesied the doom that awaited him. Cassandra and Agamemnon were subsequently murdered by Clytemnestra. Thus it is that a modern-day Cassandra is someone whose predictions of doom are fated to go unheeded.

Catherine wheel

The kind of firework that spins as it burns is known as a **Catherine wheel** and is named after a princess, **St Catherine of Alexandria**. A martyr for her Christian faith, she is said to have been sentenced to death in about AD 307 by being broken on a spiked wheel. Legend has it that she survived this torture as it was the wheel, not her body, that was miraculously broken. Catherine was then beheaded, her body, it is thought, being carried by angels to Mount Sinai where it was found in about the year 800. On the site of the discovery a monastery was built to honour her resting-place. In 1969 the Roman Catholic Church ceased to recognize St Catherine because of doubts about her existence. St Catherine's symbol is a spiked wheel.

A Catherine wheel is also the name given to a circular window that has spokes radiating from its centre, and to the sideways handspring more commonly known as a cartwheel.

cattleya

 Cattleya is the name of a genus of tropical American orchids that are grown for their showy hooded flowers. The orchids are named after the English botanist and horticultural patron **William Cattley** (died 1832). The **Cattleya fly** and the subtropical fruit **Cattley guava** also honour this patron of botany.

Celsius

 Celsius is the name of the temperature scale for which 0° is the freezing point of water and 100° the boiling point. The scale is named after the Swedish astronomer and scientist **Anders Celsius** (1701–1744), who devised it in 1742. The new scale simplified the earlier Fahrenheit scale by dividing the temperature between boiling point and freezing point into a hundred equal parts.

Originally, Celsius set 0° as the boiling point of water, and 100° as the freezing-point; later the designations were reversed.

The Celsius scale was formerly called centigrade, but this name was officially changed in 1948 to avoid confusion with centigrade meaning 'a hundredth part of a grade'. Centigrade is, however, still sometimes used in non-technical contexts.

cereal

It may seem unlikely, but the origin of **cereal**, for many people a familiar sight on the breakfast table, lies ultimately in the name of a Roman goddess. Originally an adjective meaning 'of edible grain', cereal comes from Latin *cerealis*, 'relating to the cultivation of grain', which in turn derives from **Ceres** the goddess of grain and agriculture. Originally a Roman goddess, Ceres, became identified with the Greek goddess Demeter.

Chagas' disease

Chagas' disease is a disease found in South and Central America that is caused by a protozoan parasite transmitted by bloodsucking insects and is characterized by fever, oedema and cardiac disturbances. It was named after **Carlos Ribeiro Justiniano Chagas** (1879–1934), the Brazilian physician who first described it.

chaptalize

To **chaptalize** wine is to add extra sugar to the grape juice or must during its fermentation in order to increase the alcohol content. This process is named after **Jean-Antoine Chaptal** (1756–1832), the French chemist, industrialist and statesman who originated it. Chaptal was professor of chemistry at Montpellier, and was actively involved in gunpowder production during the French Revolution. He later served as minister of the interior (1801–1809) and as Director General of Commerce and Manufactures (1815) under Napoleon I. Chaptal pioneered the application of chemical principles to industrial processes, including wine-making.

See also **gallize**.

Charles's law

 Charles's law states that the volume of a gas at constant pressure expands by 1/273 of its volume at 0°C for each degree Celsius increase in

> **Charles is also famous as the inventor of the hydrogen balloon, in which he made the first ascent in 1783.**

temperature. The law is named after the French scientist **Jacques Alexandre César Charles** (1746–1823). His law was the result of experiments that began in about 1787.

See also **Gay-Lussac's law**.

charlotte

 A **charlotte**, the baked dessert made of fruit (commonly apples) layered with bread, sponge, etc, is thought to come originally from the name of **Princess Charlotte** (1796–1817), the only daughter of King George IV. The French chef Marc-Antoine Carême (1784–1833) is said to have created a sumptuous pastry in honour of the princess.

Carême's culinary preparations were so highly regarded that it is said they were taken from the table of the king's court to the marketplace where they were sold for a lot of money.

While serving Tsar Alexander I in Russia, Carême created the **charlotte russe** (*russe* being French for 'Russian'): the dessert consisting of a mixture of whipped cream and custard set in a crown of sponge fingers.

chateaubriand

 The large, thick, fillet steak known as a **chateaubriand** comes from the name of the French writer and statesman **François René Vicomte de Chateaubriand** (1768–1848).

Chateaubriand fought in the Royalist army in France, living in exile in England from 1793 to 1800. On returning to France in 1800, he achieved great fame with his writings, notably *Le Génie du Christianisme* (1802), and is generally considered as one of the significant leaders of early French Romanticism. Under Louis XVIII, he was French ambassador in London.

It is probable that the steak named in Chateaubriand's honour was created by his chef, Montmirel, and was first prepared at the French embassy in London.

chauvinism

The word **chauvinism**, referring to an excessive unthinking devotion to one's country, comes from the name of the French soldier **Nicolas Chauvin of Rochefort**.

A soldier in Napoleon's army and wounded many times, Chauvin was ridiculed by his fellow-soldiers for his fanatical devotion to Napoleon. Even when Chauvin was released from the army with a meagre pension, his patriotic zeal continued unabated.

It was the dramatists Charles and Jean Cogniard who made the name Chauvin famous in their comedy *Le Cocarde Tricolore* (1831). In this, Chauvin is a young recruit who sings several songs with the chorus that includes the lines, *Je suis français, je suis Chauvin*. The character of Chauvin later featured in a number of other French comedies and as a result became widely known. The word chauvinism soon became familiar in English to describe fanatical patriotism. In more recent years, the sense of the word has widened to include an unreasoned and prejudiced belief in the superiority of one's group or cause, as in the expression male chauvinism.

> **Chauvin's pension consisted of a medal, a ceremonial sabre and 200 francs a year.**

Chesterfield

 Chesterfield is used to refer to two items: a padded, often leather, sofa with upright armrests which are the same height as the back, and a man's overcoat with concealed buttons and a velvet collar. Both the sofa and the coat are generally thought to be named after a nineteenth-century **Earl of Chesterfield** (probably not the famous eighteenth-century 4th Earl of Chesterfield, Philip Dormer Stanhope), but it is uncertain which.

Chippendale

The gracefully decorative English furniture style known as **Chippendale** takes its name from its originator, the English cabinet-maker and furniture designer **Thomas Chippendale** (c. 1718–1779).

The son of a Yorkshire picture-frame maker, Chippendale set up a furniture factory in London in 1749, five years later publishing *The Gentleman and Cabinet Maker's Director*. Illustrating some 160 designs in Louis XV, Chinese and Gothic styles, this was the first extensive furniture catalogue and was significant in furniture design in both England and America. Chippendale's son, also Thomas (1749–1822), continued his father's business.

Christian

The word **Christian** occurs in the New Testament in Acts 11:26: 'And the disciples were called Christians first in Antioch.' From this, its two other occurrences in the New Testament and a reference in the writings of the Roman historian Tacitus, it can be inferred that Christian was a generally recognized title for a follower of **Jesus Christ** in the time of the New Testament.

The word Christ itself comes from the Greek *christos*, meaning 'the anointed one', translated from the Hebrew *Mashsah* (Messiah). The name of Christ is also used in other words such as **christen, Christianity** and **Christendom**. The name of the festival of **Christmas** comes from the Old English *Cristes maesse* (Christ's mass).

Chubb lock

Chubb is a trademark used to describe a kind of patent lock with a device that fixes the bolt immovably so that it cannot be picked. It is named after **Charles Chubb** (1772–1846), the English locksmith who invented it. Along with his brother Jeremiah, Chubb founded a lock company, originally in Wolverhampton. In 1832, Charles Chubb issued a challenge to a local picklock and locksmith called Thomas Hart to pick a Chubb lever lock at the New Hotel in Wolverhampton. The prize was to be £100, plus free pardon by the government. After three months, Hart was forced to admit defeat.

churrigueresque

The word **churrigueresque** (pronounced chure-rig-a-resk) is used to describe a Spanish style of baroque architecture of the late seventeenth and early eighteenth centuries. Marked by highly detailed ornate surface features, this style takes its name from the Spanish architect and sculptor **José Churriguera** (1650–1725).

cicerone

A person who acts as a guide to sightseers is sometimes called a **cicerone**. The word comes from the name of the Roman orator and statesman **Marcus Tullius Cicero** (106–43 BC). Guides take their name from Cicero because he typifies the eloquence and knowledge that is expected of them. In short, they are required to point out items of local interest to visitors in the style of the orator Cicero.

> The name Cicero means literally 'chick-pea'.

cinchona

Cinchona is the name of a genus of South American trees and shrubs that contains some 40 species. One of the most important species is calisaya as its bark produces a drug that can be used in the treatment of malaria.

The genus is named after the Spanish vicereine of Peru, **Countess Ana de Chinchón** (1576–1641). In about 1638 the countess was afflicted by a tropical fever that could not be cured by European doctors. The powdered bark of a native Peruvian tree restored her to health, however. The bark was taken back to Spain where it was called Peruvian bark or Countess bark. The modern name *Cinchona* was given the genus by Linnaeus in honour of the Countess, but he must have inadvertently misspelled her name: what should really have been *Chinchona* was called *Cinchona*.

Cinderella

A person or thing described as a **Cinderella** is one that is regarded as being unjustifiably neglected: 'For too long distribution has been the

Cinderella of the publishing industry.' The expression comes from the well-known fairytale in which the heroine **Cinderella** is cruelly treated by her stepmother and her two stepsisters but with the help of a fairy godmother finally marries a prince.

clarence

 A **clarence** was a closed, four-wheeled, horse-drawn carriage for four passengers, the driver's seat being outside the carriage. It was named after the **Duke of Clarence**, later to become King William IV (1765–1837).

See also **silly-billy**.

Claude Lorraine glass

 A **Claude Lorraine glass** is a small black or coloured convex mirror, used especially by painters for reflecting landscapes in miniature and in subdued colours, in order to show their broad tonal values. The French painter Claude Gellée (1600–1682), known as **Claude Lorraine** after his birthplace, Lorraine, is said to have used such a glass. From the age of twelve, Claude worked as a pastry chef in the home of the Roman painter Agostino Tassi, later becoming his studio assistant. As an adult, he spent much of his life in Italy, often painting the beautiful coastline of the Gulf of Naples.

clementine

 A **clementine** is a small citrus fruit with sweet flesh, virtually no seeds, and an easily peeled rind. It is believed to have been named after **Père Clément**, a French missionary in Algeria, who first produced it by crossing a tangerine with a Seville orange c. 1900.

clerihew

 A **clerihew** is a witty four-line verse that consists of two rhymed couplets, usually biographical in content. The clerihew was invented by the English writer **Edmund Clerihew Bentley** (1875–1956).

The first clerihew was composed (according to Bentley's friend G K Chesterton) while Bentley was at school, 'listening to a chemical exposition, with his rather bored air and a blank sheet of blotting-paper before him'. On this he wrote:

> Sir Humphry Davy
> Abominated gravy.
> He lived in the odium
> Of having discovered sodium.

Under the name E Clerihew, Bentley published his first clerihews in 1905. He is also known for his journalistic writings and his detective novel *Trent's Last Case* (1913), but it is for his clerihews he is chiefly remembered. Perhaps the best known is:

> Sir Christopher Wren
> Said, 'I am going to dine with some men.
> If anybody calls
> Say I am designing St Paul's.'

Cocker

See **according to Cocker**.

Colles' fracture

A **Colles' fracture** is a fracture of the radius just above the wrist, with backward and outward displacement of the hand, which sometimes causes residual deformity. This type of fracture most commonly occurs in postmenopausal women, osteoporosis being a significant factor. The Colles' fracture was named after **Abraham Colles** (1773–1843), the Irish surgeon who first described it in 1814.

colón

The colón is the standard monetary unit of El Salvador and Costa Rica. It takes its name from

The indigenous peoples believed that Columbus had supernatural powers after he predicted an eclipse on 29 February 1504.

Cristóbal Colón, the Spanish name of **Christopher Columbus**, the Italian navigator and explorer (1451– 1506), who landed on what he named San Salvador island on 12 October 1492 and is credited with discovering America.

Also named after Columbus is the Republic of **Colombia** as well as numerous cities in the USA.

Colt

Colt is the trademark for a type of pistol with a revolving magazine. It has a single barrel with a revolving breech for six bullets. The pistol is named after its inventor, the American engineer **Samuel Colt** (1814– 1862). Born in Connecticut, Colt ran away to sea at the age of 16. While aboard ship he carved a wooden model of the revolver. On his return home, he established an arms factory, patenting his invention in 1835. The pistol was used notably in the Mexican War (1846–1848). In 1854 it was adopted by the Royal Navy, and a modified .45 calibre version was used by the US army and navy until 1945.

comstockery

Comstockery is strict censorship of literary works on the grounds of immorality or obscenity. The term comes from the name of the American moral crusader **Anthony Comstock** (1844–1915).

Comstock devoted most of his life to suppressing plays and books that he considered immoral. He founded a number of moralistic causes, notably the New York Society for the Suppression of Vice in 1873, the year in which he also secured the passing of the so-called **Comstock Laws** through Congress to prevent objectionable books and magazines from being sent by the post. As a guardian of the post, he is said to have arrested about 3000 people and destroyed some 50 tons of books that he considered to be immoral. Comstock objected greatly to *Mrs Warren's Profession*, the play by George Bernard Shaw, and it was Shaw who in 1905 coined the word comstockery.

Confucianism

Confucianism is the ethical system of the Chinese philosopher **Confucius** (551–479 BC). Born in Lu, a small state in what is now Shandong province, Confucius became a minor official, later rising to prime minister of Lu, being well known for his wise, just government. After his advice was ignored, however, he left Lu, returning only in the last years of his life.

From an early age he gathered a group of disciples round him and continued to teach his ethical ideas. (His name in Chinese is Kong Zi, meaning 'Kong the Master'.) In his final years he edited the books now known as the *Classics*. After his death, his disciples collected his sayings, which became known as the *Analects*. Confucius's ethical system is sometimes summed up in the rule, 'What you do not want others to do to you, do not do to them.'

'**Confucius, he say ...**' is a humorous expression sometimes used to introduce a maxim or thought that is considered wise.

Corbett

Originally, a **Corbett** was any Scottish hill between 2500 and 2999 feet high, with a 500-foot separation on all sides – there are 219 such peaks. More recently, the designation 'Corbett' has been extended to apply to any hill in the British Isles that fulfils these criteria. **John Rooke Corbett** (1876–1949) compiled the first list of Corbetts, though it was not published until after his death. Corbett not only climbed all the Corbetts, but he was also the fourth person to 'bag' all the Munros.

> **Corbett's father set up one of Britain's first day nurseries for working mothers.**

See also **Munro**.

cordoba

The **cordoba** is the basic monetary unit of Nicaragua. The word derives ultimately from the name of the Spanish soldier and explorer

Francisco Fernandez de Córdoba (c. 1475–1526). It was Córdoba who in 1522 took possession of Nicaragua for the Spanish.

Couéism

'Every day, in every way, I am getting better and better.' This was the formula advocated by the French psychologist and chemist **Emil Coué** (1857–1926) in the treatment of his patients. Establishing a clinic at Nancy in 1910, Coué practised his system of psychotherapy. He believed that by means of autosuggestion – summed up in the formula above – ideas that lead to illness could be removed from the realm of the will.

coulomb

A **coulomb** is the basic metric unit of electric charge. The term honours the name of the French physicist **Charles Augustin de Coulomb** (1736–1806).

Originally a French military engineer, Coulomb was forced because of bad health to retire from the army; subsequently he developed his interests in electricity and magnetism. Coulomb is remembered for his invention of the torsion balance to measure the force between two charged particles and his formulation of what is now known as **Coulomb's law**.

Cox's orange pippin

A **Cox's orange pippin** is a variety of eating apple with a green-and-red skin and a sharp taste, which is one of the most popular apples in Britain. It was first grown in 1825 by **Richard Cox** (c. 1776–1845), an English retired brewer and amateur fruit-grower.

Creutzfeldt–Jakob disease

Creutzfeldt–Jakob disease, more commonly known as **CJD**, is a fatal disease that affects the brain. Believed to be caused by an abnormal protein called a prion, it causes premature dementia and loss of muscular coordination. CJD was named after two German psychiatrists, **Hans Gerhard Creutzfeldt** (1885–1964) and **Alfons Maria Jakob**

(1884–1931). Creutzfeldt first described the disease in 1920; in the following year Jakob published his description of it, which became better known.

New variant CJD is a strain of the disease that was discovered in the late 1980s and that appears to be related to BSE (or 'mad cow disease'). There is some concern that an increased incidence of new variant CJD in Britain could have been caused by eating infected beef.

Crockford

Crockford is the name often used to refer to *Crockford's Clerical Directory*, the reference book giving facts about the Church of England and its clergy, first published in 1860. It is called Crockford after **John Crockford** (1823–1865), managing clerk to serjeant-at-law Edward Cox, who first published the directory. It seems that Cox preferred to use his clerk's name because of his own official position.

Croesus

Croesus was the last king of Lydia, a region of Asia Minor, who reigned from 560 to 546 BC. As a result of his conquests, Croesus became extremely rich. Indeed, he was considered by the Greeks to be the wealthiest person on earth, hence the contemporary expression '**as rich as Croesus**' meaning very rich.

Legend has it that the Athenian statesman Solon once told Croesus that no man should be considered happy, despite his riches, until he died. Later, when Cyrus the Great defeated Croesus, he condemned Croesus to be burnt alive. It is said that Croesus shouted out Solon's words from the stake. Cyrus intervened, demanding an explanation of Croesus' words, and, being so moved by what his prisoner said, reprieved him and became his friend.

Crohn's disease

Crohn's disease is a chronic inflammatory disease of the gastro-intestinal tract, which

Some scholars now believe that Beethoven suffered from Crohn's disease.

causes diarrhoea, abdominal pain and loss of appetite, resulting in weight loss. It was named after **Burrill Bernard Crohn** (1884–1983), the American pathologist who first identified it in 1932.

Crookes tube

A **Crookes tube** is the name given to several types of sealed vacuum tube used in electronics. If an object is placed near the cathode of such a tube and bombarded with electrons, it is possible to observe spectacular fluorescent effects. The tube is named after **Sir William Crookes** (1832–1919), the English scientist who invented it.

Crookes's name is also attached to **Crookes glass**, a type of glass containing cerium, which inhibits ultraviolet light from passing through it and is used in the manufacture of sunglasses.

CS gas

CS gas is a powerful irritant gas that affects vision and respiration, and which is used in riot control. It takes its name from the initials of the surnames of two American chemists, **Ben Corson** (1896–1987) and **Roger Stoughton** (1906–1957), who synthesized it in 1928.

Cuisenaire rods

Cuisenaire rods is a trademark used to describe a set of rods that have different colours and lengths. The rods are named after the Belgian educationalist **Emil-Georges Cuisenaire** (c. 1891–1976). Standing for various numbers, the rods are used to teach arithmetic to young children.

Cupid

The expression 'to **play Cupid**', meaning to play the role of match-maker, alludes to the Roman god of love. Identified with the Greek god Eros, **Cupid** is usually represented as a winged naked boy holding a bow and arrow.

The shape of the bow that Cupid is traditionally shown as carrying is referred to in the expression **Cupid's bow**, used to describe the shape of the upper human lip.

curie

The **curie** is a unit of radioactivity, now largely displaced by the becquerel (qv). It is named after the French physicist and chemist **Marie Curie** (1867–1934). The curie is equal to 3.7×10^{10} becquerels.

> **Marie Curie was the first woman to win a Nobel prize.**

Curzon line

The **Curzon line**, marking the border between Poland and the Soviet Union, was confirmed at the Yalta Conference of 1945. The boundary was named after the British politician George Nathaniel, 1st **Marquis Curzon of Kedleston** (1859–1925). Curzon served the British government in many capacities, among them viceroy of India (1899–1905), lord privy seal (1915–1916) and foreign secretary (1919–1924).

> **Curzon is quoted as saying, 'Gentlemen do not take soup at luncheon.'**

The Curzon line was proposed in the Russo-Polish War (1919–1920); Lord Curzon suggested that the Poles – who had invaded Russia – should retreat to this line while awaiting a peace conference.

Cushing's disease

Cushing's disease is a condition caused by excessive secretion of certain steroid hormones such as cortisone; its symptoms include obesity, muscular weakness and high blood pressure. The disease is named after the American neurosurgeon **Harvey Williams Cushing** (1869–1939), who was the first to identify and describe the condition.

Cyrillic

 Cyrillic is the name of the alphabet used in writing Slavonic languages such as Russian and Bulgarian. The alphabet is traditionally thought to have been developed by two Greek brothers, **St Cyril** (hence Cyrillic) (826–869) and St Methodius (c.

> The feast day of St Cyril and St Methodius is 7 July.

815–885), during the course of the translation of the Bible and liturgy into Slavonic. The Cyrillic alphabet is derived from the Greek alphabet and is supplemented by Hebrew letters for non-Greek sounds.

czar

See **tsar**.

daguerrotype

One of the earliest practicable photographic processes was the **daguerrotype**, named after its inventor, the French painter and pioneering photographer **Louis Jaques Mandé Daguerre** (1789–1851). In the daguerrotype process, an image is produced on iodine-sensitized silver and developed in mercury vapour.

Daguerre, an officer for the French inland revenue and a landscape and theatrical scenery painter, had been involved in producing the diorama, a method of exhibiting pictures by using special lighting effects. In 1829 Daguerre met the physicist Joseph Niepce (1765–1833), who had been experimenting with different photography methods for some years. Daguerre continued the work after Niepce's death, producing his results in 1839, for which he was awarded the French Legion of Honour.

At about the same time the British botanist and physicist William Henry Fox Talbot (1800–1877) was perfecting a photographic process using negatives. Although Fox's system became the basis of modern photography, it was Daguerre's invention that aroused widespread public interest in photography.

dahlia

Dahlia is a genus of herbaceous perennial plants that have showy, brightly coloured flowers and tuberous roots. Originally cultivated as a food crop, dahlias are now grown commonly as ornamental plants.

The dahlia was discovered by the German explorer and naturalist Alexander von Humboldt (1769–1859) in Mexico in 1789. It was sent to the Botanic Garden in Madrid, where Professor Cavanilles named it in honour of the Swedish botanist **Anders Dahl** (1751–1789), who had died that same year.

daltonism

Daltonism is another word for colour blindness, especially the inability to distinguish between red and green. It is named after the English scientist **John Dalton** (1766–1844), who himself suffered from this disability. He was the first person to give a detailed description of this condition, in *Extraordinary Facts Relating to the Vision of Colours* (1794).

> Dalton began teaching at the age of twelve.

It is for his work in physics and chemistry that Dalton is better known. He is regarded as the originator of the modern atomic theory of matter and he formulated the law relating to the pressure of gases that is known as **Dalton's law**.

Dandie Dinmont terrier

Dandie Dinmont is the name of a breed of Scottish terrier characterized by short legs, a long coat and drooping ears. The breed is named after **Dandie Dinmont**, a character in the novel *Guy Mannering* (1815) by the Scottish writer Sir Walter Scott (1771–1832). Andrew Dinmont was a sturdy farmer who lived in Liddesdale in the Scottish Lowlands and owned a pack of such dogs.

Daniel come to judgement

The expression 'a **Daniel come to judgement**' refers to someone who makes a wise decision about something that has puzzled others. It alludes to the biblical **Daniel** (Daniel 5:14–16 and, perhaps more specifically, the devout and upright young man of the apocryphal book of Susanna), but the source of the actual quotation is Shakespeare's *Merchant of Venice* (Act 4, Scene 1):

> *A Daniel come to judgement! yea a Daniel!*
> *O wise young judge, how I do honour thee!*

The phrase **Daniel in the lions' den**, referring to someone who is in a place where he or she is exposed to intense personal danger, alludes to the Book of Daniel, chapter 6.

darbies

 The word **darbies**, slang for handcuffs, is a shortening of the phrase 'Father Derby's [or Darby's] bands'. This was a sixteenth-century expression alluding to the rigid agreement binding a debtor to a moneylender. **Derby** (or **Darby**) may well have been the name of a notorious usurer of the period.

Darby and Joan

 A happily married elderly couple are sometimes known as **Darby and Joan**: 'One summer afternoon we drove to my aunt and uncle's home for tea. They were a real old Darby and Joan – as much in love at 80 as they were at 18.' These names first appeared in a song by Henry Woodfall published in *The Gentlemen's Magazine* (1735).

The original Darby and Joan are thought to have been the London printer **John Darby** (died 1730), to whom Woodfall served as an apprentice, and his wife **Joan**.

The names are further remembered in the 'Darby and Joan' club, a club for elderly people.

davenport

 A **davenport** is a small compact writing desk with a vertically folding writing surface and side drawers. The word derives from the name **Davenport** between 1820 and 1840, but sources differ as to whether Davenport was a furniture maker or a captain who first commissioned its manufacture. The sense of the word common in America for a large sofa, especially one that can be converted into a bed, came later.

David and Goliath

The **David** in the expressions **David and Goliath** and **David and Jonathan** is the Old Testament king of Israel (c. 1000–962 BC). The youngest son of Jesse, David was anointed by Samuel as the successor to Saul as king of Israel. David's successes against the Philistines included the slaying of Goliath. **Goliath**, as is well known, was the Philistine giant who was dealt a fatal blow by the seemingly insignificant David –

Goliath, the armoured champion, bearing a javelin and a spear; David, the mere shepherd boy, bearing a staff, five smooth stones in his shepherd's bag and a sling. Yet it was David who slung a stone that killed the giant (1 Samuel 17). The expression David and Goliath is used, therefore, to refer to a contest between someone who is apparently weak and someone who seems to possess overwhelmingly superior strength.

David became a close friend of **Jonathan**, Saul's eldest son, and the Bible records their mutual loyalty and affection (1 Samuel 20) – hence the expression 'David and Jonathan' to refer to close friends of the same sex.

Davy Crockett hat

 The American frontiersman, politician and soldier **Davy Crockett** (1786–1836) is one of the most popular of American heroes. His fearless deeds have been widely described, and his name is still remembered for the **Davy Crockett hat**, the style of fur hat with a characteristic extended tailpiece that he is said to have worn. Crockett died defending the Alamo during the war for Texan independence.

Davy Jones' locker

The bottom of the sea, thought of as the grave of those drowned or buried at sea, is known as **Davy Jones' locker**. **Davy Jones** is seen as a personification of the devil who rules over the evil spirits of the sea, and the expression has been part of sailor slang for over two hundred years; there are several different theories as to how it originated.

Some suggest that Jones is a corruption of the name of the biblical Jonah, thrown overboard from a ship and swallowed by a great fish. The name Davy is said to have been added by Welsh sailors, David being the patron saint of Wales.

Other sources say that Davy is an anglicization of the West Indian word *duffy* or *duppy* meaning a malevolent ghost.

Still others hold that **Davy Jones** was originally the owner of a sixteenth-century London public house that was popular with sailors.

The pub is said to have also served as a place for press-ganging unwary citizens into service: Davy Jones was thought to store more than just ale in the lockers at the back of the pub. The victims would be drugged and transferred to a ship, to awaken only when the ship had put to sea. Thus Davy Jones' locker came to be feared.

Davy lamp

The **Davy lamp** (also known as the safety lamp) takes its name from the British chemist **Sir Humphry Davy** (1778–1829). Davy invented the

Michael Faraday worked for Davy as a laboratory assistant and valet.

safety lamp for miners in 1816; its flame is enclosed in metal gauze to prevent the possible ignition of explosive gas. His other notable achievements included the isolation of the elements potassium, sodium, calcium and magnesium.

Debrett

Debrett – in full **Debrett's Peerage** – is the name of a directory of the British aristocracy. The listing bears the name of the London publisher who first issued it, **John Debrett** (c. 1752–1822). The original compilation, published in 1802, was titled *A Peerage of England, Scotland, and Ireland*; it was followed six years later by *A Baronetage of England*.

decibel

The **decibel** is a unit that is used to compare two power levels, especially of the intensity of sound, on a logarithmic scale. The decibel is one-tenth of a bel, but 'decibel' is much more commonly used than 'bel'. Both units are named after the Scottish-born American scientist **Alexander Graham Bell** (1847–1922).

Bell is famous for his invention of the telephone (1876); the first, historic, words that Bell spoke to his assistant Thomas Watson on the telephone were, 'Watson, come here, I want you.'

De Clerambault's syndrome

De Clerambault's syndrome, also called erotomania, is a psychiatric
disorder in which the patient becomes fixated on someone, often a
person they do not know, such as a celebrity. The patient is convinced
that the object of their obsession welcomes their attentions and returns
their love but that there is a conspiracy to keep them apart. Often the
patient believes that the 'love object' is communicating with them using
a secret code; for example, they may interpret comments, or even
gestures, made during a television interview as having some special
secret significance for them. This type of obsession can result in violence
when the patient's approaches are persistently rejected. This syndrome
was first discovered c. 1910 by a French psychiatrist called **Dr De
Clerambault** (1872–1934).

Delia

Delia Smith (born 1941) is
a British cookery writer
and 'celebrity chef',
probably best known for
her cookery programmes on
television, particularly the *How to
Cook* series, which featured 'back-to-basics' cooking with simple
ingredients and basic techniques, starting with how to boil an egg. Her
name has become synonymous with good basic British cooking, so that
'to **do a Delia**' means to cook in this style.

> A young Delia Smith baked the
> cake that appeared on the
> cover of The Rolling Stones'
> 1969 album *Let It Bleed.*

Delia Smith's other great passion is football. She is a director of Norwich
City FC.

Delilah

A **Delilah** is a treacherous and seductive woman, especially a mistress or
wife. The use of this name alludes to the story of the biblical character
Delilah who was bribed by the Philistine rulers to discover the secret of
Samson's great strength (Judges 16:4–22). Samson lied to her on three
occasions, but when she continued to ask him, he grew so weary of her
nagging that he told her the truth – that the source of his power lay in

his long hair. Delilah then betrayed this secret to the Philistines, and while Samson slept upon her lap, his hair was shaved off, so depriving him of his strength.

See also **Samson**.

demijohn

 A **demijohn** is a large narrow-necked bottle made of glass or stoneware. Usually having small handles at the neck, demijohns are often encased in wickerwork. The word demijohn probably derives from the French **dame-jeanne**, 'Lady Jane', from the resemblance between the shape of the large bulging bottle and that of a particular buxom French housewife or, more likely, with portly women in general.

Derby

 The **Derby** is the name of the annual flat race for three-year-old horses run at Epsom Downs, Surrey. It is probably named after Edward Stanley, 12th **Earl of Derby** (1752–1834), who founded the horse-race in 1780. The American counterpart is the Kentucky Derby, founded in 1875.

Derby is also the American and Canadian word for a bowler hat (its first syllable being pronounced to rhyme with 'fur'). It is said that some Americans, noticing the distinctive shape of the style of hat worn by English sportsmen, took some of the hats back to American manufacturers, asking them to copy the narrow-brimmed felt hats with a rounded crown that came to be sold as 'hats like the English wear at the Derby'.

derrick

The word **derrick**, now referring to a hoisting apparatus or crane, formerly described a gallows. The word derives from the seventeenth-century English hangman surnamed **Derrick**.

Derrick served under the command of Robert Devereux, 2nd Earl of Essex, in the sacking of Cadiz (1596), where he was charged with rape and found guilty. He was sentenced to death by hanging but was pardoned by Essex when he agreed to become executioner at Tyburn gallows, London, near what is now Marble Arch. A few years later, Essex was found guilty of treason after instigating a riot in London (1601) and was sentenced to death, and it fell to Derrick to execute him. On this occasion Derrick used an axe, requiring three attempts to cut off Essex's head. In all, Derrick is said to have carried out more than 3000 executions in his service as hangman, his name being applied to the gallows itself and then to the crane that the gallows resembled.

derringer

A **derringer** is a small, short-barrelled pistol of large calibre. It is named after its inventor, the American gunsmith **Henry Deringer** (1786–1868). Deringer's invention meant that he became one of America's largest manufacturers of arms. There were, however, many imitations of his gun, one of which was the European make of derringer – i.e. Deringer's name adapted with an additional 'r' to avoid patent laws – and it is the spelling derringer that has become generally accepted.

deutzia

Deutzia is the name of a genus of ornamental shrubs of the saxifrage family that bear white or pink bell-like flowers. It is named after the Dutch patron of botany **Jean Deutz** (c. 1743–c. 1784).

Dewar flask

A **Dewar flask** is the name given to a kind of vacuum flask used in scientific experiments to store a liquid or gas at a constant temperature. It is also known by the trademark Thermos flask or, non-technically, as a vacuum flask. A Dewar flask has two thin glass walls that are separated by a vacuum to reduce loss of heat by conduction. The inner surface is silvered to reduce loss of heat by radiation, and the vessel has a tight stopper to prevent evaporation.

The Dewar flask takes its name from the Scottish chemist and physicist **Sir James Dewar** (1842–1923), who invented this prototype of the modern vacuum flask in about 1872. Dewar is known for his research into gases – he was the first person to produce liquid hydrogen – and, with the British chemist Sir Frederick Augustus Abel (1827–1902), he invented the explosive cordite.

Dewey Decimal System

The book classification system known as the **Dewey Decimal System** is named after the American librarian **Melvil Dewey** (1851–1931). Dewey devised his book-classification system in 1876, while working as acting librarian at Amherst College, Massachusetts. In Dewey's system, books are classified according to their subject matter by a three-digit number showing the main class, followed by numbers after a decimal point, to show subdivisions. The Dewey system is widely used by libraries throughout the world, the classification being constantly revised.

Dickensian

The adjective **Dickensian** has a number of meanings: it suggests poverty, misery and the squalor of urban or industrial life in Victorian England; it suggests conviviality ('an old-fashioned Dickensian Christmas') and it means vividly caricatured, when used in connection with the figures he created. The word Dickensian comes of course from the name of the English novelist **Charles Dickens** (1812–1870). It was memories of his painful childhood – he himself had to go to work in a blacking warehouse at the age of twelve – that inspired a great deal of his writing. Some of the characters in his writings have also become eponymous, for example, Scrooge (qv) from *A Christmas Carol* and gamp (qv), an umbrella, from Mrs Sarah Gamp in *Martin Chuzzlewit*.

It is a mistake, however, to consider that '**the dickens**', in expressions such as 'what the dickens' and 'the dickens only knows' comes from the name of Charles Dickens. The dickens referred to here is a euphemism for the devil. In fact the expression was used centuries before Dickens; Shakespeare used it in *The Merry Wives of Windsor* (Act 3, Scene 2): 'I cannot tell what the dickens his name is.'

> **Dickens was commemorated on Bank of England £10 notes until being replaced by Charles Darwin in 2000.**

diddle

The word **diddle**, meaning informally to cheat or swindle, comes from the name of the character **Jeremy Diddler** in the farce *Raising the Wind* (1803) by the Irish-born English dramatist James Kenney (1780–1849). Diddler, the chief character of the play, has the habit of constantly borrowing small sums of money that he never pays back. The play's success led to the quick acceptance of the verb diddle into the language.

diesel

A **diesel** engine is an internal-combustion engine in which fuel is ignited by highly compressed air. The word diesel comes from the name of the German mechanical engineer **Rudolf Diesel** (1858–1913), who

> Diesel vanished from a mail steamer between Antwerp and Harwich in 1913, and was presumed drowned.

invented the diesel engine in 1892. Diesel's design followed up earlier ideas of the French scientist Sadi Carnot (1796–1832). Diesel developed the engine at the Krupp factory in Essen; and he not only invented a new kind of engine, he also found the best kind of fuel, the relatively cheap semi-refined crude oil, to power the engine. Today the diesel engine is widely used in industry and road, rail and maritime transport.

Dionysian

Dionysus was the Greek god of wine, also of fruitfulness and vegetation; he is identified with the Roman god Bacchus. He was worshipped in five annual dramatic festivals (the Dionysia) by the people of Athens. **Dionysian** feastings were scenes of wild, orgiastic licentiousness and it is in allusion to such ecstatic frenzy that the words Dionysian (or Dionysiac) are sometimes used today.

See also **bacchanalia**.

Dioscorea

Dioscorea is the botanical name of the genus of plants in the yam family. This name was given by Linnaeus in honour of the Greek physician **Dioscorides Pedanius** (c. AD 40–c. 90). As a surgeon in the Roman army, Dioscorides travelled widely and he collected information about nearly six hundred plants and their medicinal properties, which he recorded in *De materia medica* (c. AD 77). He is commonly regarded as one of the founders of the science of botany.

Disneyfication

The **Disneyfication** of something, such as history or culture, means the trivialization of it by presenting it in a oversimplistic, commercialized manner, especially in order to appeal to mass-market tourism. This is a reference to the world-famous theme parks opened by the Walt Disney Corporation in California, Florida, Tokyo and Paris.

> **Alfred Hitchcock said of Disney, 'If he didn't like an actor, he could just tear him up.'**

Walter Elias Disney (1901–1966) was an American animator and film producer, who created Mickey Mouse and produced many of the best-loved children's films of all time, including the first ever full-length cartoon, *Snow White and the Seven Dwarfs*, in 1937.

Dives

Dives is the name given to the rich man in the story about the rich man and Lazarus told by Jesus (Luke 16:19–31). In the story, Dives pays no attention to the plight of Lazarus, the beggar at his gate. After death Lazarus is carried to 'Abraham's bosom' (qv) and Dives to hell, but it is not possible for there to be any contact between them.

It is interesting to note that the rich man is not actually named in the English Bible text. It is in the Latin version of the New Testament that he is called *dives*, meaning 'rich', hence 'a rich man', and the word has come to be thought of as a proper noun.

The name of **Dives** has thus become proverbial for a very rich person, especially one who is unconcerned and hardened to others' needs.

Doberman pinscher

A **Doberman pinscher** is a breed of short-haired, medium-sized dog with a short tail. The name of the dog derives from the German **Ludwig Dobermann** (1834–1894) and the German word *Pinscher*, a breed of hunting dog. A tax collector as well as a dog breeder, Dobermann developed in the 1880s a particularly ferocious breed of dog to help him in his duties. Nowadays Dobermans are widely used as guard dogs.

Doe

See **John Doe and Richard Roe**.

doily

The word **doily**, for a small ornamental openwork mat made of paper, cloth or plastic that is laid under dishes of food, comes from the name of a London draper. His name is variously spelt **Doily**, **Doiley** or **Doyley** – and he owned a London shop around the year 1700 in The Strand, where fabrics trimmed with embroidery or crochet work were sold. The decorative cloths were originally known as Doily napkins, then doilies.

Dolby

 Dolby is a trademark for an electronic circuit that reduces extraneous noise on audio tape recordings. This system was devised in 1966 by **Raymond Dolby** (born 1933), an American engineer.

Dolby's company sued 1980s pop star Thomas Dolby (real name Thomas Morgan Robertson) for using the name.

Dollywood

 Dolly Parton (born 1946) is an American country singer and songwriter. Her best-known songs include 'Jolene' (1974), 'I Will Always Love You' (1974) and '9 to 5' (1981). Dolly Parton has also acted in several films, including *9 to 5* (1980), *The Best Little Whorehouse in Texas* (1982) and *Steel Magnolias* (1989). In 1986, she opened her own very successful theme park, **Dollywood**, in Pigeon Forge, Tennessee. It is based on her own life, from her impoverished childhood in Locust Ridge, Tennessee, right through her successful career.

Dolly Parton insured her breasts for $600,000.

dolomite

Dolomite is the name given to the mineral calcium magnesium carbonate, which has a hexagonal crystal structure and is used in the manufacture of cement and as a building stone. The term is also used to refer to a rock containing a high ratio of magnesium carbonate that is used as a building material. The word dolomite comes from the name of the French geologist **Déodat de Dolomieu** (1750–1801) who discovered the mineral.

Don Juan

A **Don Juan** is a man who tries to seduce many women, a man with an insatiable desire for women. The name is based on the legendary fourteenth-century Spanish aristocrat and womanizer, **Don Juan Tenorio**. According to the traditional Spanish story, Don Juan Tenorio of Seville kills the father of Doña, the young girl he is attempting to seduce. On visiting the tomb, Don Juan scornfully invites the statue to a feast; the statue accepts, seizes Don Juan and delivers him to hell.

Don Juan is the subject of numerous plays and operas: Molière's *Don Juan* (1665), Mozart's *Don Giovanni* (1787), Byron's *Don Juan* (1819–1824) and Shaw's *Man and Superman* (1903).

Don Quixote

See **Quixotic**.

Doppler effect

The **Doppler effect** is the technical name for the change in the apparent frequency of the waves of sound, light, etc, when there is relative motion between the source and the observer. For instance, the sound of a low-flying aeroplane seems to drop in pitch as the plane passes the observer although it in fact remains constant.

> **Doppler originally tried to apply his principle to explain the coloration of stars.**

The phenomenon is named after the Austrian physicist **Christian Johann Doppler** (1803–1853), who first explained it in 1842.

doubting Thomas

A **doubting Thomas** is someone who is sceptical, particularly someone who refuses to believe until he has seen proof of something or has been otherwise satisfied as to its truth. The expression alludes to one of Jesus' apostles, **Thomas**, who refused to believe in Christ's resurrection until he had seen and felt Christ's body for himself (John 20:24–9).

Douglas fir

The **Douglas fir** is a very tall evergreen American tree that is grown both for ornament and for its high-quality timber. With needle-like leaves and large cylindrical hanging cones, the Douglas fir is named after the Scottish botanist **David Douglas** (1798–1834).

> **Douglas suffered an unusual death: he was gored by a wild bull while working in Hawaii.**

Sent to North America at the age of 23, Douglas crossed Canada on foot and travelled as far south as California. When he came across the tall trees (which are second in height only to the giant sequoias and redwoods), Douglas had to shoot some seeds down with a gun – and in the process was chased by American Indians. In all, Douglas collected over two hundred plants and seeds that were unknown in Europe.

Dow–Jones average

The **Dow–Jones average** (or **index**) is a daily index of the relative prices of shares on the New York Stock Exchange. Based on the prices of a representative number of shares, the index takes its name from two American financial statisticians, **Charles Henry Dow** (1851–1902) and

Edward D Jones (1856–1920). Dow and Jones founded Dow, Jones and Co. in 1882 to provide information to Wall Street finance houses. Since 1884 indexes of movements of selected stocks and shares have been calculated.

Downing Street

 Downing Street is the name of the road in Westminster, London, that houses the official residences of the British prime minister (Number 10) and the chancellor of the exchequer (Number 11). The street is named after the English statesman **Sir George Downing** (1623–1684). A nephew of a Massachusetts governor, Downing graduated from Harvard and returned to England where he served under both Cromwell and King Charles II. His warning to Charles II in 1657 that Cromwell wanted to capture him saved Charles's life. Downing was later given a grant of land in what is now Downing Street.

Down's syndrome

 Down's syndrome is a congenital disease typically marked by mental retardation and the physical features of slanting eyes, a broad short skull and short fingers. Associated with the presence of one extra chromosome in each cell, the condition is named after the English physician **John Langdon-Down** (1828–1896) who first adequately described it in 1866. The disease was formerly called mongolism because the characteristic facial appearance of the affected children was commonly thought to resemble that of the people of Mongolia.

draconian

 Draconian means 'very harsh or severe' and is used to describe laws, measures or regulations. The word comes from **Draco**, the seventh-century-BC Athenian law-giver. In 621 BC he drew up what was probably the first comprehensive code of laws in Athens; before that time the laws had been interpreted arbitrarily by members of the city's governing body.

Draco's code of laws was so severe – almost every named crime carried the death sentence – that draconian came to be used to describe laws of unreasonable cruelty. In 590 BC the Athenian statesman Solon formulated a more lenient legal code.

Druse

The **Druses** (or **Druzes**) are members of a religious sect centred on the mountains of Syria and Lebanon. The name probably derives from the name of one of the sect's founders, **Ismail al-Darazi**, Ismail the tailor (died 1019). The Druses' scriptures are based on the Bible, the Koran and Sufi writings. Druses believe in the deity of Al-Hakim, a caliph of Egypt.

dryasdust

A boring pedantic person is sometimes called a **dryasdust**. The name is that of the fictitious character the **Reverend Dr Jonas Dryasdust**, to whom the Scottish writer Sir Walter Scott (1771–1832) addressed the prefaces of some of his novels.

Duchenne muscular dystrophy

Duchenne muscular dystrophy is a form of muscular dystrophy, an inherited disease that causes progressive weakness and disability, which usually affects boys only and results in an early death. It was named after **Guillaume-Benjamin-Amand Duchenne** (1806–1875), the French neurologist who first described it. Duchenne is widely acknowledged to be the founder of electrotherapy, having treated patients with faradic currents from 1830.

dunce

The word **dunce**, 'a person who is stupid or slow to learn', derives originally from the name of the Scottish theologian **John Duns Scotus** (c. 1265–1308). (The Duns in his name comes from his supposed birthplace near Roxburgh, Scotland.) A Franciscan, his teaching combined elements of Aristotle's and Augustine's doctrines, but he was opposed to the theology of St Thomas Aquinas, he being nicknamed 'the Subtle Doctor' and Aquinas 'the Angelic Doctor'. His teachings ('Scotism') were accepted by the Franciscans and were influential in the Middle Ages but were ridiculed in the sixteenth century by humanists and reformers who considered his followers (called Dunsmen or Dunses) reluctant to accept new theological ideas. The word dunce then came to refer to a person resistant to new ideas, hence to someone who is dull or stupid.

Dupuytren's contracture

Dupuytren's contracture is a condition in which one or more fingers, most often the ring finger and the little finger, are caused to be bent in towards the palm of the hand by the contraction of a fibrous chord in the tissue of the palm, so that the affected fingers cannot be extended. This condition is named after **Baron Guillaume Dupuytren** (1777–1835), the French surgeon who first described it in 1831.

> **Former US president Ronald Reagan and former British prime minister Margaret Thatcher both suffered from Dupuytren's contracture.**

E

Earl Grey

Earl Grey is a black tea that is scented with bergamot oil and has a musky taste. It was named after the British prime minister and diplomat, Charles Grey, the 2nd **Earl Grey** (1764–1845), who is believed to have been presented with the recipe by a mandarin on a diplomatic mission to China in 1830.

E. coli

E. coli is an abbreviation of *Escherichia coli*, which is an aerobic rod-shaped Gram-negative bacterium that occurs naturally in the intestines of vertebrates. Although usually harmless, occasionally it can cause severe food poisoning, especially in susceptible individuals such as children and elderly people. **Theodor Escherich** (1857–1911), the German paediatrician and bacteriologist, first described this bacterium in 1886.

eggs Benedict

Eggs Benedict is a popular breakfast dish consisting of a toasted split English muffin topped with poached eggs, grilled bacon or ham, and hollandaise sauce. There are several versions of the origin of this dish. According to one version, it was named after **LeGrand Benedict**, a Wall Street financier and regular at Delmonico's restaurant in Manhattan, for whom the chef created this dish in the 1920s when Mr Benedict complained about the restricted choice on the menu. An alternative story is that eggs Benedict was named after **Lemuel Benedict**, a Wall Street broker, who invented and ordered it at the Waldorf Hotel in Manhattan in 1894, whereupon the chef, Oscar Tschirky, added it to the menu.

einsteinium

Einsteinium is the name of a radioactive chemical element that is produced artificially; its atomic number is 99. The element, originally

identified by the American physicist
Albert Ghiorso and others in
1952 in fall-out from the first
hydrogen bomb explosion, is
named after the German-born
American physicist **Albert Einstein**
(1879–1955). Einstein is most famous for his
formulation of the special theory of relativity (1905) and the general
theory of relativity (1916) and was awarded the Nobel prize (qv) for
physics in 1921.

> **Einstein said of his
> involvement in developing
> the nuclear bomb, 'If only I
> had known, I would have
> become a watchmaker.'**

See also **boson**.

Electra complex

The term **Electra complex** is used to refer to cases when a female
child is attracted to her father and shows hostility to her mother.

In Greek mythology, **Electra** was the daughter of Agamemnon and
Clytemnestra. After Clytemnestra and her lover, Aegisthus, had
murdered Agamemnon, Electra persuaded her brother Orestes to avenge
their father's murder by killing Clytemnestra and Aegisthus.

See also **Oedipus complex**.

Elizabethan

The reign of **Queen Elizabeth I** (1533–1603; reigned 1558–1603) was
marked by great achievements in literature, exploration and many other
areas, for instance, by the life and work of poets such as Shakespeare
and Spenser, the adventurers Raleigh and Drake and musicians such as
William Byrd. It is this spirit of outstanding
creativity and bold adventure that is
evoked by use of the term
Elizabethan. The adjective may also
be applied to **Queen Elizabeth II** (born
1926), alluding to the possibility of a similarly
great and imaginative age.

> **Elizabeth I banned
> football from the streets
> of London in 1572.**

éminence grise

An **éminence grise** refers to someone who exercises power unofficially by influencing another person or group who appear to have authority. **Éminence grise** (French for 'grey eminence') was originally the nickname given to the French friar and diplomat Père Joseph (François le Clerc du Tremblay 1577–1638), private secretary and confidant to the French statesman Cardinal Richelieu. The nickname referred to the colour of Père Joseph's garments and also to the authority he wielded over the unsuspecting Richelieu.

eonism

Eonism is another name for transvestism, the practice of adopting the dress, and sometimes the manner, of the opposite sex. This name is based on that of the **Chevalier Charles Éon de Beaumont** (died 1810), a French diplomat and transvestite.

epicure

A person who cultivates a discriminating taste in food or wine is known as an **epicure**. The word derives from the name of the Greek philosopher **Epicurus** (341–270 BC). Epicurus taught that the highest good was pleasure, but because every joy entailed some pain, he taught his disciples (**Epicureans**) to exercise moderation in all things. Epicurus also taught that pleasure was gained not through sensual indulgence but by self-control and achieving tranquillity of mind. His teachings have been misunderstood at times, however, and some have seen them as defending the unashamed pursuit of bodily pleasure.

Epstein–Barr virus

The **Epstein–Barr** virus is a virus belonging to the herpes family that causes glandular fever and is associated with Burkitt's lymphoma (qv). It was named after two British virologists, **Michael Anthony Epstein** (born 1921) and **Yvonne M Barr** (born 1932), who isolated this virus in cultured Burkitt's lymphoma cells in 1964.

Erastianism

The theory that the state should have authority over the church in ecclesiastical matters is known as **Erastianism**. This term comes from the name of the Swiss theologian **Thomas Erastus** (1524–1583), to whom such a theory was attributed. In fact, however, Erastus limited his argument only to 'the case of a state where but one religion is permitted'.

erotic

The word **erotic**, 'of or tending to arouse sexual desire', derives from **Eros**, the Greek god of love, and the Greek word *eros*, meaning love; (sexual) desire. The god Eros – whose Roman counterpart was Cupid (qv) – was the son of Aphrodite and was usually portrayed as a winged, blindfolded youth with a bow and arrows.

eschscholtzia

Eschscholtzia is the name of a genus of plants in the poppy family and is applied particularly to the California poppy (*Eschscholtzia californica*), grown for its yellow and orange flowers. The term Eschscholtzia honours the name of the Russian-born German naturalist **Johann Friedrich von Eschscholtz** (1793–1831), who accompanied the German navigator and explorer Otto von Kotzebue on his expeditions (1815–1818, 1823).

Esperanto

Esperanto is the name of the artificial language invented by the Polish doctor and linguist Lazarus Ludwig Zamenhof (1859–1917) in 1887. The language takes its name from the pseudonym **Doctor Esperanto** which Zamenhof adopted when he wrote his first book on the subject, *Linguo Internacia de la Doktoro Esperanto*. The word Esperanto itself comes from Latin *sperare* (to hope), thus his pseudonym means 'the hoping doctor'. The language's grammar is completely regular and each letter represents only one sound. It is the world's most successful artificial language.

Euclidean geometry

Euclidean geometry is a system of geometry based on the axioms of the third-century-BC Greek mathematician **Euclid**. These axioms are recorded in Euclid's books, *Stoicheia* (Elements),

Euclid is said to have warned King Ptolemy I that 'there is no royal road to geometry' when asked if there was a quicker and easier way to learn the subject.

which remained the standard work on geometry for over 2000 years. It was not until the nineteenth century that the possibility of a non-Euclidean geometry was seriously contemplated.

Besides referring to geometry, the adjective Euclidean is also sometimes used to mean clear and orderly in presentation and explanation.

euhemerism

Euhemerism is the theory that the gods described in mythology are in fact historical heroes who have come to be regarded as divine. The word euhemerism derives from the name of the fourth-century Sicilian Greek philosopher **Euhemerus** who advanced this theory in his philosophical romance *Sacred History*. Euhemerus asserted that he had come across an inscription that supported his theory on a gold pillar in a temple on an island in the Indian Ocean.

euphorbia

Euphorbia is the name of the genus of plants of the spurge family that have a milky sap and small flowers surrounded by conspicuous bracts. As well as being used for ornamentation, some of the species have been used medicinally. The description euphorbia derives ultimately from the name of the first-century-AD Greek physician **Euphorbus**. Euphorbus was physician to King Juba II of Mauritania, who is said to have named the plant after him.

euphuism

Euphuism – not to be confused with euphemism – is used to describe an artificial and highly ornate style of writing or speaking. Fashionable in the late sixteenth and early seventeenth centuries, euphuism derives from **Euphues**, a character in the prose romance in two parts *Euphues: The Anatomy of Wit* (1578) and *Euphues and his England* (1580) by the English writer John Lyly (c. 1554–1606).

An example of this style is: 'Be valiant, but not too venturous. Let thy attire by comely, but not costly.'

Euphues is Greek for 'well endowed by nature' and Lyly's prose romance, marked by excessive use of antithesis, alliteration, historical or mythological allusion and other figures of speech, has given us the word euphuism to describe this elaborately embellished style.

Eustachian tube

The **Eustachian tube** is the name of the canal connecting the pharynx (throat) to the middle ear. Known also as the pharyngotympanic tube, it had already been discovered by the fifth-century-BC Greek physician Alcmaeon of Croton, but it was the Italian physician **Bartolommeo Eustachio** (c. 1520–1574) who first adequately described it. As well as undertaking anatomical research into the ear, Eustachio studied the heart, kidneys and nervous system.

Everest

The name of the world's highest mountain, **Mount Everest**, on the Nepal–Tibet border (8848 m; 29,028 ft), honours the surveyor-general of India, **Sir George Everest** (1790–1866). Everest was the first to undertake detailed mapping of the subcontinent, including the Himalayas.

Since 1920–1921 expeditions to climb Mount Everest have been undertaken, the first successful one being the expedition led by Colonel John Hunt when the New Zealander Edmund Hillary and the Sherpa Tensing Norkay became the first to reach the summit on 29 May 1953.

In a derived application of the word, **Everest** is sometimes used to refer to the highest point of achievement.

everyman

Everyman is the name sometimes given to the typical or average person, 'the man in the street'. The description comes from the allegorical character **Everyman** in the sixteenth-century morality play of the same title. In the play, which is based on a slightly earlier Dutch counterpart *Ellckerlijc*, Everyman is summoned by Death, but he finds that none of his friends will go with him except Good Deeds. The lines of Knowledge in the play have become legendary:

> *Everyman, I will go with thee and be thy guide,*
> *In thy most need to go by thy side.*

F

Fabergé eggs

Fabergé eggs are intricate decorative Easter eggs made of gold and enamel and often jewel-encrusted, which were designed for members of the Russian and other European royal families by **Peter Carl Fabergé**, born Karl Gustavovich Fabergé (1846–1920), a Russian goldsmith and jeweller.

Fabergé's business was ruined by the Russian revolution, and he died in exile in Switzerland.

Fabian

The adjective **Fabian** is sometimes used to mean cautious in politics; avoiding direct confrontation. This sense derives from the policies of the Roman general **Quintus Fabius Maximus** (also known as Cunctator, the delayer; died 203 BC). As a commander against Hannibal in the Second Punic War, Fabius continually harassed Hannibal's armies without ever risking a pitched battle. Fabius's cautious tactics contributed to Hannibal's eventual defeat.

The **Fabian Society**, an association of British socialists, took its name from Quintus Fabius Maximus. Founded in 1884 to establish democratic socialist principles gradually rather than by adopting revolutionary methods, its prominent personalities included George Bernard Shaw.

Fagin

The name **Fagin** is sometimes used to describe an adult who teaches others, especially children, to steal goods, and also to describe a person who receives stolen goods. The allusions are to the fictional character **Fagin**, the head of a gang of thieves in the novel *Oliver Twist* (published in 1837–1838) by Charles Dickens.

Fahrenheit

Fahrenheit is the scale of temperatures in which 32° represents the freezing point of water and 212° the boiling point of water. It is named after its inventor, the German scientist **Gabriel Daniel Fahrenheit** (1686–1736), who set 0° as the lowest temperature he could scientifically derive, by mixing ice and common salt. The Fahrenheit scale is no longer in general use, having been replaced by the Celsius (qv) scale.

Fahrenheit was born in Danzig (modern Gdansk) and lived most of his life in Holland and England. His father wanted him to be a merchant, but after a brief and unsuccessful attempt at this career, he turned to physics. Before he was 20, Fahrenheit manufactured meteorological instruments. He initially used alcohol in his thermometers, but he soon substituted mercury, inventing the first mercury thermometer. He was elected to the Royal Society in 1724.

Fallopian tubes

The **Fallopian tubes** are the two tubes that connect the uterus to the ovaries in female mammals. They are named after the Italian anatomist **Gabriel Fallopius** (1523–1562) who first described them. A pupil of the Flemish anatomist Andreas Vesalius (1514–1564), Fallopius was professor of anatomy at Pisa (1548–1551), after which he taught at Padua University. He described features of the ear as well as the reproductive system in his *Observationes anatomicae* (1561).

Falstaffian

The adjective **Falstaffian** is sometimes used to describe someone who is plump, witty and self-indulgent. The word derives from the character **Sir John Falstaff** in Shakespeare's *Henry IV, Parts I* and *II* (1597 and 1598) and *The Merry Wives of Windsor* (1602).

Fanconi's anaemia

Fanconi's anaemia is a rare inherited form of anaemia, which leads to bone-marrow failure, short stature and increased susceptibility to cancer, especially leukaemia. This disease is named after **Guido Fanconi** (1892–1979), the Swiss paediatrician who first described it in 1927.

farad

The English physicist and chemist **Michael Faraday** (1791–1867) was born into a poor London family and was apprenticed at an early age to a bookbinder. The books he came

> Faraday appeared on the Bank of England's £20 notes between 1991 and 1999, before being supplanted by Sir Edward Elgar.

across having aroused his interest in science, he attended lectures at the Royal Institution and persuaded Sir Humphry Davy to engage him as his assistant (1813), eventually succeeding Davy as professor of chemistry there (1833). Faraday made many notable discoveries in different areas of the physical sciences, but it is particularly with electricity and electrochemistry that his name is perpetually linked.

Two scientific units are named after him: a **farad** is the basic metric unit of electrical capacitance; a **faraday** is a quantity of electricity used in electrolysis. Faraday is known for his laws of electrolysis (1813–1814) and his pioneering work on electromagnetic induction, hence the terms **faradic** and **faradism**.

Fata Morgana

Fata Morgana is the name given to a mirage that traditionally is seen in the Straits of Messina from the Calabrian coast. In a derived sense, the term may be applied to any mirage or to a figment of the imagination. The name Fata Morgana (in English, Morgan le Fay) comes from the Italian *fata*, 'fairy', and **Morgana**, who was the queen of Avalon, half-sister of King Arthur and evil sorceress of Arthurian legend. It was believed by the Norman settlers in England that she lived in Calabria, hence the application of the name to the apparition.

faun

A **faun** is a figure in Roman mythology that has the body of a human and the horns and legs of a goat. The word derives from **Faunus**, the Roman god of pastures and forests who was later identified with the Greek god Pan.

The name **fauna**, referring to animal life in general or that of a particular area or period (and often complementing flora (qv)), was adopted by Linnaeus in 1746, Fauna being the sister of the god Faunus.

Faustian

Faust is the name of the semi-legendary medieval German scholar and magician who allegedly sold his soul to the Devil in exchange for knowledge and power. Stories of conjurors working with the Devil, linked with the historical figure of the wandering conjuror **John Faust** (c. 1488–1540), have inspired many literary works including Marlowe's *Dr Faustus* (1604) and Goethe's *Faust* (1808, 1832). The adjective **Faustian** has thus come to describe different characteristics of Faust and Faustus, including the abandonment of spiritual values in order to gain material benefits, the relentless pursuit of knowledge and enjoyment, and spiritual disillusionment and dissatisfaction.

fedora

A **fedora** is a soft felt hat with a brim and a creased crown. It takes its name from *Fedora*, a tragedy by the French playwright Victorien Sardou (1831–1908), which was first produced in 1882. In the title role of **Fedora Romanoff**, a Russian princess, the French actress Sarah Bernhardt made a triumphant comeback to the stage and the hat that she wore for the part started a fashion trend for both men and women.

fermium

Fermium is an artificially produced radioactive element. Like einsteinium (qv), it was first detected by the American physicist Albert Ghiorso in fall-out after the first hydrogen-bomb explosion (1952). It was named after the Italian-born American physicist **Enrico Fermi** (1901–1954).

Fermi's early work in Italy was concerned with quantum statistics – the **Fermi–Dirac statistics** are named after himself and the British physicist Paul Adrien Maurice Dirac (1902–1984). Fermi is best known for his work on nuclear physics: he was awarded the Nobel prize (qv) for physics in Stockholm in 1938. Owing to his anti-Fascism and because his wife was Jewish, Fermi sailed directly from Stockholm with his family to the United States. In Chicago he led the group that produced the first controlled nuclear chain reaction (1942). As well as being known for a chemical element, Fermi's name is also honoured by the **fermi** (a former unit of length in nuclear physics), the so-called **Fermi level** and **fermion** (an elementary particle).

Ferris wheel

A **Ferris wheel** is a large upright fairground wheel with seats that hang freely from its rim; the seats remain more or less horizontal as the power-driven wheel turns. It is named after the American engineer **George Washington Gale Ferris** (1859–1896) and was introduced at the World's Columbian Exposition in Chicago (1893). The first Ferris wheel measured 250 feet (76 m) in diameter, and had 36 cars, each holding up to 40 people. The 'big wheels' of today are more modest attractions, seating six to eight people in each car.

fiacre

A **fiacre** was a small, four-wheeled, horse-drawn carriage of the seventeenth and eighteenth centuries. The name of the cab derives from the townhouse where they were first hired out in 1648, the Hôtel de St Fiacre in Paris. Fiacre is the French version of the name of the Irish **Prince Fiachrach** (or **Fiachra**), who founded a monastery at Breuil, near Paris, in about 670.

Fibonacci sequence

The **Fibonacci sequence** is the name given to the sequence of numbers in which each number after the first two numbers is the sum of the previous two in the series. The sequence begins with the numbers (known as Fibonacci numbers) 0, 1, 1, 2, 3, 5, 8, 13, 21, 34. It is named after the Italian mathematician **Leonardo Fibonacci** (c. 1170–c. 1250), who is said to have invented it in 1225 in order to solve a puzzle about the breeding rate of rabbits. The sequence has been found to occur in

> **Fibonacci is also credited with popularizing the Arabic numerical notation in his *Book of the Abacus* (1202).**

nature, such as in the number of leaf buds on a plant stem and the number of spirals of seeds on the head of a sunflower.

filbert

The **filbert** (*Corylus maxima*) is a tree that is closely related to the hazel. It is named after the Frankish abbot **St Philibert** (died 684), because his feast day (22 August) falls in the nutting season.

fink

The word **fink** is used chiefly in US and Canadian slang for a strikebreaker, informer or a contemptible or unpleasant person. There are a number of different theories as to the word's origin. One possible suggestion is that fink is an altered form of pink, which is short for **Pinkerton**, the name of the strikebreakers in the Homestead steel strike of 1892.

flora

The word **flora** refers to plant life in general or that of a particular area or period; it often complements fauna (qv). The term derives from **Flora**, the Roman goddess of flowers, youth and spring, whose name comes from the Latin *flos* (flower). The spring festival (Floralia) in her honour was established in 283 BC and provided an excuse for wild, uninhibited conduct.

Foley artist

In the film industry, a **Foley artist** is a technician who adds post-production sound effects to a film. During filming, the actors' dialogue is virtually all that is picked up by the microphones. All other sounds, such as footsteps or a door closing, are recreated afterwards by Foley artists in sound studios. **Jack Foley** (1891–1967) was an American film technician who, in the early days of sound on film, invented the techniques used to produce these sound effects.

forsythia

Forsythia is the name given to a genus of ornamental shrubs of the olive family that have bright yellow bell-shaped flowers which appear before the leaves in early spring. The name honours the British botanist **William Forsyth** (1737–1804). A Scottish gardener and horticulturist, Forsyth became superintendent of the Royal Gardens of St James's and Kensington. He may have personally brought the forsythia shrub from its native China and introduced it to Britain.

Fosbury flop

Dick Fosbury (born 1947) was an American high-jumper who invented a revolutionary new technique. Instead of the traditional 'straddle' method, which involves jumping while facing the bar and then swinging one leg and then the other over the bar, in the **Fosbury flop** the jumper throws his or her body backwards over the bar with arched back. This method proved so successful for Fosbury that he won the gold medal at the 1968 Olympic Games in Mexico City. Subsequently, the Fosbury flop became the standard method used in the high-jump event.

> After Fosbury won his gold medal, an American coach said, 'Kids imitate champions. If they try to imitate Fosbury, he'll wipe out an entire generation of high jumpers because they all will have broken necks.'

Foucault pendulum

A **Foucault pendulum** is a heavy free-swinging weight suspended from a long wire, whose plane of motion appears to change in relation to the rotation of the earth. By means of this pendulum, its inventor, the French physicist **Jean-Bernard Léon Foucault** (1819–1868), demonstrated, in 1851, the rotation of the earth on its axis. Foucault also invented the gyroscope in 1852.

Franciscan

Franciscans are members of the Order of Friars Minor founded by **St Francis of Assisi** in 1209. In its original form, the distinctive feature of this order was its insistence on complete poverty of individual friars and corporately of the whole order.

St Francis (original name Giovanni di Bernardone; 1182–1226) was the son of a wealthy merchant, who renounced his worldly possessions in 1205, turning to a life of prayer. By 1209 he had gathered a band of disciples around him. He composed for himself and his associates a Primitive Rule – now lost, but it seems to have been composed mainly of passages from the Gospels. In 1212 he presented this rule to Pope Innocent III, who gave his approval to the new order. St Francis later travelled widely, retiring in 1220 from leadership of his order, and, according to tradition, receiving the stigmata of Christ in 1224. He is remembered for his deep humility and generosity, his simple faith and his love of God, his fellow-men and nature.

The Franciscan Order has known decline and division since St Francis' time, but has remained a missionary and charitable part of the church.

frangipane

Frangipane is a pastry filled with cream and almonds. The name (often spelt **frangipani**) is also applied to the shrub *Plumeria rubra* of the periwinkle family (red jasmine) and to a perfume prepared from this plant or resembling the odour of its flowers.

The origin of frangipane is uncertain. It seems that the word came via French from the sixteenth-century Italian nobleman, the **Marquis Muzio Frangipani**, who first invented a perfume for scenting gloves. It may well have been the marquis or a relative of his who originally prepared the pastry named in his honour.

Frankenstein

A **Frankenstein's monster** is the product of an inventor that then destroys its creator. The expression comes originally from the name **Baron Frankenstein** in the novel *Frankenstein, or the Modern Prometheus* (1818) by the English novelist Mary Wollstonecraft Shelley (1797–1851). The novel describes how the hero, the philosopher Baron Frankenstein, creates an immense and

> Frankenstein's monster was memorably played on screen by Boris Karloff in *Frankenstein* (1931) and its sequels.

repulsive monster out of inanimate matter; the monster gets out of control and eventually murders its creator. In contemporary usage, the name Frankenstein is often applied to the monster itself rather than its creator.

Fraunhofer lines

Joseph von Fraunhofer (1787–1826) was a German physicist and optician. In 1814 he observed numerous dark lines in the sun's spectrum, now known as the **Fraunhofer lines**. He also made significant improvements to the design of telescopes and other optical instruments.

Fraunhofer's success was due in part to a great misfortune. The son of a lens-maker, he was orphaned as a boy and apprenticed to an apothecary in Munich; but he was to be the only survivor when the dilapidated tenement in which he lived collapsed. Watching the rescue was the Elector of Bavaria, Charles Theodore, who was so moved by the boy's predicament that he bought him out of the apprenticeship, so enabling him to develop his knowledge and skills.

freesia

Freesia is the name of a genus of ornamental sweet-scented South African plants of the iris family, grown for their yellow, pink or white flowers. The plants are named after the German physician **Friedrich Heinrich Theodor Freese** (died 1876).

Fresnel lens

In the field of applied optics, a **Fresnel lens** is a type of compound lens that consists of several smaller lenses arranged in a flat surface of short focal length. Fresnel lenses are used in lighthouses, to produce two parallel beams of light, and in theatrical spotlights.

The French physicist **Augustin Jean Fresnel** (1788–1827), an adherent of Huygens' wave theory of light, was the first person to establish that the wave motion of light is transverse rather than longitudinal, and the first person to produce circularly polarized light.

Freudian slip

A **Freudian slip** is a slip of the tongue that is considered to reveal an unconscious thought of the speaker's mind. The expression is often used to describe a word that is uttered unintentionally but which is thought nearer to the truth than the word the speaker originally had in mind.

The expression 'Freudian slip' comes from the teachings of the Austrian psychiatrist **Sigmund Freud** (1856–1939), who pioneered psychoanalysis. Freud developed the method of free association – he encouraged his patients to pursue verbally a particular train of thought. His *Interpretation of Dreams* (1899) analysed dreams in terms of unconscious childhood experiences and desires. His insistence that mental disorders had sexual causes that originated in childhood led to his estrangement from many of his colleagues.

> Freud conceded that not everything has to have a deep or inner meaning, saying, 'Sometimes a cigar is just a cigar.'

In basic psychoanalytic terms, a Freudian slip is seen as a momentary lapse in a person's defensive position; thoughts or feelings that have been repressed are then unintentionally expressed.

Friday

The name of the sixth day of the week comes from the Old English *Frigedaeg*, the day of the Norse goddess **Frig** (or **Frigga**), the wife of

Woden and goddess of married love. In some legends she is identified with Freya, the Norse goddess of love and fertility and the counterpart of the Roman goddess Venus. It is said that as Wednesday and Thursday (qqv) had been named after Frig's husband Woden and her son Thor, **Friday** was assigned to her in order to appease her.

A **man Friday** is a trustworthy, loyal male employed for general duties. The expression comes from the name of the native servant in the novel *Robinson Crusoe* (published in 1719) by the English writer Daniel Defoe (c. 1660–1731). The expression **girl Friday** is formed, on the analogy of man Friday, for female general assistant, particularly in an office.

Friedreich's ataxia

 Friedreich's ataxia is an inherited degenerative disease that affects the nervous system, causing muscle weakness, speech disorders and heart disease. It is characterized by twitching and lack of muscular coordination. This disease is named after **Nikolaus Friedreich** (1825–1882), the German clinician and neurologist who described it.

fuchsia

 Fuchsia is the name of a genus of ornamental shrubs and herbs native to Central and South America; they have showy drooping deep red, purple, pink or white flowers. The name honours the German botanist and physician **Leonhard Fuchs** (1501–1566). Fuchs's book on medicinal plants, *De historia stirpium* (1503), was widely known at the time; he was professor of medicine at the University of Tübingen from 1535. The plant was named in honour of Fuchs in 1703 by the French monk and botanist Charles Plumier (1646–1704).

furphy

In informal, chiefly Australian, usage a **furphy** is an unlikely or ridiculous rumour or story. The word probably derives from the name **Furphy**, a supplier of water and sanitation carts in Australia in World War I. The name was printed on the water tanks and the latrine buckets used by the Australian troops; they therefore came to describe news of the war obtained at these centres of gossip as furphies. An alternative, less likely, theory suggests that the origin lies with the name of the Australian writer **Joseph Furphy** (1843–1913), who wrote stories under the pseudonym of Tom Collins.

G

gadolinite

The black or brown mineral known as **gadolinite** is a silicate of the metallic elements iron, beryllium and yttrium. It is named after the Finnish chemist **Johann Gadolin** (1760–1852), who discovered and analysed it at Stockholm in 1794.

The metallic element **gadolinium**, which occurs in gadolinite, is also named after Gadolin. The element was discovered by the Swiss chemist J C G Marignac in 1880.

Galahad

In Arthurian legend, **Sir Galahad** is the most virtuous knight of the Round Table. He is the son of Lancelot and Elaine and is, in many romances, the only knight who succeeds in the quest for the Holy Grail. As one tradition has it, Galahad was added by Walter Map (c. 1140–c. 1209) to the Arthurian legends. The name of **Galahad** has come to stand for chivalrous male purity and nobility.

galenical

The ideas of the Greek physician **Galen** (AD 129–199) dominated medicine for well over a thousand years after his death. He wrote numerous treatises on medical theory and practice; and although some of his views are now known to have been mistaken, his experiments and findings – for example that the spinal cord is important in muscle activity – proved significant in the study of medicine. His name is still remembered in the adjective **galenical**, for a medicine that is prepared from plant or animal tissue rather than being chemically synthesized.

> **The name Galen was used for the ape played by Roddy McDowell in the television series *Planet of the Apes*.**

gallium

The metallic element known as **gallium** was first identified in 1875 by the French chemist **Paul Lecoq de Boisbaudran** (died 1912). It is said that the name derives from the Latin translation (*gallus*) of the French word *coq* (cock) in the name of its discoverer.

gallize

To **gallize** wine is to add water and sugar to the grape juice or must during its fermentation in order to increase the quantity of wine produced. This process is named after **Ludwig Gall** (1791–1863) of Trier, Germany, who originated it.

See also **chaptalize**.

Gallup poll

A **Gallup poll** is a survey of the views of a representative sample of the population on a particular issue; it is used especially as a means of forecasting election results. The poll is named after the American statistician **George Horace Gallup** (1901–1984), who originally devised the method for assessing public opinion in advertising. Following his successful prediction of the result of the 1936 American presidential election, his techniques have been widely used, and developed, by different organizations, not only to forecast voting patterns but also to provide the basis of many other statistical surveys.

> Gallup is reported to have said, 'I could prove God statistically.'

galvanize

Galvanize means to cover iron or steel with a protective zinc coating and, in a derived sense, to stimulate into sudden action. The word comes from the name of the Italian physician **Luigi Galvani** (1737–1798).

Galvani observed that the muscles of a frog twitched when they were touched by metal contacts. He thought this effect was caused by 'animal electricity', and it was his fellow-countryman Volta who later provided the correct explanation, that the current was produced by the contacts of the metals themselves. Nevertheless, Galvani undertook a great deal of research in the development of electricity, and his name is linked both with the verb galvanize and the noun **galvanometer**, an instrument used to measure small electric currents.

gamp

Gamp is sometimes used in informal British usage for a large umbrella, especially one that is loosely tied. The word comes from the name of the nurse **Mrs Sarah Gamp** in the novel *Martin Chuzzlewit* (1843–1844) by Charles Dickens who is known for her large, untidily tied umbrella.

Garamond

The style of type known as **Garamond** derives its name from its designer, the French type founder **Claude Garamond** (died 1561). Garamond was largely responsible for the move away from Gothic or 'black-letter' printing fonts towards the modern 'roman' fonts. Although his designs were highly influential, he was a failure as a businessman and died in poverty.

Some modern type designs that bear the name Garamond are not in fact closely

A modern Garamond typeface:
ABCDEFGHIJKLMNOPQRSTUVWXYZ
abcdefghijklmnopqrstuvwxyz

related to his designs, but are based on types that were mistakenly attributed to him.

gardenia

Gardenia is the name of a genus of ornamental tropical shrubs and trees cultivated for their large, fragrant, often white, flowers. The name does not come from the word garden, as might be thought, but from the name of the Scottish-American botanist **Alexander Garden** (1730–1791). Dr Garden was a physician who spent much of his life in Charleston, South Carolina. He not only practised medicine but devoted a great deal of his time to collecting specimens of different plants and animals. He is said to have discovered the conger eel and several snakes and herbs. He pursued a vigorous correspondence with Linnaeus and other European naturalists, even seeking to persuade Linnaeus to name a plant after him. Dr Garden's wishes were eventually fulfilled: in 1760 Linnaeus named the genus in his honour.

gargantuan

The word **gargantuan** means 'enormous or colossal'; it derives from the name **Gargantua**, the gigantic king in the novel *Gargantua* (1534) by the French satirist François Rabelais (c. 1494–1553). Gargantua's appetite was so enormous that he once ate six pilgrims in a salad, and it is to food and appetites that the adjective gargantuan is most often applied.

garibaldi

A **garibaldi** is a woman's loose, long-sleeved blouse or, alternatively, a kind of biscuit containing a layer of currants. The word derives from the name of the Italian patriot and soldier **Giuseppe Garibaldi** (1807–1882). The blouse was so named because it resembled the red shirt worn by Garibaldi and his thousand Redshirt followers in the Risorgimento – the nineteenth-century Italian nationalist movement. Garibaldi led his thousand volunteers to conquer Sicily and Naples, so enabling South Italy to be reunited with the North (1860–1861). It is said that the red shirts worn by Garibaldi and his men were presented to him by the government in Uruguay, while he was gathering troops there.

It is uncertain how the biscuit came to be named after him, although it may be that he was fond of such delicacies.

Gatling gun

A **Gatling gun** was an early type of machine-gun. Mounted on wheels, it had a revolving cluster of barrels, the gunner controlling its rate of fire by means of a hand crank. The gun is named after its inventor, the

American **Richard Jordan Gatling** (1818–1903). Patented in 1862, the Gatling was used in the later stages of the American Civil War (1861–1865); it was discarded before the beginning of World War I.

The name survives in the word **gat**, slang for a revolver or pistol.

Gaullism

Gaullism refers to the French political movement devoted to supporting the principles and policies of General, later President, **Charles de Gaulle** (1890–1970). Promoted to general in World War II (1940), he became leader of the French forces organized in London and a symbol of French patriotism. After the war he was president of a provisional government

> De Gaulle said, 'The French will only be united under the threat of danger. How else can one govern a country that produces 246 different types of cheese?'

(1945–1946), and later, of the Fifth Republic (1958–1969). As president of the Fifth Republic, de Gaulle emphasized the status of the presidency and the supremacy of national interest; his independent foreign policy was aimed at re-establishing France as a world power. Gaullist principles continue to be a dominant influence in contemporary French politics.

gauss

The **gauss** is the unit of magnetic flux density in the centimetre–gram–second system of measurement. The unit is named after the German mathematician **Karl Friedrich Gauss** (1777–1855). Gauss – who is regarded as one of the greatest mathematicians of all time – is known for significant mathematical work in the fields of probability theory and number theory; he also applied mathematics to electricity, magnetism and astronomy.

Gauss's name is also remembered in the word **degauss**, meaning 'to demagnetize'. During World War II, Germany developed a magnetic mine for use at sea, the mine being detonated by the magnetism of an approaching ship. Equipment was then designed to degauss the ship: to neutralize the magnetic field of the ship's hull.

Gay-Lussac's law

The law of expansion of gases known as Charles's law (qv) is also sometimes known as **Gay-Lussac's law** after the French scientist **Joseph Louis Gay-Lussac** (1778–1850). Gay-Lussac held a number of senior academic posts in France, including professor of physics at the Sorbonne (1808–1832) and professor of chemistry at the National Museum of Natural History (from 1832). In 1808 he independently published findings about the expansion of gases that were more accurate than Charles's.

Geiger counter

A **Geiger counter** is an electronic instrument that is used to measure the presence and intensity of radiation. The instrument is named after the German physicist **Hans Geiger** (1882–1945), who developed it with the help of the German scientist Walter M Müller (1905–1979). Research by Geiger and Müller built on investigations undertaken by the British physicist Ernest Rutherford (1871–1937). Geiger later became professor of physics at the Universities of Kiel (1925–1929) and Tübingen (1929–1936), and the Technische Hochschule, Berlin (from 1936).

gentian

Gentian is the name of a group of plants (genus: *Gentiana*) with showy, mainly blue, flowers; many alpine perennials are gentians. The name of the plant is said to derive from **Gentius**, a second-century-BC king of Illyria, an ancient region on the Adriatic. Gentius is believed to have discovered the medicinal properties of the plant now known as yellow gentian (*Gentiana lutea*).

georgette

Georgette (or **georgette crêpe**) is a fine, thin, strong, silk crêpe used in clothing, especially for blouses and gowns. The fabric is named after the late-nineteenth-century Parisian dressmaker **Madame Georgette de la Plante**.

Georgian

The **Georgian** style of architecture is that which was dominant in the reigns of the kings **George I** to **George IV** (1714–1830). The style is marked by well-proportioned gracefulness.

Georgian is also a term applied in a literary sense to the writers, especially poets, during the reign of **King George V** (1910–1936).

The American state of **Georgia**, on the south-east coast of the USA, is named after **King George II** (1683–1760; reign 1727–1760). Founded in 1732, it was the last of the 13 original states.

The **George Cross** (GC) is a decoration awarded for bravery, especially to civilians, instituted in 1940 by **King George VI** (1894–1952; reign 1936–1952). It is equivalent in status to the Victoria Cross.

See also **Victorian**.

gerbera

Gerbera is a tropical plant of the daisy family with large, brightly coloured flowers. It is native to South Africa, but is now grown in greenhouses in cooler climates. It was named in honour of **Traugott Gerber** (died 1743), the German naturalist who started the first botanical garden in Moscow in the 1700s.

Geronimo

'**Geronimo**', an exclamation of delight or surprise, was originally the cry of American airborne paratroopers as they jumped from their planes into battle. The name shouted is that of the American Apache Indian chief **Geronimo** (1829–1909), but there are different theories as to how the expression was adopted. One suggestion is that the cry was inspired by paratroopers in training seeing a film featuring the Apache Indian

> **Geronimo was finally captured in 1886, and became something of a celebrity when he visited the St Louis World's Fair and other expositions.**

chief. Others suggest that Geronimo, being hotly pursued by the cavalry, shouted out his name as he plunged on horseback down an almost vertical cliff into a river below.

gerrymander

To **gerrymander** means to divide an area into new electoral districts in order to give one party an unfair advantage. It is also used in a derived sense to mean to manipulate to obtain an

> **Gerry went on to become the vice-president of the USA from 1813 to 1814.**

unfair advantage for oneself. The word comes from the name of the American politician **Elbridge Gerry** (1744–1814). While governor of Massachusetts (1810), Gerry sought to rearrange the electoral boundaries in favour of his own party in the forthcoming elections. It is said that one day the painter Gilbert Stuart came into the offices of the *Boston Sentinel* newspaper, and, seeing the newly redrawn district on a map, proceeded to draw a head, wings and claws round the district that was already in the shape of a salamander. 'That will do for a salamander,' declared the artist. 'A Gerrymander, you mean,' replied the editor, Benjamin Russell, and so the word was born.

Gideon

The **Gideons** are an interdenominational Christian group who have the aim of making the Bible freely available. Originally founded in Wisconsin, USA, in 1899, the organization places Bibles in hotel rooms, hospital wards, etc. The name derives from the Old Testament judge **Gideon**, who was noted for his leadership of a small army who triumphed over the Midianites (Judges 6–7).

gilbert

A **gilbert** is the unit of magnetomotive force in the centimetre–gram–second system of measurement. It is named after **William Gilbert** (1544–1603), English physicist and physician to Queen Elizabeth I. Gilbert is noted for his pioneering work on magnetism, especially his treatise *De Magnete* (1600), and he has come to be known as the father of electricity. Gilbert was responsible for introducing many new terms into the language, including electricity, electric force and magnetic pole.

Gilbertian

Gilbertian is used to refer to the satirical light humour of the English comic dramatist **Sir William Schwenk Gilbert** (1836–1911). Originally a barrister, in 1869 Gilbert met the composer Arthur Sullivan (1842–1900), for whom he wrote the librettos of 14 operettas for the impresario Richard D'Oyly Carte, including *Trial by Jury* (1873), *HMS Pinafore* (1878), *The Pirates of Penzance* (1879), *Iolanthe* (1882), *The Mikado* (1885), *Rudigore* (1887), *The Yeoman of the Guard* (1888) and *The Gondoliers* (1889). Thus the adjective Gilbertian has come to mean 'fanciful, wittily humorous', in the style of these ever-popular operas.

Gill

The style of type known as **Gill** derives its name from its designer, the British typographer **Eric Gill** (1882–1940). Gill trained as an architect, but then took up letter-cutting and masonry and later engraving. He was a founder member of Artists International, a group set up in 1933 to oppose Fascism.

A Gill typeface:
ABCDEFGHIJKLMNOPQRSTUVWXYZ
abcdefghijklmnopqrstuvwxyz

girl Friday

See **Friday**.

Gladstone bag

A **Gladstone bag** is an article of hand luggage: a bag that has flexible
sides set on a rigid frame, it opens into two equal-sized compartments.
The bag is named after the British statesman and prime minister
William Ewart Gladstone, known as the Grand Old Man
(1809–1898), but he did not invent it. It seems that the article of hand
luggage was named in Gladstone's honour because he undertook so
much travelling in the course of his public career. The bag was designed
for the purpose of being particularly convenient for travellers.

godetia

 Godetia is a North American garden plant, closely related to the
evening primrose, that is valued for its showy red or lilac flowers. It
takes its name from **Charles Henri Godet** (1797–1879), the Swiss
botanist.

Goethian

The German **Johann Wolfgang von Goethe** (1749–1832) was not
only a great poet and writer; he was also a scholar and scientist. His
powerful writings, notably *Götz von Berlichingen* (1773), *The Sorrows of
Young Werther* (1774), *Iphigenie auf Tauris* (1787) and *Faust* (1808; 1832),
have inspired the adjective **Goethian**, 'intellectual, yet kind and
benevolent'.

His scientific work, for example *The Theory of Colours* (1810) and
Metamorphosis of Plants (1817–1824), led to a mineral being named after
him: **goethite**, the yellow-brown mineral that is formed as a result of
the oxidation and hydration of iron minerals.

Goldwynism

> Goldwyn is reported as saying, 'Any
> man who goes to a psychiatrist
> should have his head examined.'

**Samuel
Goldwyn** (born
Samuel Goldfish;
1882–1974) was a very distinguished Hollywood film producer, who
was born in Poland but emigrated as a child first to England and then to

the USA. His frequent misuse of English, his adopted language, often to humorous effect, became known as **Goldwynisms**. Some examples of Goldwynisms are 'Gentlemen, kindly include me out' and 'A verbal contract isn't worth the paper it's written on.'

Gongorism

Gongorism is used to refer to an artificial literary style whose chief characteristics include elaborate constructions and obscure allusions and comparisons. It is named after the Spanish priest and lyric poet **Luis de Góngora y Argote** (1561–1627). Góngora's earlier works are not written in such a style, but his later works, including notably *Soledades* (1613), show many Gongoristic elements. The style resembles euphuism (qv).

Good Samaritan

A **Good Samaritan** is a kind person who selflessly helps people in distress. The allusion is to the biblical story told by Jesus (Luke 10:25–37); the **Good Samaritan** has come to stand for a helpful person who assists others, often to the point of inconvenience and without the slightest thought of personal gain.

By extension, the name **Samaritans** has been given to those who man the voluntary telephone service set up to help those in need. Established in Britain in 1953, the Samaritans provide a confidential and anonymous service to anyone in despair.

goon

In American slang, a **goon** is a bully or a hired thug, particularly one who was hired to terrorize workers during industrial disputes in the USA in the late 1930s. The word gained currency following the creation by Elzie C Segar (1894–1938), the American cartoonist, of a cartoon character called **Alice the Goon** in the late 1920s. Alice the Goon was a subhuman but good-hearted character in Segar's comic strip called *Thimble Theater*, which is better known today as *Popeye*. However, the word goon probably predates Alice; it may have originally come from the dialect word *gooney*, meaning 'a simpleton'.

Gordian knot

The expression 'cut the **Gordian knot**' means to solve a complex problem by a single decisive, brilliant action. The phrase alludes to the story of **Gordius**, the peasant king of Phrygia in Asia Minor. Gordius dedicated his chariot to Jupiter, fastening the yoke to the beam of his chariot with such an intricate knot that no one could untie it. The legend developed that whoever could untie the knot would reign over the whole empire of Asia. When Alexander the Great passed through the town (333 BC) he is said to have simply cut the knot with his sword and so claimed fulfilment of the legend in himself.

Gordon Bennett

The name **Gordon Bennett** is used as an exclamation to express great surprise: 'Gordon Bennett! It's Jack – how are you? It must be years since I've seen you!' The expression probably comes from

> **Gordon Bennett's engagement to a New York socialite ended abruptly after he turned up at his fiancée's family's mansion in an inebriated state and proceeded to urinate in the living-room fireplace in front of his astonished hosts.**

James Gordon Bennett (1841–1918), an American journalist and playboy. He is famous for his sponsorship of balloon races at the beginning of the twentieth century. Like the slang expression 'gorblimey', Gordon (Bennett) was originally used as a euphemism to avoid using the name of God directly.

Gordon setter

The black-and-tan breed of dog known as the **Gordon setter** originated in Scotland. The breed was developed by the Scottish nobleman **Alexander Gordon** (1743–1827), who was also a sportsman and a writer of folk ballads.

Gore-Tex

Gore-Tex is a trademark for a breathable water-repellent windproof fabric made of two or three layers laminated together, which is used mainly to make outerwear and footwear. This fabric, whose scientific name is polytetrafluoroethylene (or PTFE), is produced by W L Gore & Associates, a company that was started in 1958 by **Wilbert and Genevieve Gore** and is world-famous for fluoropolymer technology and manufacturing.

Graafian follicle

A **Graafian follicle** is one of the small liquid-filled sacs in the ovary of a mammal that contains the developing egg. The name Graafian follicle honours their discoverer, the Dutch physician and anatomist **Regnier de Graaf** (1641–1673).

gradgrind

A hard, utilitarian person who remorselessly pursues facts and statistics is sometimes known as a **gradgrind**. The word derives from **Thomas Gradgrind**, a character in the novel *Hard Times* (1854) by Charles Dickens. Gradgrind is a hardware merchant in Coketown, a drab northern industrial centre. Considering himself to be an 'eminently practical man', he suppresses the imaginative and spiritual aspects of the education of his children, Tom and Louisa.

In the novel, Gradgrind says, 'Now what I want is facts. Teach these boys and girls nothing but facts. Facts alone are wanted in life. Plant nothing else and root out everything else.'

graham flour

Graham flour is a Northern American term for wholemeal flour. The name derives from the American dietary reformer **Sylvester Graham** (1794–1851). Originally a Presbyterian minister, Graham advocated temperance and also campaigned widely for changes in Americans' diets, especially the use of unbolted wheat flour. His efforts were rewarded by the emergence in the 1830s of Graham food stores and Graham Societies. He is still remembered in America by **graham crackers** and **graham bread** as well as graham flour.

grangerize

The verb **grangerize** means to illustrate a book with pictures taken from other books or publications. The word comes from the name of the English writer and clergyman **James Granger** (1723–1776), who in 1769 published a book entitled *Biographical History of England from Egbert the Great to the Revolution, Consisting of Characters Dispersed in Different Classes, and Adapted to a Methodical Catalogue of Engraved British Heads*. The book contained blank pages that were to be filled by cutting illustrations out of other books. A craze (**Grangerism**) developed, leading to the mutilation of many other valuable books.

> Granger is said to have cut 14,000 engraved portraits from other books.

Granny Smith

Granny Smith is the name of a variety of hard green apple that can be cooked or eaten raw. It is named after the Australian gardener **Maria Ann Smith**, known as Granny Smith (died 1870). Granny Smith first grew the apple at Eastwood, Sydney in the 1860s.

Graves' disease

Graves' disease (exophthalmic goitre) is a disorder of the thyroid gland accompanied by protrusion of the eyeballs. It is named after the Irish physician **Robert James Graves** (1796–1853) who first identified it in 1835.

> Graves was a friend of the artist J M W Turner, and travelled around Europe with him before starting to practise medicine.

Great Scott

The expression of great surprise, '**Great Scott!**' probably alludes to **General Winheld Scott** (1786–1866). Scott was a hero of the Mexican War (1846–1848) and candidate in the US presidential election in 1852. The exclamation may originally have been applied in praise of the hero's achievements.

greengage

The variety of greenish or greenish-yellow plums known as **greengage** comes from a combination of the word green and the name Gage. It was the English botanist **Sir William Gage** (1777–1864) who introduced the variety of plum to England from France about 1725.

Interestingly, the French word for a greengage is also eponymous. This variety of plum was brought in the early sixteenth century from Italy to France, where it was named *reine-claude* (Queen Claude) in honour of Queen Claudia, wife of King Francis I of France, the reigning monarch of the time.

Gregorian calendar

In the old-style Julian calendar (qv), the average length of the year was 365¼ days. This was approximately eleven minutes longer than the actual time it takes for the earth to rotate around the sun, as calculated from astronomical and seasonal data. In order to rectify this error **Pope Gregory XIII** introduced a new system in 1582, which became law in Britain and the colonies in 1752 and is now used throughout most of the world. Under the new-style **Gregorian** system, named in the Pope's honour, leap years are every year that is divisible by four and century years divisible by 400 (thus 2000 was a leap year, but 1900 was not). To allow for the alteration to the new system, eleven days were omitted, 2 September in 1752 being followed by 14 September.

Gregorian chant

The **Gregorian chant** is the official liturgical plainsong of the Roman Catholic Church. The term derives

> Gregory I was known as Gregory the Great.

from the name of **Pope Gregory I** (c. AD 540–604). It was under his papacy (590–604) that the whole subject of plainsong was reviewed, and the vocal, unaccompanied chant now known as the Gregorian chant was introduced.

Gresham's law

Sir Thomas Gresham (c. 1519–1579) was the English financier who founded the Royal Exchange (1568). He is perhaps better known for the so-called **Gresham's law**, attributed to him in the mid-nineteenth century. Gresham's law, usually formulated as 'Bad money drives out good money', means that if two different types of coin are in circulation, the less valuable will remain in circulation, while the more valuable will be hoarded and will eventually disappear from circulation.

Grimm's law

Grimm's law is a rule that describes the change of consonants in the Germanic and Indo-European languages. Named after its formulator, the German philologist **Jakob Ludwig Karl Grimm** (1785–1863), Grimm's law explains, for example, the change from Latin p-sounds to English f-sounds, as in the progression from Latin *piscis* to English *fish*.

Jakob Grimm is also known with his brother Wilhelm Karl (1786–1859) for their *Kinder und Hausmärchen*, a collection of German folk tales, published 1812–1814, which came to be known in English as *Grimm's Fairy Tales*.

grog

Grog is the term for diluted spirits, usually rum, as formerly given to sailors. The word comes from **Old Grog**, the nickname of the British

Vernon became a rear-admiral at the tender age of 24.

admiral Sir Edward Vernon (1684–1757). Old Grog began the issue of diluted alcoholic spirits in 1740, in order to put an end to drunken brawling aboard his ship, and soon the sailors were calling the drink grog. The nickname Old Grog arose from the fact that in rough weather the admiral wore a cloak made of grogram – a coarse fabric, usually of wool and mohair or silk.

grundyism

See **Mrs Grundy**.

Guillain–Barré syndrome

Guillain–Barré syndrome, which is also known as Landry's paralysis, is an inflammatory disorder of the nerves outside the brain and the spinal cord. It causes weakness and often strange sensations in the extremities or paralysis. This is a long-term and disabling, but not usually fatal, illness. It was named after **Georges Charles Guillain** (1876–1961) and **Jean-Alexandre Barré** (1880–1967), the two French neurologists who first described this syndrome in 1916.

It is now widely believed that President Franklin D Roosevelt may have suffered from Guillain–Barré syndrome.

guillotine

The device for beheading people known as a **guillotine** consists of a heavy blade that slides down between two grooved upright posts. The name of the machine derives from the French physician **Joseph Ignace Guillotin** (1738–1814). Contrary to popular belief, Guillotin did not invent the device; it was designed as a development of similar instruments in use elsewhere in Europe by a colleague of Guillotin, Dr Antoine Louis (1723–1792). Guillotin advocated the use of this machine on humanitarian grounds: it was a speedier and more efficient method than the former practice of putting common criminals to death by means of a clumsy sword. Guillotin therefore proposed to the French National Assembly that this device should be used as a means of capital punishment. The first person to be decapitated by the guillotine was a highwayman in April 1792.

gun

The word **gun**, first recorded in the fourteenth century, may come originally from the Old Norse female name Gunhildr, both elements of which mean 'war'. The list of weapons in the English Exchequer Accounts of 1330–1331 records 'a large ballista [a catapult used to hurl stones] called **Lady Gunhildr**'. With the passage of time, the name became shortened to gunne and then to gun, the word's application also changing, on the invention of the cannon, from a weapon that threw missiles to one that discharged missiles by explosion.

Gunter's chain

A **Gunter's chain** is a measuring device 66 feet (20 m) long used, especially formerly, in surveying. The term derives from the name of the English mathematician and astronomer **Edmund Gunter** (1581–1626).

Gunter's name is also honoured in the **gunter rig**, a kind of ship's rig with a sliding topmast, so called because it resembled a slide-rule invented by Gunter that was used in solving navigational problems.

guppy

A **guppy** is the name of a kind of freshwater fish that is popular in aquariums. The fish is named after the Trinidadian naturalist and clergyman **Robert John Lechmere Guppy** (1836–1916). Guppy sent specimens of the fish to the British Museum in 1868. The male guppy is brightly coloured – hence the alternative name rainbow fish; the female is a prolific breeder and produces live young, rather than eggs, every four weeks.

guy

The word **guy** referring in informal use to a man or fellow (or in contemporary usage, in the plural, any group of people) comes from the first name of the English conspirator **Guy Fawkes** (1570–1606). Fawkes served as a mercenary in the Spanish army in the Netherlands and when he returned to England in 1604 became involved in the Gunpowder Plot. A convert to Roman Catholicism, Fawkes was outraged by the harshness of the anti-Catholic laws imposed by King James I. Together with a group of other Catholics, Fawkes plotted to blow up James I and Parliament on 5 November 1605. The conspirators were informed on and Fawkes was caught red-handed, with the gunpowder in a cellar of the Palace of Westminster. Guy Fawkes and six of the other conspirators were executed the following year. The anniversary of 5 November continues to be remembered in Britain, with firework displays and guys, stuffed effigies of Fawkes, being burnt on bonfires.

H

hahnium

Hahnium is a name that was formerly used for two different artificially produced radioactive transuranic elements: dubnium and hassium. Hahnium was named in honour of the German nuclear physicist and chemist **Otto Hahn** (1879–1968). Together with the Austrian-Swedish physicist Lise Meitner, Hahn discovered the chemical element protactinium in 1917 and, in collaboration with the German physicist Fritz Strassmann (1902–1980), they discovered nuclear fission in 1938. Hahn was awarded the Nobel prize (qv) for chemistry in 1944.

See also **meitnerium**.

Halley's comet

The British astronomer **Edmund Halley** (1656–1742) was the first to realize that comets do not appear haphazardly but have orbital periods. Following his observations in 1682 of the comet that has been named after him, he correctly predicted it would reappear in 1758. Halley was a friend of Sir Isaac Newton and financed the publication of Newton's *Principia* (1686–1687). Halley was appointed to the post of astronomer royal in 1720. The last appearance of **Halley's comet** was in 1985–1986.

Hamitic

A **Hamitic** person, or a **Hamite**, is a member of a group of North African peoples supposedly descended from Noah's son **Ham** from the Old Testament. This group of peoples includes the ancient Egyptians and the Berbers.

See also **Semitic**.

Hammond organ

 A **Hammond organ** is the trademark for a kind of electronic organ that usually has two manual keyboards and a pedal keyboard. The sound is produced electronically to simulate that of a pipe organ ten times its size. The Hammond organ was invented c. 1934 by **Laurens Hammond** (1895–1973), and manufactured by the Hammond Organ Company in Chicago. Hammond was not a musician, but an ex-watchmaker and engineer with a degree in mechanical engineering. The Hammond organ has been used by jazz, blues and rock musicians (such as Jimmy Smith and Booker T), as well as being written for by modern composers (such as Karlheinz Stockhausen).

Hansard

 Hansard is the official verbatim report of debates in the Houses of Parliament in the United Kingdom. The reports are so called after the name of the London printer **Luke Hansard** (1752–1828) who printed the *Journal of the House of Commons* from 1774 onwards. His eldest son, Thomas Curson Hansard (1776–1883), printed the first reports of parliamentary debates in 1803, and the Hansard family continued to print parliamentary reports up to the end of the nineteenth century. Now printed by HM Stationery Office, the official record of the debates is still known as *Hansard*.

Hansen's disease

 Hansen's disease is another name for leprosy. This term was introduced in an attempt to remove the stigma that has been associated with the word leprosy. Hansen's disease is named after **Gerhard Henrik Armauer Hansen** (1841–1912), the Norwegian physician who, in 1873, discovered the bacillus, now known as **Hansen's bacillus**, that causes leprosy. Prior to this discovery, leprosy had been believed to be largely hereditary.

hansom cab

 The **hansom cab**, a light two-wheeled covered carriage, in which the driver sits high up at the back, is named after its designer, the English

architect **Joseph Aloysius Hansom** (1803–1882). Noted for his designs of public buildings and churches, Hansom designed the town hall of Birmingham in 1833. A year later he registered a 'Patent Safety Cab'. These hansom cabs – or hansoms –
quickly became popular and were manufactured in various designs. It seems that Hansom was not so skilled at handling

> **Disraeli called hansom cabs 'the gondolas of London'.**

financial arrangements as designing buildings and vehicles. He is said to have sold his patent rights for a mere £300, while the manufacturers of his designs made fat profits.

See also **brougham**.

Harlequin

The stock character of pantomime, **Harlequin**, has a shaved head, a mask over his face and a diamond-patterned tight-fitting costume. The name may come from the Old French Hellequin, the name of a devil-horseman riding by night, which in turn may derive ultimately from Old English **Herla Cynnig**, King Herle, a legendary king who is identified with the god Odin (Woden).

The Harlequin has its origins in the Italian *commedia dell'arte*. In traditional English pantomime, Harlequin is the mute character who is the foppish lover of the beautiful Columbine. He is supposedly invisible to both the clown and pantaloon and rivals the clown in the affections of Columbine.

Harley-Davidson

Harley-Davidson is a trademark for a large powerful motorcycle manufactured by the Harley-Davidson Motor Company. This American company was launched in 1903 by **William S Harley** (1880–1943) and **Arthur Davidson** (1881–1950). The Harley-Davidson has become an American icon, especially since it was featured in the cult film *Easy Rider* (1969).

Hashimoto's disease

Hashimoto's disease is a chronic inflammation of the thyroid gland, which causes goitre and often results in hypothyroidism, a condition in which there is deficient activity of the thyroid gland. This disease was named after **Hakaru Hashimoto** (1881–1934), the Japanese surgeon who first described this condition in 1912.

havelock

A **havelock** is the cloth cover for a soldier's cap with a long flap that extends down the back, designed to protect the wearer's head and neck from the heat of the sun. The word comes from the name of the English general **Sir Henry Havelock** (1795–1857).

Havelock served for over 34 years with the British army in India, taking only one period of home leave during that time. He is noted for his recapture of Kanpur (Cawnpore) and his holding of Lucknow until relieved by troops under Campbell (1857). It seems unlikely that Havelock actually invented the cloth cover named in his honour, a similar covering having been known for centuries before, but it was the havelock which he devised for his brigades that became known.

> **Havelock died of dysentery just four days after the relief of Lucknow.**

Haversian canals

The **Haversian canals** are the small channels containing blood vessels and nerve fibres that form a network in bone tissue. They were named after **Clopton Havers** (1657–1702), the British physician and anatomist who published the first detailed description of them in 1691.

Hay diet

The **Hay diet** is a 'food-combining' diet, the main rule of which is that carbohydrates and proteins should not be combined in the same meal, with the aim of aiding digestion and achieving weight loss. This diet was introduced in 1911 by the American physician **William Howard Hay** (1866–1940).

Heath Robinson

A **Heath Robinson** device or contraption is one that is absurdly complex in design. The description comes from the name of the English artist **William Heath Robinson** (1872–1944). Known for his drawings depicting ingenious devices used to perform trivial tasks, Robinson was also a serious artist whose illustrations accompanied poems in several books of verse. He also designed stage scenery.

Heaviside layer

The **Heaviside layer** is a former name for the E-layer of the earth's atmosphere – the charged level of the upper atmosphere that reflects medium-frequency radio waves. This layer is 90–150 km above the earth's surface. The Heaviside layer was so called because it was predicted and then discovered by the British physicist **Oliver Heaviside** (1850–1925).

> Heaviside lived the life of an eccentric hermit in Devon. Even after gaining public recognition for his scientific achievements, he was still so poor that at times he could not even afford to pay his gas bills.

The American electrical engineer Arthur Edwin Kennelly (1861–1939), working independently of Heaviside, made a similar prediction in 1902, the same year as Heaviside's prediction, and so the layer is also known as the **Heaviside–Kennelly layer**.

Heaviside is also noted for his development of the mathematical study of electric circuits and his work in vector analysis.

See also **Appleton layer**.

hector

The word **hector** may be used as a noun to refer to a bully or as a verb to mean 'to bully or torment'. The word alludes to the Greek legendary character **Hector**, son of Priam and Hecuba, the Trojan hero of Homer's *Iliad* who was killed by Achilles.

Homer, and English literature up to the seventeenth century, depicted Hector as a gallant warrior. It seems that the derogatory meaning derives from a gang of disorderly youths in London at the end of the seventeenth century. This band of young men took the name Hectors, fancying themselves as models of bravery. In reality, however, their bullying, terrorizing behaviour became infamous and the unfavourable meaning of the word hector became predominant.

Hegelianism

Hegelianism is the system of logic and philosophy of the German idealistic philosopher **Georg Wilhelm Friedrich Hegel** (1770–1831). Hegel's philosophy equates mind and nature, holding that whatever is rational is real and whatever is real is rational. Hegel influenced the thinking of many philosophers, including Karl Marx and Friedrich Engels, and is said to have been an inspiration in Adolf Hitler's view of national socialism. *The Phenomenology of Mind* (1807) and *Encyclopedia of the Philosophical Sciences in Outline* (1817) are among Hegel's major works.

> Hegel said, 'We do not need to be shoemakers to know if our shoes fit.'

Heimlich manoeuvre

The **Heimlich manoeuvre** is a method of dislodging a foreign object from a choking person's windpipe by applying sudden upward pressure to the upper abdomen in a series of thrusts. By lifting the diaphragm, this manoeuvre forces air up from the lungs to make the person cough and force out the obstructing object. The Heimlich manoeuvre was named after **Henry Jay Heimlich** (born 1920), the American surgeon who developed it in 1976. Heimlich also devised an operation to replace the oesophagus.

henry

 The **henry** is the derived metric unit of electric inductance; it is named after the American physicist **Joseph Henry** (1797–1878). Henry is famous for his contributions to electromagnetism, inventing the first electromagnetic motor; he discovered electromagnetic induction independently of the English scientist Michael Faraday.

The US Weather Bureau was established as a result of Henry's meteorological work while he was the first director of the Smithsonian Institute, Washington DC. He is considered the founder of weather forecasting from scientific data in the USA.

Hepplewhite

Hepplewhite is used to describe an eighteenth-century style of English furniture. The style is noted for its graceful, elegant curves, especially in chairs with straight tapering legs and oval or heart-shaped backs with openwork designs. The name of the style honours the English cabinet-maker **George Hepplewhite** (died 1786). Probably originally a Lancastrian, Hepplewhite worked from a shop at St Giles, Cripplegate, in London.

herculean

A **herculean** task is one that requires immense effort or strength. The word comes from **Hercules** (in Greek, Heracles), the son of Zeus and Alcmena and the greatest and strongest of the Greek demigods. While in the service of his rival Eurystheus, Hercules completed twelve supposedly impossible labours: he killed the Nemean lion and the Lernean water-snake Hydra; he captured the Arcadian stag and the Erymanthian boar; cleaned the Augean (qv) stables; killed the ferocious Stymphalian birds; captured the white Cretan bull; caught the man-eating mares of Diomedes; stole the girdle of the Amazon Queen Hippolyte; captured the oxen of Geryon; took the golden apples of Hesperides; and finally brought the three-headed dog Cerberus to its master, Hades. This last task was seen as representing victory over death itself.

hermaphrodite

 A **hermaphrodite** is an animal or plant that has both female and male reproductive organs. The word comes from **Hermaphroditos**, the Greek mythical son of Hermes and Aphrodite, goddess of love. Hermaphroditos refused the love offered by the nymph Salmacis, in whose pool he was bathing. She embraced him, however, and prayed to the gods to make them indissolubly one. The gods answered her prayer and the body of both the nymph and Hermaphroditos grew together as one. From this story of the union of these two beings comes the word hermaphrodite.

hermetic

A **hermetic** seal is one that is airtight, the word hermetic deriving ultimately from the name **Hermes Trismegistus** ('Hermes, thrice-greatest'). This is the Greek name given to the Egyptian god of learning, Thoth, and also the name given after the third century AD to the author of certain writings on alchemy and mysticism. Hermes Trismegistus is traditionally believed to have invented a seal to keep containers airtight by using magical powers.

hertz

 A **hertz** is the derived metric unit of frequency, equal to one cycle per second. (The term may be more familiar in the word **kilohertz**, meaning one thousand hertz or one thousand cycles per second.) The terms honour the German physicist **Heinrich Rudolph Hertz** (1857–1894). Developing the work of the Scottish scientist James Clerk Maxwell, Hertz was the first person to detect radio waves (1888). The type of electromagnetic wave known as the **hertzian wave** is also named after him.

Hilary term

 The term that begins in January at Oxford University and certain other educational institutions is known as the **Hilary term**. The name is chosen because the feast day of St Hilary falls on 13 January. **St Hilary of Poitiers** (c. 315–c. 367) was converted to Christianity from

Neoplatonism and became
Bishop of Poitiers in
about 353. The most
highly regarded Latin
theologian of his time,
he was a leading critic of
the heretical doctrine of Arianism.

> **St Hilary's bed was kept on display in Poitiers Cathedral after his death. It was said that if a madman were to spend a night in it, he would be cured.**

His defence of orthodox beliefs led to his exile for four years. St Hilary's
works include *De Trinitate* (a criticism of Arianism) and *De Synodis*.

Hippocratic oath

The Greek physician **Hippocrates** (c. 460–c. 377 BC) is commonly
regarded as the father of medicine. He has given his name to the
Hippocratic oath traditionally taken by a doctor before commencing
medical practice. The oath comprises a code of medical ethics probably
followed by members of the school of Hippocrates.

Born on the island of Cos, Hippocrates was the most famous physician
of the ancient world. Some of his writings still survive, including his
Aphorisms, of which the most famous reads, in Chaucer's translation,
'The life so short, the craft so long to learn.'

Hitler

A person showing ruthless dictatorial characteristics may be described as
a **Hitler**, with reference to the German dictator **Adolf Hitler** (1889–
1945). Born in Austria, Hitler served in World War I and became
president of the National Socialist German Workers' (Nazi) Party in
1921. After an abortive coup (the Munich Putsch, 1923), Hitler spent
several months in prison, during which
time he wrote *Mein Kampf*, which
expressed his political
philosophy based on the innate
superiority of the Aryan race
and the inferiority of the Jews.

> **Hitler said, 'The broad mass of a nation will more easily fall victim to a big lie than a small one.'**

Hitler was appointed chancellor of Germany in 1933 and a year later
assumed the title of *Führer* (leader). Germany became a totalitarian state,

with Hitler establishing concentration camps to exterminate the Jews. World War II was precipitated by his invasion of Austria (1938), and Czechoslovakia and Poland (1939). He narrowly escaped assassination in 1944 and, in the face of an Allied victory in April 1945, committed suicide.

Hobson's choice

If you were in seventeenth-century England and wanted to hire a horse from **Thomas Hobson** of Cambridge, you would have had no choice at all over which horse you could take. The liveryman Thomas Hobson (1544–1631) is said not to have allowed his customers any right to pick one particular horse, insisting that they always choose the horse nearest the door. Hence the expression **Hobson's choice**, a situation in which there appear to be alternatives but, in fact, no real alternative is offered and there is only one thing you can do.

Hodgkin's disease

Hodgkin's disease (also known as lymphoma or lymphadenoma) is a cancerous disease marked by an enlargement of the lymph nodes, liver, etc. The disease is named after the English physician **Thomas Hodgkin** (1798–1866), who first described it in 1832. A physician at Guy's Hospital, London, Hodgkin was one of the most distinguished pathologists of his time.

Homeric

The adjective **Homeric** is used to mean heroic, majestic or imposing. **Homer** is the presumed author of the great epic poems the *Iliad* and *Odyssey*, but little is in fact known about his life. He is believed to have lived in the eighth century BC and, according to legend, was blind.

The expression '**Homer sometimes nods**' means that even the wisest of people make mistakes. The source of the expression is Horace: 'If Homer, usually good, nods for a moment, I think it shame' (*Ars Poetica*) and Byron (*Don Juan*):

> *We learn from Horace, 'Homer sometimes sleeps';*
> *We feel without him, Wordsworth sometimes wakes.*

hooker

Hooker is a slang word for a female prostitute. The word is popularly associated with the American Civil War general **Joseph Hooker**, known as 'Fighting Joe' (1814–1879). The story goes that Hooker regularly received prostitutes into his camp, and when people asked who these women were, they received the reply, 'They're Hooker's'. This story may have popularized the use of the word, but in fact the word has been recorded in this meaning as early as 1845.

hooligan

The origin of the word **hooligan**, meaning a rough lawless young person, seems to lie with the name **Patrick Hooligan**, an Irish criminal who was active in London in the 1890s. It is said that Pat Hooligan and his family – their real name may have been Houlihan – basing themselves at the Lamb and Flag, a public house in south London, attracted a gang of rowdy followers.

Hoover

Hoover is a trademark used to describe a type of vacuum cleaner. The name comes from the American **William Henry Hoover** (1849–1932). Hoover, however, did not invent this cleaner; he was a perceptive businessman who saw the possible sales of a new kind of cleaner that had been made by a J Murray Spangler, a caretaker in an Ohio department store. Hoover persuaded Spangler to sell his rights to the invention and so, in 1908, it was the Hoover Suction Company that produced the first Hoover – selling for $70. Four years later vacuum cleaners made by Hoover were exported to Britain, where, in fact, the vacuum cleaner had been invented in 1901 by the Scotsman Hubert Cecil Booth (1871–1955). However, it is neither Booth's nor Spangler's name that is remembered today, Hoover now being used not only generically as a noun to refer to a vacuum cleaner but also as a verb to mean 'to clean with a vacuum cleaner'.

hotspur

The word **hotspur**, meaning a rash or fiery person, was originally applied to the English rebel Sir Henry Percy (1364–1403), known as **Harry Hotspur**. Together with his father, also Sir Henry Percy, 1st Earl of Northumberland, he led a revolt against King Henry IV, whom earlier he and his father had supported. Impetuous and headstrong – hence his nickname – he was killed at the Battle of Shrewsbury. Shakespeare featured the rash, fearless character of Hotspur in *Richard II* and *Henry IV*.

Houdini act

Someone who does a **Houdini act** succeeds in performing an astonishing act of escape or disappearance. The expression honours **Harry Houdini**, the stage name of the American magician and escapologist Ehrich Weiss (1874–1926). Of Hungarian-Jewish descent, Weiss assumed the name of Harry Houdini to echo the name of the great French magician Jean Eugene Robert Houdin (1805–1871). Houdini became world-famous for his ability to escape from handcuffs, straitjackets, locked chests, etc, even when under water.

> **Houdini is said to have given Joseph 'Buster' Keaton his nickname after watching him fall down a flight of stairs as a child.**

Hoyle

See **according to Hoyle**.

Hubble Space Telescope

The **Hubble Space Telescope** is a telescope mounted on a satellite that was launched into orbit around the Earth at an altitude of 610 km by the space shuttle *Discovery* in 1990. Various technical faults discovered after the launch were corrected in 1994 by five astronauts. Because of its position in space, the Hubble Telescope is able to produce images of distant parts of the universe that are far superior to those produced by any ground-based instrument.

The Hubble Space Telescope was named in honour of **Edwin Powell Hubble** (1889–1953), an American astronomer who investigated nebulae and the galaxies. Hubble proved that the universe was both larger and older than had previously been believed and that it was still expanding. He devised **Hubble's constant**, a measure of the rate of expansion of the universe.

Huguenot

The **Huguenots** were Calvinist French Protestants, especially in the sixteenth and seventeenth centuries. The name of this religious movement comes from the Middle French dialect word *huguenot*, which is an alteration of the Swiss–German *eidgnoss*, 'confederate', influenced by the name of the Swiss political leader **Besançon Hugues** (died 1532). Hugues was a Protestant syndic and party leader in Geneva.

Huntington's chorea

Huntington's chorea is a rare hereditary disorder of the brain in which there is progressive involuntary spasmodic movement (chorea) and gradual mental deterioration. It is named after the American neurologist **George S Huntington** (1851–1916) who described it.

> The American singer and songwriter Woody Guthrie is probably the most famous victim of Huntington's chorea.

hyacinth

The **hyacinth**, the fragrant plant of the lily family that bears clusters of typically blue, pink or white flowers takes its name from **Hyacinthus**, a youth in Greek mythology. Hyacinthus was so attractive that he was loved by both Apollo, god of the sun, and by Zephyrus, god of the west wind. Hyacinthus' preference for Apollo made Zephyrus intensely jealous, and while the three of them were playing games one day, Zephyrus hurled Apollo's quoit of iron at Hyacinthus, hitting him on the head and killing him. It is said that a flower grew from the blood of the wound.

> Milton describes the hyacinth as 'that sanguine flower inscribed with woe'.

hygiene

The word **hygiene**, the science of maintaining good health and the clean conditions that lead to good health, comes from **Hygeia**, the Greek goddess of health. Hygeia was worshipped with Aesculapius, the god of medicine, and is sometimes identified as his wife or daughter. Hygeia was typically depicted as feeding a serpent from a dish in her hand.

Immelmann turn

The **Immelmann turn** is an aircraft manoeuvre consisting of a simultaneous loop and roll, which is used to gain height while reversing flight direction. This manoeuvre was invented by **Max Immelmann** (1890–1916), a German aviator who joined the German Army Air Service in 1914. In 1915 Immelmann won the Iron Cross First Class and in 1916 he was awarded the Ordre pour le Mérite (the Blue Max), Prussia's highest award for bravery. In 1916 Immelmann was killed in aerial combat with a British aircraft.

iris

Iris is the name of a genus of plants that have sword-shaped leaves and large showy flowers made up of three upright petals and three drooping petals. The name of the plant comes from **Iris**, the Greek goddess of the rainbow, because of the flower's bright and varied colours. Messenger of Hera (the queen of the Olympian gods), Iris travelled along the colours of the rainbow to bring her messages to earth.

The name of **iris** is also used for the coloured part of the eye surrounding the pupil.

isabelline

The adjective **isabelline**, meaning greyish-yellow, comes from the name of the colour isabel or isabella. It is said that these words are derived from the colour of the underwear of **Isabel Clara Eugenia**, daughter of King Philip II of Spain, who in 1598 married Albert, Archduke of Austria. Tradition has it that at the siege of Ostend, she vowed not to change her underwear until the city was captured. The siege lasted for three years, so the colour of her under-garments must have been truly isabelline when the city was finally taken.

Other sources relate a similar story about **Queen Isabella of Castile** (1451–1504) and the siege of Granada.

Ishmael

An **Ishmael** is a social outcast. The expression comes from the Bible figure of **Ishmael**, the son of Abraham and Hagar, the Egyptian maidservant of Sarah. According to the biblical narrative (Genesis 16–25), when Sarah realized that she could not conceive children, she gave her maidservant to Abraham to conceive in her stead. When Hagar became pregnant, she began to despise her mistress who then drove her out of her home. An angel of Jehovah met Hagar and told her to return and submit to Sarah, also saying that her descendants through Ishmael

> **'Call me Ishmael' is the famous opening sentence of Herman Melville's *Moby Dick*.**

would be innumerable. God assured Abraham that Ishmael would be the father of twelve rulers and ultimately of a great nation. When in due course Sarah bore a son, Isaac, by Abraham, she insisted that Ishmael and Hagar be expelled from the home. In the desert, the outcasts nearly perished for lack of water, but God provided them with a well to drink from. Ishmael grew up to become an archer and, Hagar having found him a wife, he did indeed become the father of twelve sons.

J

jackanapes

The word **jackanapes** is sometimes used to refer to an impudent or conceited person or a mischievous child. There are two theories of the origin of the word. Some suggest that it is an alteration of Jack Ape, a term of endearment for a pet monkey. Other sources suggest that it derives from **Jack Napes**, the nickname of William de la Pole, 1st Duke of Suffolk (1396–1450), whose symbol showed an ape with a ball and chain. In 1450 de la Pole was arrested and beheaded at sea, while being sent into exile for conspiring against King Henry VI. He was later nicknamed Jack Napes or Jackanapes.

Jack Ketch

Jack Ketch was a seventeenth-century English public executioner who was notorious for his barbarism. He was appointed hangman in 1663 and was particularly infamous for his executions of Lord William Russell, a conspirator in the Rye House Plot against King Charles II (1683), and the Duke of Monmouth (1685).

Ketch was known for his bungling, cruel, work – he is said to have required several blows to sever Russell's head. The Duke of Monmouth's last words are reputed to have been, 'Do not hack me as you did my Lord Russell!' but it seems that he was slaughtered as ineptly if not even more clumsily than the earlier victim.

After his death in 1668, the name of **Jack Ketch** came into common use to refer to a public executioner, and it was later used for the hangman of the Punch and Judy puppet shows.

Jack Russell terrier

A **Jack Russell terrier** is a breed of dog with a stocky body, small drooping ears, short legs and a short white, black and tan coat. The

breed of terrier is named after the English clergyman **John** (Jack)
Russell (1795–1883) who developed the breed from the fox terrier.
Russell was curate of Swimbridge, near Barnstaple, and was also master
of the local foxhounds.

Jacky Howe

The expression **Jacky Howe** is used in Australian English for a
sleeveless shirt, as worn by sheep-shearers. It is named after **John**
(Jacky) **Howe** (1855–1922). Howe was the world sheep-shearing
champion for many years; in 1892 he sheared 321 merinos in one day.

Jacobean

Jacobean refers to the styles of furniture and architecture current at
the time of **King James I** of England, from the New Latin *Jacobaeus* for
James. He was the first Stuart king of England and Ireland (1603–1625)
and, as **King James VI**, ruled Scotland (1567–1625). The Jacobean
style of furniture is particularly noted for its use of dark brown carved
oak. In architecture, the Jacobean style
stands between the Elizabethan and
the classical Palladian style of the
English architect and designer
Inigo Jones (1573–1652). It is
marked by a combination of Renaissance
forms, such as ornamental gables, and the late Gothic preference for
mullioned windows.

> **King James was known
> as 'The Wisest Fool in
> Christendom'.**

Jacobite

The **Jacobites** were followers of the Stuart **King James II** (New
Latin, *Jacobus*) after his overthrow in 1688 (the Glorious Revolution),
and of his descendants. The Jacobites made several attempts to enable the
House of Stuart to regain the throne. Two Jacobite rebellions – in 1715;
led by James Edward Stuart (James II's son, known as the Old Pretender)
and in 1745, led by Charles Edward Stuart (the son of James Edward
Stuart, known as the Young Pretender or romantically as Bonnie Prince
Charlie) – were suppressed. At the Battle of Culloden (April 1746),

Bonnie Prince Charlie was defeated by the Duke of Cumberland, so
concluding the Jacobite rebellion.

Jacob's ladder

Jacob's ladder is the name given to two items – a ladder used on
board ship and a plant. The Jacob's ladder that is used on board ship is
made of rope or cable; it has wooden or metal rungs and is dropped over
the side of a ship to allow people to ascend from or descend to small
boats positioned alongside. The plant known as Jacob's ladder
(*Polemonium caeruleum*) has blue or white flowers and a ladder-like
arrangement of its light–green leaves.

The origin of the expression Jacob's ladder is to be found in the Bible
(Genesis 28:12); it is the ladder, which rested on the earth and reached to
heaven, that **Jacob** saw in a dream.

Jacquard loom

The **Jacquard loom** was a loom for weaving patterned fabrics. It is
named after the French weaver and inventor **Joseph Marie Jacquard**
(1752–1834), who completed its design in 1801. When first introduced
in France, it was very unpopular, because it was so efficient that it made
thousands of people redundant. Within eleven years of its introduction,
however, over ten thousand Jacquard looms were in use in France.
Napoleon bought the loom for the state, declaring it to be public
property; he paid Jacquard a yearly pension of 3000 francs and also a
small sum for each machine sold. The revolutionary loom was the first
automatic machine that could weave patterns into fabrics. It was
controlled by punched cards – a method that was later applied by the
British mathematician Charles Babbage (1792–1871) in his development
of the calculator and subsequently in the development of computers.

Jacuzzi

Jacuzzi is a trademark used to describe a system of underwater jets of
water that massage the body. The name derives from its creator, the
Italian-born **Candido Jacuzzi** (c. 1903–1986). Candido was born the

youngest of seven brothers and six sisters. When the family emigrated to California early in the twentieth century, it seemed that they would prosper from aviation engineering. But in 1921, when the first Jacuzzi monoplane crashed on its first flight, the Jacuzzi boys were forbidden by their mother to develop these skills.

The brothers also worked in the field of fluid dynamics, patenting a jet pump, originally for use in ornamental gardens. When one of the children of the family was stricken by rheumatoid arthritis, they developed a pump that could be used to produce the therapeutic effects of swirling bubbly water in a home bath tub. In 1968, Roy Jacuzzi, a third-generation member of the Jacuzzi family, saw the commercial potential of the whirlpool bath: a pump was fixed to the bath's outer walls to force the water and air through four jets – and so the modern Jacuzzi came into being.

Jansenism

Jansenism was a Roman Catholic movement in the seventeenth and eighteenth centuries based on the teaching of the Dutch theologian **Cornelius Otto Jansen** (1585–1638). First director of the episcopal college in Louvain, and consecrated Bishop of Ypres (1636), Jansen is noted for his treatise *Augustinus* (1640), which he wrote after reading St Augustine's works many times. The teaching of Jansenism, as expressed in *Augustinus*, emphasized the more strictly predestinarian points of St Augustine's doctrines. The teaching brought the followers of Jansenism into conflict with the Jesuits and was condemned by Pope Innocent X as heretical (1653).

January

January, the first month of the year, comes from the name of the Roman god **Janus**. Janus was the god of doors, thresholds and bridges. He is usually portrayed as having two faces, one looking forwards and the other backwards. January is therefore seen as providing an opportunity for looking back to take stock and of gazing into the future to wonder what lies ahead. From the representation of Janus as having two faces also comes the expression **Janus-faced**, meaning two-faced or hypocritical.

JCB

A **JCB** is the trademark for a type of mechanical earth-mover. At the front of the vehicle is a hydraulically operated shovel and at the back, an excavator arm. The name of the earth-mover comes from the initials of its English manufacturer **Joseph Cyril Bamford** (1916–2001).

A skilled welder and fitter, Bamford built a farm trailer using materials surplus to war use in 1945. Various types of trailer were then constructed, and by the late 1940s and the early 1950s hydraulics were introduced in tipping trailers and loaders. The JCB company is currently headed by Sir Anthony Bamford, the eldest son of the original Bamford.

> **Bamford's first vehicle was made using a £1 welding set.**

Jekyll and Hyde

The phrase **Jekyll and Hyde** is used to describe a person who has two separate personalities, one good and the other evil. The expression derives from the name of the main character in the novel *The Strange Case of Dr Jekyll and Mr Hyde*, published 1886, by the Scottish writer Robert Louis Stevenson (1850–1894).

In the story **Doctor Jekyll** discovers a drug that will change him into an evil dwarf, whom he calls **Mr Hyde**. At first, Doctor Jekyll is able to change from one personality to the other at will, but gradually the personality of Mr Hyde begins to predominate, and Hyde later commits murder. In the trial that follows the secret is made known and Hyde commits suicide. The expression is often used in front of a noun; for example, 'a Jekyll-and-Hyde personality'.

jeremiad

A **jeremiad** is a lengthy lamentation or complaint. The word comes, via French, from the name **Jeremiah**, the Old Testament prophet. His book contains many prophecies of judgement, particularly against idolatry, immorality and false prophets, and he is sometimes known as the Prophet of Doom. Thus a **Jeremiah** has come to be used to refer to a pessimistic person who foresees a gloomy future or one who condemns the society he lives in.

jeroboam

A **jeroboam** is a very large wine bottle, one that holds the equivalent of four standard bottles. It seems that the expression was first humorously applied to such bottles in the nineteenth century, alluding to **Jeroboam**, the first king of the northern kingdom of Israel, whom the biblical text describes as 'a mighty man of valour' (1 Kings 11:28) and who 'did sin, and who made Israel to sin' (1 Kings 14:16). The bottle is without doubt 'mighty' and the alcoholic drink contained in it could certainly lead to 'sin'.

See also **jorum**; **methuselah**; **nebuchadnezzar**; **rehoboam**.

jerry-built

A building that is **jerry-built** is one that has been poorly built with cheap, low-quality materials. There are various theories of the origin of the expression. According to some sources jerry could refer to the tumbling walls of Jericho in the Bible (Joshua, chapter 6). An alternative theory states that jerry comes from the name of the prophet **Jeremiah**, who predicted decay and destruction. Still others suggest that jerry is a corruption of *jury-mast*, a makeshift wooden mast in use in English shipbuilding yards in the mid-nineteenth century.

Jesuit

A **Jesuit** is a member of the Society of Jesus, a Roman Catholic religious order founded by St Ignatius Loyola in 1534. Its original aims were to defend Catholicism in the face of the Reformation and to under-take missionary work amongst the unbelieving world. The word Jesuit comes from **Jesus** and the suffix *–ita* meaning follower or supporter.

Because of a tendency of a few Jesuits, especially in the seventeenth century, to be concerned with politics, the word Jesuit and the adjective **Jesuitical** are sometimes used to refer to a person who is involved in subtle intrigue or cunning deception.

Jezebel

A **Jezebel** is a shameless, scheming or immoral woman. The word comes from the biblical figure of **Jezebel**, daughter of Ethbaal, king of Tyre and Sidon, who married Ahab, the king of Israel. Jezebel's notorious wickedness is described in 1 and 2 Kings. She worshipped the fertility god Baal and persuaded Ahab and his people to follow her religion. Under her orders, God's prophets were killed, and were replaced by the prophets of Baal. In answer to Elijah's prayer, God defeated Baal at Mount Carmel. Jezebel then resolved to kill Elijah, who was forced to go into hiding. After the incident over Naboth's vineyard, Elijah predicted Jezebel's violent end, and some time later she was thrown down from a high palace window.

jim crow

The phrase **jim crow** (or **Jim Crow**) was used in American English to refer to a Black person, and also to racial segregation imposed by Whites on Blacks. The phrase was very common in the 1880s and 1890s, but has been dated back to 1730, when Black people were first described as crows. In 1828 a White blackface minstrel Thomas D Rice wrote the song 'Jim Crow', which was widely sung and danced in both Britain and the United States in the 1830s. **Jim Crow** was the Black person of the song-and-dance act. The song popularized the expression Jim Crow to mean a Black, a Jim Crow store being a shop with provisions that would be sold only to Blacks, and, later, Jim Crow laws being discriminatory laws against Black Americans.

Job

The Old Testament character of **Job** was a man of upright character who lost his wealth, his ten children and his health. Satan brought these disasters on him with God's permission. The book of Job tells how Job kept his faith in God in the midst of all his afflictions. Thus, **the patience of Job** has become proverbial to stand for the enduring of difficulties, misfortunes or laborious tasks with supreme patience, courage and tolerance.

Job was visited by three friends who gave him the advice of popular opinion, emphasizing particularly that his misfortunes were brought about by his own disobedience to God. From these friends, whom Job refers to as 'miserable comforters' (Job 16:2), comes the expression 'a **Job's comforter**', used to describe someone whose attempts to bring encouragement or sympathy have the opposite effects of discouragement and distress in reality.

Joey

The traditional name of a circus clown, **Joey**, comes from the famous English clown **Joseph Grimaldi** (1779–1837). He is said to have been only one year old when he made his début at the Drury Lane Theatre in London. He began as a dancer, and later became well known as a clown and pantomime artist.

Grimaldi's memoirs were edited by Charles Dickens.

The word **joey**, for a young kangaroo, is not related to the name, but comes from a native Australian language.

John Barleycorn

John Barleycorn is a personification, usually in humorous usage, of alcoholic drink. The expression may have originated in the early seventeenth century, but it was popularized by the Scottish lyric poet Robert Burns (1759–1796) in his narrative poem *Tam o'Shanter*:

> *Inspiring bold John Barleycorn*
> *What dangers thou canst make us scorn!*

John Bull

John Bull is a personification of the English nation or a typical Englishman. The expression was first used in the satirical pamphlet by the Scottish writer and physician John Arbuthnot (1667–1735), 'Law is a Bottomless Pit', published in 1712. The pamphlet was designed to ridicule the Duke of Marlborough and to express disgust at the continuing war against France.

In the pamphlet **John Bull** is an allegorical character representing England. He is straightforward, honest, independent, bold and quarrelsome. Other characters in the pamphlet are Humphrey Hocus (the Duke of Marlborough), Lewis Baboon (Louis XIV of France), Nicholas Frog (the Dutchman) and Lord Strutt (Philip of Spain). The pamphlet was originally one of a series and later the collection was reissued under the title *The History of John Bull*.

John Doe and Richard Roe

 John Doe and Richard Roe are the names sometimes given to the two parties to legal proceedings. It seems unlikely that men by these names actually existed, the forenames being apparently chosen randomly because of their frequent occurrence. The surname **Doe** was probably chosen with reference to the gentle and pleasant character of a doe and **Roe** seems to have been chosen because it rhymes with Doe.

The names were used in legal documents since at least the fourteenth century – one source suggests that the names may even date back to Magna Carta (1215).

Originally, prosecutors are said to have used these names when they could not find two genuine witnesses or when the true witnesses did not wish to disclose their real names. Later, the names came to be used instead of the real names of the parties to legal proceedings, John Doe usually being the plaintiff and Richard Roe the defendant.

John Dory

A **John Dory** is a golden yellow food fish, *Zeus faber*, with an oval compressed body, long spiny dorsal fins and a black spot on each side. The name John may have been chosen arbitrarily, and dory is probably simply derived from the Middle French *dorée*, 'gilded one'. An alternative theory suggests that the fish is named after a certain **John Dory**, an infamous privateer in the sixteenth century and the subject of a popular song, but this seems unlikely.

John Hancock

The expressions **John Hancock** or **John Henry** are used particularly in American English to refer to a person's signature. **John Hancock** (1737–1793) was the Boston merchant and revolutionary patriot who not only was the first to sign the American Declaration of Independence but also was the one who wrote his signature the most prominently and apparently the most aggressively, 'so big no Britisher would have to use his spectacles to read it'. Hancock later became president of the Continental Congress and governor of Massachusetts.

The alternative expression **John Henry** came originally from the cowboy slang of the American west.

joliotium

Joliotium is a former name for dubnium, an artificially produced radioactive transuranic element. It was named in honour of the French nuclear physicists **Jean-Frédéric Joliot-Curie** (1900–1958) and **Irène Joliot-Curie** (1897–1956). While Frédéric Joliot was Marie Curie's assistant at the Radium Institute in Paris, he worked with and later married her daughter Irène (both used the name Joliot-Curie after their marriage). In collaboration, the Joliot-Curies discovered artificial radioactivity and were jointly awarded the Nobel prize (qv) for chemistry in 1944.

Jonah

A **Jonah** is a person who is believed to bring bad luck. The expression derives from the biblical **Jonah**, the Hebrew prophet who was held responsible for the storm that struck the ship he was travelling on (Jonah 1:4–7). Jonah was running away from God, disobeying his command to go to Nineveh to denounce its people.

Joneses

The idiomatic expression 'keeping up with the **Joneses**' means trying to maintain the same living standards as one's richer neighbours. The expression derives from a comic strip by Arthur R Momand with the title '**Keeping up with the Joneses**' which began in the New York

Globe in 1913 and was based on the experience of the author and his wife trying to maintain the same material standards as those living around them.

> **Momand originally thought of calling the cartoon strip 'Keeping up with the Smiths', but 'Keeping up with the Joneses' was eventually chosen as being more euphonious.**

jorum

A **jorum** is a large drinking bowl. It is named after the Old Testament character **Joram**, who brought to King David 'vessels of silver, and vessels of gold, and vessels of brass' (2 Samuel 8:10).

See also **jeroboam**; **methuselah**; **nebuchadnezzar**; **rehoboam**.

joule

A **joule** is the metric unit of work or energy. The unit is named after the English physicist **James Prescott Joule** (1818–1889). Born in Salford, Joule was a student of Dalton and performed experiments in the

> **Joule's day job was to run the family brewery.**

1840s to determine the mechanical equivalent of heat. He is also known for his work on the heating effects of an electric current (**Joule's law**), his work on the effect on temperature that occurs when a gas expands under certain conditions (the **Joule–Thomson effect** or **Joule–Kelvin effect**), and his research that formed the basis of the theory of the conservation of energy.

Jove

Jove was a form of the name of the Roman god Jupiter and the word is sometimes used in the exclamation 'by **Jove**' to express surprise or agreement, for example, 'By Jove, you're right!' Originally a euphemism for 'by God', the first recorded use of 'by Jove' is 1570.

Jovial, with its contemporary meaning of good-humoured, originally meant to have been born under the influence of the planet Jupiter, which astrologers considered to be the source of good humour.

Judas

A **Judas** is a traitor, a person who betrays a friend. The word comes from the name of Christ's betrayer, **Judas Iscariot**.

The name Judas occurs in a number of expressions that allude to betrayal or cunning. A **Judas kiss** is a show of affection that conceals treachery. A **Judas slit** is a peep-hole in a door through which guards can observe their prisoners. A **Judas tree** is an ornamental shrub or tree of the genus *Cercis*; its pinkish-purple flowers bloom before the leaves appear. The genus is so called because it is traditionally thought that Judas hanged himself on such a tree.

juggernaut

In contemporary English, a **juggernaut** is a large articulated lorry: 'Huge juggernauts roaring through country villages.' The original meaning of the word is an irresistible, overwhelming force or object: 'The inexorable juggernaut of government.' The word comes from Hinduism: **Jagannath**, Lord of the World, is one of the titles of the Hindu god Vishnu. At an annual festival, an idol of this god is carried in an enormous wheeled vehicle; devotees, it is said, formerly threw themselves under its wheels.

Julian calendar

The **Julian calendar** was the name given to the system introduced by **Julius Caesar** in 46 BC in which three years, each of 365 days, were followed by a leap year of 366 days. The system was used for centuries until it was replaced by the more accurate Gregorian calendar (qv), formulated in 1582.

juliet cap

A **juliet cap** is a small round close-fitting skullcap, usually made of lace or netting and worn by brides. This is named after **Juliet**, the heroine of William Shakespeare's tragedy *Romeo and Juliet* (published in 1594), because such a cap usually forms part of the costume of the character.

See also **Romeo**.

July

The seventh month of the year is named after **Julius Caesar** (100?–44 BC). When Caesar reformed the Roman calendar in 46 BC, he decided to rename the month of Quintilis (so called because it was originally the fifth, the first month originally being March), and chose to name it after himself.

See also **August**; **Caesarean section**; **Caesar's wife**.

jumbo

The adjective **jumbo** means enormous or very large, as for example in a jumbo packet of washing powder. Originally, **Jumbo** was the name of a very large, 62-ton African elephant exhibited at London Zoo from 1865 to 1882.

Despite an outcry, which included a personal protest from Queen Victoria, Jumbo was bought by the American showman P T Barnum in 1881. In the USA, Jumbo was exhibited in the Barnum and Bailey Greatest Show on Earth. Jumbo lived for three and a half years in America and during this time it is estimated that he carried a million children on his back. He died in 1885, when a railway train hit him while he was trying to rescue Tom Thumb, Barnum's smallest attraction.

There are several different theories as to the origin of Jumbo's name. Some believe it comes from mumbo-jumbo, others that it is derived from the Swahili *jumbe*, meaning chief, while still others claim that its origin lies in *gullah jamba*, meaning elephant.

Whichever theory is correct, P T Barnum's showmanship resulted not only in the celebration of an outsize animal, but also in the introduction of a new word into the language, now seen also in the compound **jumbo jet**.

June

 The name of the sixth month of the year may come from **Junius**, the name of the Roman family to which the murderers of Julius Caesar belonged. Other sources suggest that **June** derives from the name of the goddess of the moon, women and marriage, **Juno**, whose festival fell in this month. She was both the wife and sister of Jupiter.

The adjective **Junoesque** derives from the name Juno and means beautiful in a stately or regal manner.

Kafkaesque

The adjective **Kafkaesque** is used to describe a nightmarish sense of unreality and helplessness in the face of an impersonal and sinister bureaucracy. The word derives from the name of the Czech–born Austrian novelist **Franz Kafka** (1883–1924).

Virtually unknown as an author in his own lifetime, Kafka wanted his manuscripts to be destroyed at his death. However, his friend Max Brod undertook to publish his works posthumously. Among his best known writings are *Metamorphosis* (1912), *The Trial* (1925) and *The Castle* (1926).

kaiser

See **tsar**.

kalashnikov

A **kalashnikov** is a Russian–made semi-automatic assault rifle, which was used by the Soviet army from 1951 and is also favoured by many terrorists and guerrillas. As it produces virtually no vibration when fired on full automatic, the kalashnikov is a very accurate weapon at ranges of up to 300 metres. Its inventor was **Mikhail Timofeyevich Kalashnikov** (born 1919), a former NCO armour commander in the Soviet army.

Kaposi's sarcoma

Kaposi's sarcoma is a sometimes-fatal disease resembling cancer, which mainly affects the skin but can also attack the linings of the mouth, nose or eyes. This disease was initially thought to be a type of cancer, but later research discovered that it was caused by a herpes virus. Kaposi's sarcoma was originally found in equatorial Africa but it now affects about 20% of all AIDS patients, predominantly men. It usually manifests itself as lesions on the skin of the face, arms and legs. Kaposi's sarcoma was named after **Moritz Kohn Kaposi** (1837–1902), a Hungarian dermatologist who first described it.

kelvin

The **kelvin** is the metric unit of thermodynamic temperature. The kelvin scale is a scale of temperature in which the hypothetically coldest temperature (absolute zero) is 0°K and the freezing-point of water is 273.16°K. It is named after the Scottish physicist **William Thomson Kelvin**, 1st Baron Kelvin (1824–1907), who was a professor at Glasgow University for 53 years.

As well as suggesting the temperature scale, Kelvin is noted for his work on electricity and the conservation of energy, his many inventions of instruments, including the modern compass, and his personal supervision of the laying of the first transatlantic cable in 1866.

Keynesianism

Keynesianism is the economic thinking of **John Maynard Keynes**, 1st Baron Keynes of Tilton (1883–1946), the influential British economist and government adviser. In *The General Theory of Employment, Interest and Money* (1935) he argues that insufficient demand

> Keynes said, 'In the long term we are all dead.'

causes unemployment and excessive demand causes inflation and that governments should therefore adjust their expenditure and taxation in order to manipulate the aggregate demand.

King Charles spaniel

> Charles II was first British monarch to allow women to perform on the stage.

The **King Charles spaniel** is a toy breed of spaniel with a short turned-up nose, a domed head, floppy ears, and a tan-and-white or black-and-white coat. This breed was named after **Charles II** (1630–1685), king of England, Scotland and Ireland from 1660 to 1685, who was particularly partial to it.

King Edward potato

The **King Edward potato** is a variety of potato with a white-and-reddish skin and creamy-white floury flesh that tends not to discolour when cooked. It was named after **Edward VII**, king of Great Britain and Ireland (1841–1910; reign 1901–1910).

See also **Prince Albert**.

King James Bible

The **King James Bible** is an alternative name for the Authorized Version of the Bible, written under the patronage of **King James I** (1566–1625; reign 1603–1625) and published in 1611.

At a conference at Hampton Court (1604) a suggestion was made by a Dr John Reynolds (1549–1607), a Puritan and president of Corpus Christi College, that a new translation of the Bible be undertaken. The proposal appealed to the king, who wanted a uniform translation written by scholars from Oxford and Cambridge Universities, to be considered by bishops and to be ratified by his authority. The translation was based on the earlier Bishops' Bible (1568), and other versions, especially the Geneva Bible (1560), and work by William Tyndale. The style and wording of the Authorized (King James) Version has had a unique influence on the English language, becoming the familiar version of the Bible for generations of English-speaking people. Many of its phrases have become part of the language, including 'an eye for an eye', 'a fly in the ointment', 'the powers that be' and 'the salt of the earth'.

kir

Canon Félix Kir (1876–1968) was the mayor of Dijon, France (1945–1968). During World War II, Kir was a leader of the French Resistance in the province of Burgundy. In celebration of his heroic efforts, the people of Burgundy invented a drink made from the local dry white wine and crème de cassis (a blackcurrant liqueur), and called it **kir** in honour of the mayor. A **Kir Royale** is made from champagne, or other sparkling wine, and crème de cassis.

Klieg lights

Klieg lights are intense carbon-arc lamps used for lighting on film sets. They are bright enough to enable filming on a dull day, and even to make night appear to be day. Originally they were called kliegl lights, after **John H Kliegl** (1869–1959) and his brother **Anton Tiberius Kliegl** (1872–1927), the German-born American lighting experts who invented them. In 1896, the Kliegl brothers established a company, called the Kliegl Brothers Universal Electric Stage Lighting Company, for the design and production of theatrical lighting equipment. They originated many innovative lighting effects both for the stage and for the new film industry.

knickerbockers

Knickerbockers are short, baggy breeches gathered in at the knee. The word comes from the name **Dietrich Knickerbocker**, the pseudonym under which the American author Washington Irving (1783–1859) wrote his *History of New York from the Beginning of the World to the End of the Dutch Dynasty*, published in 1809.

The name Knickerbocker came to stand for the typical, solid Dutch burgher, who was a descendant of the original Dutch settlers in New York. The

> New York's professional basketball team is called the New York Knickerbockers – usually shortened to 'Knicks'.

word knickerbockers is said to have been used for the baggy breeches considered to have been the traditional dress of the Dutch settlers in America. This tradition arose from illustrations by the caricaturist George Cruikshank (1792–1878) in a British edition of Irving's book in the 1850s. Cruikshank portrayed the Dutch settlers as wearing baggy breeches and so the name knickerbockers came to be used.

See also **bloomers**.

Köchel number

A **Köchel number** (or **K number** for short) is a serial number in a catalogue of the works of Mozart, for example Mozart's Clarinet

Concerto in A major is K.622. Köchel numbers are named after the Austrian botanist and cataloguer **Ludwig von Köchel** (1800–1877), whose catalogue of Mozart's works was first published in 1862. The letter K (or in German KV, for *Köchelverzeichnis*, 'Köchel index') followed by a number, shows the chronological order of Mozart's works.

Korsakoff's psychosis

Korsakoff's psychosis (or **Korsakoff's syndrome**) is a serious mental illness, usually the result of chronic alcoholism, in which there is disorientation and a loss of memory of recent events, for which there is a tendency to invent explanations. This condition was first described by the Russian neuropsychiatrist **Sergei Sergeyevich Korsakoff** (1854–1900), who was one of the founders of the Russian school of psychiatry.

L

Lady Bountiful

A **Lady Bountiful** is a woman who is noted for her generous bestowing of charity or favours in a condescending, patronizing manner, as for example in: 'We don't need her coming round here to play Lady Bountiful; we can afford to buy our own food and clothes, thank you very much.' The expression comes from the character in the comedy *The Beaux' Stratagem* (1707) by the Irish dramatist George Farquhar (1678–1707). In the play, **Lady Bountiful** gives half her money to charity.

Lalique glass

 Lalique glass is decorative glassware produced by the French designer **René Lalique** (1860–1945). It is lead-based and usually has stylized motifs in the form of flowers, figures, birds, etc. Lalique created over 250 perfume bottles for most of the top French perfumers. In addition to his glassware, Lalique is famous for his Art Nouveau jewellery, particularly brooches and combs.

Lamaze

 Lamaze is a method of childbirth in which the expectant mother learns to suppress pain through relaxation exercises and breathing techniques in order to give birth without the use of drugs. This method was developed by the French obstetrician **Fernand Lamaze** (1891–1957) after a visit to the USSR in 1951, during which he was impressed by the psychologist Ivan Pavlov's work on conditioning. The Lamaze method was promoted in the USA by Elisabeth Bing, and became very popular there.

lambert

 Born the son of an impoverished tailor, the German scientist **Johann Heinrich Lambert** (1728–1777) is noted for his work in several disciplines, such as mathematics, physics, astronomy and philosophy. Lambert proved that pi was an irrational number; he derived the trigonometric hyperbolic functions; and he measured the amount of light emitted by stars and planets.

It is for his work in physics that Lambert is particularly honoured: the unit of illumination in the centimetre–gram–second system of measurement is named after him.

lamington

 In Australia and New Zealand, a **lamington** is a very popular cake. It consists of a square piece of sponge cake coated in soft chocolate icing and desiccated coconut, and is often served with afternoon tea. The lamington is named after Charles Wallace Baillie, **Lord Lamington** (1860–1940), who was Governor of Queensland from 1895 to 1901.

The cake is said to have originated when a clumsy maid at the governor's residence dropped a plain sponge cake into a bowl of chocolate.

lawrencium

 Lawrencium is a short-lived radioactive chemical element that is artificially produced from the element californium. It is named after the American physicist **Ernest Orlando Lawrence** (1901–1958). As physics professor at the University of California (1930), Lawrence invented the cyclotron, a type of particle accelerator that produces high-energy particles, for which he was awarded the Nobel prize (qv) for physics in 1939.

lazaret

 A **lazaret** or **lazaretto** is a hospital for people with contagious diseases, a building or ship used for quarantine, or a ship's storeroom. The terms derive from a combination of the words lazar and Nazaret. Lazar is an archaic word for a poor diseased person, especially a leper, and comes from **Lazarus**, the name of the beggar in Jesus' parable (Luke 16:20; *see also* **Dives**). Nazaret is short for Santa Maria di Nazaret, a church in Venice that maintained a hospital.

Legg–Calvé–Perthes disease

See **Perthes' disease**.

Leninism

The word **Leninism** is used to refer to the political, economic and social theories of communism propounded by the Russian statesman **Vladimir Ilyich Lenin** (1870–1924), whose original surname was Ulyanov. It was the close study of Marxism and the execution of his elder brother Aleksandr that set Lenin on his political career. In exile in Siberia for his revolutionary activities (1897–1900) he wrote his first book, and married a fellow Marxist, Nadezhda Krupskaya. He was one of the leaders of the unsuccessful revolution of 1905. After the Russian Revolution broke out in 1917, Lenin led the Bolsheviks in the overthrow of the provisional government. He made peace with Germany (1918) and fought off opposition in the civil war (1918–1921). As head of state, he founded the Third International (1918) and instituted the New Economic Policy (1921) which allowed a small degree of free enterprise. After a series of strokes, he died in 1924. His embalmed body was put on display in a tomb in Red Square, Moscow.

> The name Lenin means literally 'Man of Iron'.

The former capital of Russia known as St Petersburg (1703–1914) and Petrograd (1914–1924) was renamed **Leningrad** after Lenin's death. It has since reverted to the name St Petersburg.

See also **Marxism**; **Stalinism**; **Trotskyism**.

leotard

A **leotard** is a close-fitting, one-piece garment worn by acrobats, ballet dancers and others performing physical exercises. It is named after the French acrobat **Jules Léotard** (1842–1870), who designed and

introduced the original costume for the circus. Léotard was one of
France's most famous acrobats, starring in circuses in Paris and London.
He perfected the first aerial somersault and invented the flying trapeze;
he inspired the popular song 'That Daring Young Man on the Flying
Trapeze' (1860) by George Leybourne. He died of smallpox at the age of
just 28.

Levis

Levis is a trademark for a kind of jeans, from the name of **Levi
Strauss** (1830–1902), a Bavarian immigrant to the USA and a San
Francisco clothing merchant at the time of the Gold Rush. Strauss started
to make durable jeans in the 1850s. He added rivets to the corners of the
pockets in the mid-1870s, so that, it is said, the pockets would not tear
when they were loaded with ore samples. As he became more well
known, so these hard-wearing jeans came to be called Levis.

lewisite

The colourless, poisonous liquid known as **lewisite** causes blistering of
the skin. It was developed (1917–1918) by the American chemist
Winford Lee Lewis (1878–1943), after whom it is named, as a gas to
be used in chemical warfare.

Leylandii

The **Leylandii**, or **Leyland cypress**, is a fast-growing conifer, which
is widely grown for hedging. In the USA, they are also very popular as
Christmas trees. The tree takes its name from the British horticulturalist
Christopher J Leyland (1849–1926). In 1888, Leyland discovered six
seedlings at his brother-in-law's estate, Leighton Hall, near Powys in
South Wales, and planted them on his own land at Haggerston Castle
estate in Northumberland, where they quickly grew into large trees.
These seedlings were the result of an accidental hybridization involving
the female flowers, or cones, of the macrocarpa being fertilized by pollen
from the Nootka cypress. Being a hybrid, the Leylandii is sterile, and has
to be propagated by individual cutting. This means that all Leylandii
trees have originated from the trees that grew from those six seedlings.

life of Riley

A person who enjoys an easy, lazy and luxurious life may be said to be 'living the **life of Riley**'. There are a number of different theories as to the origin of this expression. Some sources state that the original Riley was the American poet **James Whitcomb Riley** (1849–1916), whose writings often concerned boys spending summer days in a carefree manner; others suggest that the phrase originates with the song 'The Best In the House is None Too Good for Reilly' by Lawlor and Blake; still others say that the original Riley was an **O'Reilly** of the song 'Are You the O'Reilly?' popularized by Pat Rooney in the 1880s: O'Reilly would one day strike it rich, and everyone would be prosperous.

Linnaean

Carolus Linnaeus (original name Carl von Linné; 1707–1778) was the Swedish botanist who established the system of naming living organisms. In his **Linnaean** system, all organisms have two names, the first identifies the genus to which the organism belongs, the second its species. For example. Linnaeus classified members of the human race as belonging to *Homo sapiens* ('wise man'), *Homo* being the genus, and *sapiens* the specific species.

The son of a Lutheran clergyman, Linnaeus had an early interest in nature – he was nicknamed 'the little botanist' at the age of eight. He became assistant professor of botany at Uppsala University, studied medicine in Holland, and later became professor of medicine and botany at Uppsala University in 1741.

Linnaeus' system is outlined in his books, especially *Systema naturae* (1735), *Genera plantarum* (1737) and *Species plantarum* (1753). His was the first significant attempt to bring all living things together in a systematic classification.

> **It is said that Linnaeus believed he had been chosen by God to name and classify plants and animals.**

Not only did he indeed name more living organisms than any other person in history, but also his system of nomenclature formed the basis of modern classification.

Linux

Linux is a computer operating system similar to Unix that is suitable for use on personal computers. It was named after **Linus Torvalds** (born 1969), a Finnish computer programmer, who, as a 21-year-old student at Helsinki University, wrote his own operating system. Rather than copyrighting his computer code for financial gain, Torvalds released the first versions of his operating system on the Internet in 1991, inviting other programmers to suggest improvements to him by e-mail. As a result, only about 2% of the current version of Linux was actually written by Torvalds himself.

listeria

Listeria is a type of rod-shaped bacterium that causes infections in human beings and in various other mammals and birds. Although listeria is widespread in the environment, it affects only about one to three per million of the population per year.

One of the most serious infections caused by this bacterium is **listeriosis**, an often fatal form of food poisoning that can cause meningitis, septicaemia and encephalitis. It can also cause pregnant women to have miscarriages.

> **Lister was the first medical practitioner to be created a lord.**

Both listeria and listeriosis were named after the British surgeon **Joseph Lister**, 1st Baron Lister (1827–1912). Having studied the germ theory of the French bacteriologist Louis Pasteur, in 1865 Lister introduced the use of carbolic acid as an antiseptic during operations, greatly reducing the surgical mortality rate.

lobelia

Lobelia is the name of a genus of flowers bearing showy lipped blue, red, yellow or white flowers. The genus is named after the Flemish botanist and physician **Matthias de Lobel** (1538–1616), who was physician to King James I.

loganberry

The **loganberry**, the large sweet purplish-red berry of the upright-growing raspberry plant (*Rubus loganobaccus*) takes its name from an American lawyer. It was judge **James Harvey Logan** (1841–1928) who developed the plant in his experimental orchard at his home in California in about 1881.

See also **boysenberry**.

Lolita

If a girl is described as a **Lolita**, she is an adolescent who is regarded as being sexually precocious and seductive. **Lolita** is the main character in the novel of the same name (1955) by the Russian-born American writer Vladimir Nabokov (1899–1977). This story tells of a middle-aged man's obsessive and destructive desire for his precocious twelve-year-old stepdaughter.

Lonsdale belt

The belt awarded as a trophy to professional boxing champions is known as a **Lonsdale belt**. It is named after Hugh Cecil Lowther, 5th **Earl of Lonsdale** (1857–1944), who originated the awards. The Earl of Lonsdale was an all-round sportsman; he was president of the National Sporting Club. Not only was he a sparring partner to the heavyweight fighter John Lawrence Sullivan (1858–1918), he was also an expert huntsman, steeplechaser and yachtsman.

Lothario

A **Lothario** is a man who makes a practice of seducing women. **Lothario** is a character in *The Fair Penitent* (1703), a play by the English dramatist Nicholas Rowe (1674–1718). In the play, 'the gay Lothario' seduces Calista, an unfaithful wife, as well as the fair penitent of the title.

Lou Gehrig's disease

Lou Gehrig's disease is another name for amyotrophic lateral sclerosis, a form of motor neurone disease. This is a chronic degenerative disease of the nervous system that causes progressive muscle weakness and atrophy, resulting in paralysis and, usually, death within two to five years. **Lou Gehrig** (1903–1941) was a famous American baseball player. He played

> **Lou Gehrig's story was made into the film *The Pride of the Yankees* (1942), in which he was played by Gary Cooper.**

2130 consecutive games for the New York Yankees and still holds the record for hitting the most grand slam home runs (23), but his career was cut short by amyotrophic lateral sclerosis in 1939.

Lucullan

The Roman general **Lucius Licinus Lucullus** (c. 110–57 BC) was a Roman general and administrator. He waged war in the East against Mithridates, gaining both riches and success. He retired to private life in Rome in about 66 BC to enjoy a life of luxury; and his **Lucullan** (or **Lucullian**) feasts became proverbial for their lavishness.

Lucy Stoner

In America, a **Lucy Stoner** is a woman who retains her maiden name after she marries. The expression comes from the name of **Lucy Stone** (1818–1893), who was a prominent figure in the movement to gain women the vote in America and called the first national Women's Rights Convention in 1850. In 1851, she married Henry Brown Blackwell, but, with her husband's agreement, retained her maiden name as a symbol of their equality.

The Lucy Stone League was founded in the 1920s to campaign for women to have the same rights as men to use and modify their birth names. It has been disbanded and reformed several times, its most recent revival being in 1997.

Luddite

A **Luddite** is a person who is opposed to industrial innovation. It is said that the name derives from a **Ned Ludd**, an eighteenth-century English labourer who in about 1779 destroyed labour-saving stocking frames at his workplace. The name Luddite was adopted by a group of workers between 1811 and 1816 who tried to destroy new mechanical textile appliances in the Midlands and the north of England. The workers saw the new machines as a threat to their livelihood. The movement was suppressed and some Luddites were hanged or transported. Distrust of innovation continues and the word Luddite is still used to refer to someone who opposes the latest technological changes.

Luger

 Luger is a trademark for a German-made automatic pistol of bottleneck design. Also known as the Parabellum, the Luger was designed by **Georg Luger** (1849–1923), a German firearms expert, and introduced in 1900 by the German firm DWM.

lush

 Lush, slang for intoxicating liquor and also a drunken person, is said to have originally been a shortening of the name of an actors' drinking club in London, the City of Lushington. The club, founded in the mid-eighteenth century, met in the Harp Tavern in Great Russell Street until the 1890s. The name of the club may possibly have come from a chaplain, **Dr Thomas Lushington** (1590–1661), who was a drinking companion of Bishop Richard Corbet, although a number of alternative theories have been proposed, including the suggestion that the origin is *lush*, to eat and drink, in Shelta, a language used by travelling people.

Lutheran

 Martin Luther (1483–1546) was a German religious reformer who founded the movement known as the Reformation, which led to the establishment of the Protestant Church. Luther was ordained as a priest in 1507, but he was appalled at the corrupt practices he observed in the Roman Catholic Church. He began to teach that salvation is achieved by faith rather than by works. In 1517, he nailed a list of 95 theses to the door of the church at Wittenberg, denying that the Pope had any right to forgive sins. This act prompted a prolonged dispute with the ecclesiastical authorities, culminating in Luther being banned at the Diet of Worms in 1521.

Luther was subsequently arrested and held captive, primarily for his own protection. In the civil disobedience that followed over the next decade, he attempted to steer a path between lawlessness on the one hand and the tyranny of the authorities on the other. At Marburg in 1529, Luther met with Swiss Protestants led by Zwingli, but he failed to agree with them on the interpretation of the holy communion, and so Protestantism never became a unified movement.

The word **Lutheran** is now applied to any Protestant Church that follows Luther's doctrines. The Lutheran Church originally flourished in Germany and Scandinavia, but has spread worldwide as a result of immigration and missionary work.

lutz

 A **lutz** is a standard jump in figure skating, in which the skater takes off from the rear outside edge of one skate and lands on the rear outside edge of the other skate, with one, two or three turns in the air. The lutz is probably named after the Austrian skater **Alois Lutz** (1898–1918), who first executed the single lutz in 1913.

lynch

 If an angry mob of people **lynch** someone, they put that person to death without giving him or her a proper trial. The word comes from **lynch law**, the condemning and punishing of a person who has not been tried, but dictionary writers have long argued over which person with the name Lynch originated the expression. Most now agree, however, that it was probably **William Lynch** (1742–1820), an American who organized extra-legal trials in Virginia.

The evidence for this is an editorial on lynching by the American short-story writer Edgar Allen Poe (1809–1849) in an issue of the *Southern Literary Messenger*, published in 1836. Poe wrote that the expression 'lynch law' originated in 1780 when Captain William Lynch led a group of his fellow citizens in Pennsylvania County, Virginia, to deal with a group of ruffians who were disturbing public order. Lynch had an agreement with his fellow vigilantes 'to inflict such corporeal punishment … as shall seem adequate to the crime committed or the damage sustained'. Thus lynch law came to refer to the administration of mob justice using non-legal means, and on occasions men were hanged for their alleged crimes.

The expressions lynch law and lynch also, no doubt, gained currency because of the practices of another person named Lynch, the planter and justice of the peace, **Charles Lynch** (1736–1796), who took the law into his own hands and set up his own trials during the American War of Independence. However, there is no evidence that the administration of rough justice by this Lynch ever led to any hangings.

M

macabre

The adjective **macabre**, meaning 'grim or gruesome', is derived from the Old French *danse macabre*, 'dance of death', a medieval representation of a dance in which living people are taken, in order of their social standing, to their graves by a personification of death. The origin of the *danse macabre* may lie in a miracle play in which the martyrdom of the seven young **Maccabee** brothers under the Syrian (Seleucid) King Antiochus IV is depicted. This story is told in the Apocrypha in the second Book of the Maccabees, Chapter 7.

> **Maccabee comes from a Hebrew word meaning 'hammerer'.**

macadam

A **macadamized** road is one that has a surface made of **macadam**: compacted layers of small broken stones bound together with tar, asphalt, etc. The word macadam honours its inventor, the Scottish engineer **John Loudon McAdam** (1756–1836). It is said that as a small boy McAdam laid out model roads in his back garden – but it was years later, after spending some time in America, that he returned to Scotland, to discover that the roads in the estate that he had bought in Ayrshire were, like most roads, in a poor condition. McAdam set to work to improve the state of the roads, experimenting in Ayrshire and later in Falmouth. His efforts led to his appointment in 1815 to construct new roads around Bristol, and in 1827 he was made surveyor general of all British metropolitan roads.

Macadamizing – covering the earth base with a layer of large, tightly packed, broken stones that were in turn covered by a layer of smaller stones – soon became the standard road-surfacing method.

macadamia

The **macadamia** is an Australian evergreen rainforest tree with edible nutlike seeds and small white flowers. It was named in honour of the Australian chemist and physician **John Macadam** (1827–1865) by his friend, the botanist Baron Ferdinand von Mueller (1825–1896), who first described the genus in 1857. Macadam was born in Scotland and emigrated in 1855 to Australia, where he became a member of parliament of Victoria. Unfortunately, Macadam died of pleurisy at the age of 38, allegedly without ever having tasted the nut that was named after him.

McCarthyism

The name of the US Republican senator **Joseph Raymond McCarthy** (1909–1957) is remembered for **McCarthyism**, a kind

> McCarthy described his policies as 'Americanism with its sleeves rolled'.

of political witchhunting in America in the early 1950s. In February 1950, McCarthy claimed he knew of over 200 communists, or communist sympathizers, in the State Department. The investigations that followed marked a witchhunt that personally attacked individuals not only in politics but also in the television and film industries. McCarthy was, however, unable to prove his allegations. Eventually he was censured by the Senate in December 1954 and his witchhunt came to an end.

The term McCarthyism is still used, however, to refer to an obsessive opposition to individuals considered disloyal or who hold views considered to be subversive, especially when the charges against the individuals are not substantiated.

McCoy

Someone or something that is described as **the real McCoy** (or **the real Mackay**) is certainly genuine; it is not an imitation or a fake. There are, however, many different theories as to the origin of the expression.

Some say it comes from **Kid McCoy** (professional name of the American Norman Selby, 1873–1940), welterweight boxing champion 1898–1900, who was said to have proved his identity by boxing with his doubters until they conceded he was 'the real McCoy'.

Others suggest a Chicago livestock trader **Joseph McCoy** (born 1838) who changed the town of Abilene, Kansas, into a cow town in 1867 by taking cattle via the new railhead at Abilene to the cities of the north and east. It is said that he transported half a million cattle a year and he claimed that he was 'the real McCoy'.

Still further explanations of the origin of the expression include a chief of the **Mackay** clan; a Prohibition rum-runner named **Bill McCoy**; a character in an Irish ballad of the 1880s; the island of Macao (hence McCoy), where drug addicts are said to have demanded 'the real Macao' of the island's uncut heroin; and whisky dispatched from Glasgow to the United States by **A M MacKay**. This last explanation may well have increased the currency of the expression, since it seems that the phrases 'McCoy' or 'the clear McCoy' were originally (1908) used to refer to good whisky.

Machiavellian

The adjective **Machiavellian** has come to refer to cunning, double-dealing and opportunist methods and to describe a view that in politics the use of any means, however unscrupulous, can be justified in the pursuit of political ends. The term derives from the Italian political theorist **Niccolò Machiavelli** (1469–1527).

> **Machiavelli wrote, 'It is much safer for a prince to be feared than loved.'**

Machiavelli served as a statesman and secretary to the Florentine Republic from 1498 to 1512. When the Medici family were restored to power, he was forced into exile, however. His most famous work was *Il Principe* (*The Prince*; published in 1532), in which he argued that all means are acceptable in the securing and maintenance of a stable state. It seems that his views have been unfairly exaggerated in the modern connotation of unprincipled trickery in the word Machiavellian.

Mach number

A **Mach number** is a number that represents the ratio of the speed of a body to the speed of sound in the same medium. Thus Mach 1 corresponds to the speed of sound, a number less than 1 is subsonic, a number greater than 1 is supersonic, and a number greater than 5 is said to be hypersonic. The term 'Mach number' is named after the Austrian physicist and philosopher **Ernst Mach** (1838–1916) for his research into airflow.

Mach was also known as a philosopher; he propounded the theory of sensationalism – that the only things that ultimately exist are sensations. This theory influenced the philosophical movement of logical positivism in the 1920s.

McIntosh red

A **McIntosh red** is a Canadian variety of red-skinned eating apple. It was first discovered growing wild on the farm of **John McIntosh** (1777–c. 1845), who was born in the USA and moved to Canada in 1796.

mackintosh

A kind of raincoat made of rubberized cloth, a **mackintosh** (also **mac** or **macintosh**) is named after the Scottish chemist **Charles Macintosh** (1760–1843). It was, however, another Scotsman, James Syme (1799–1870), who first invented the process of making waterproof fabrics in 1823. A few months later, the fabric was patented by Macintosh, who went on to found a company in Glasgow, which produced the first mackintoshes in 1830. In Macintosh's process, a waterproof fabric was produced by sticking two layers of cloth together with rubber dissolved in naphtha. Nowadays, the word mackintosh is applied to any raincoat.

madeleine

A **madeleine** is a small, rich sponge cake that is baked in a mould. It is probably named after **Madeleine Paulmier**, the nineteenth-century

French pastrycook who is said to have been the first to concoct this delicacy.

The experience of smelling and tasting a madeleine inspired Marcel Proust's classic series of novels *Remembrance of Things Past*.

Mae West

A **Mae West** is an inflatable life jacket that was issued to airmen in World War II. When inflated, the life-jacket resembled a well-developed bust – hence the choice of the name of the American actress **Mae West** (1892–1980), renowned for her full figure.

On learning that she was honoured in the name of the life jacket, she is said to have uttered, 'I've been in *Who's Who* and I know what's what, but it's the first time I ever made the dictionary.'

magdalen

The word **magdalen** (or **magdalene**) means a reformed prostitute or a house of refuge or of reform for prostitutes. It comes from the name **Mary Magdalene**, a woman rid by Jesus of evil spirits (Luke 8:2) and the first person to whom the risen Jesus appeared (John 20:1–18). Mary Magdalene is often also traditionally identified with the sinful woman of Luke 7:36–50, and considered to have been a reformed prostitute, though the biblical text does not justify such a conclusion.

magnolia

Magnolia is the name of a genus of evergreen or deciduous shrubs or trees with showy white, yellow, rose or purple flowers. The genus is named after the French botanist **Pierre Magnol** (1638–1715). Magnol, professor of botany at Montpellier University, is known for his systematic classification of plants.

malapropism

A **malapropism** is an instance of the unintentional confusion of words that produces a ridiculous effect. The word comes from the name of the character **Mrs Malaprop** in the play *The Rivals* (1775) by the Irish dramatist Richard Brinsley Sheridan (1751–1816). In the play, Mrs Malaprop – her name comes from the French *mal à propos*, meaning inappropriate – misapplies words on numerous occasions; for example, 'If I reprehend anything in this world, it is the use of my oracular tongue and a nice derangement of epitaphs!' (Act 3, Scene 3).

> **Some examples of malapropisms are 'under the affluence of alcohol' and 'teutonic ulcers'.**

Malpighian

The name of the Italian physiologist **Marcello Malpighi** (1628–1694) is relatively unknown, but he was a pioneer in the field of microscopic anatomy. In 1661 he identified the capillary system, confirming the theory of the English physician and anatomist William Harvey (1578–1657). Malpighi made several studies of organs of the body, and the **Malpighian corpuscle**, part of the kidney, and the **Malpighian layer**, a layer of skin, are named after him. Malpighi held professorships at Bologna, Pisa and Messina; he also served as private physician to Pope Innocent XII.

Malthusian

The adjective **Malthusian** refers to the population theories of the English economist **Thomas Robert Malthus** (1766–1834). In his *Essay on the Principle of Population*, which aroused great controversy throughout the world when it was published in 1798, Malthus argued that population increases at a faster rate than the means of subsistence. The inevitable result would be that the human race would remain near starvation unless the growth in population was checked by sexual restraint or by natural controls such as disease, famine or war.

Man Booker Prize

See **Booker Prize**.

Mandelbrot set

In fractal geometry, a **Mandelbrot set** is a set of complex numbers that produces a convoluted fractal boundary when plotted on a graph. It is named after **Benoît B Mandelbrot** (born 1924), the Polish-born French mathematician who is regarded as the pioneer of fractal geometry. Mandelbrot was born in Warsaw, but studied in France and the USA. He has taught economics, engineering, physiology and mathematics at some of the most prestigious universities in the world. Fractal geometry, with its abstract approach to dimension, has many applications in science and technology, particularly in computer graphics.

man Friday

See **Friday**.

Manichaeanism

Manichaeanism is the religious movement named after its Persian founder, **Mani** (c. AD 217–c. 276). It combined elements from Buddhism, Zoroastrianism and Christianity. According to the teaching, the world and the human race are engaged in the struggle between good and evil (light and darkness, God and matter). By strict abstinence and prayer, Manichaeans believed that man could become aware of the light.

The religion spread throughout Asia and the Roman Empire and lasted until the thirteenth century. Mani, its founder, was martyred by the disciples of Zoroastrianism. St Augustine followed Manichaeanism for a brief period before his conversion to Christianity.

mansard roof

A **mansard roof** has two slopes on both sides and ends, the lower slopes being almost vertical and the upper ones nearly horizontal. It is often used to provide a high ceiling to an attic. The roof is named after

It is said that Mansart was chosen to design the Louvre, but since he would not allow his design to be changed during the building, he was not appointed.

181

the French classical architect **François Mansart** (1598–1666). Notable buildings that Mansart designed include the north wing of the Château de Blois (1635–1638) and the Maisons Laffitte near Paris (1642).

Maoism

The theory of Marxism-Leninism was developed in China by **Mao Tse-tung** (or **Mao Zedong**; 1893–1976). Born into a peasant family in Hunan province, Mao helped establish the Chinese Communist Party in 1921 and founded a Soviet republic in Jiangxi province in south-east China (1931).

He led the Long March, the flight of the Chinese communists from Jiangxi to north-west China (1934–1936), and this established him as leader of the Communist Party. He joined forces with the Kuomintang (Nationalist Party) to bring about the defeat of Japan in the Sino-Japanese War (1937–1945), but he then opposed and defeated the Kuomintang in the ensuing civil war.

> **Mao is quoted as saying, 'The more books one reads, the more stupid one becomes.'**

In 1949, he founded the People's Republic of China and was chairman of the Communist Party from 1949 until his death. He instigated the economic Great Leap Forward (1958–1960) and the Cultural Revolution (1966–1969). Mao, one of the most significant revolutionary figures of the twentieth century, is remembered for, amongst other things, his emphasis on revolutionary guerrilla warfare of the peasant armies, his courageous political and social activities in transforming China, and his stress on moral exhortation and indoctrination, typified by the *Little Red Book* of his sayings.

See also **Marxism**; **Leninism**.

marcel wave

A **marcel wave** is a deep, soft, continuous wave made in the hair with a curling iron; to **marcel** the hair is to make such a wave in the hair.

The word comes from the name of the French hairdresser **Marcel Grateau** (1852–1936). In 1875, Grateau devised the marcelling process; it is said that the hairstyle became so popular in France that Grateau amassed a great wealth, enabling him to retire before he was even 30.

March

The name of the third month of the year comes from the name of the Roman god **Mars**, the god of war. In the earliest period of Roman history, the year began in **March**. This month was considered the beginning of not only a new year but also a new season of waging war; so the month was committed to Mars and named in his honour.

Marfan syndrome

Marfan syndrome is a hereditary disorder of the connective tissue. People who have this condition are usually uncommonly tall and thin, with long thin limbs and digits. They also have cardiovascular and optical defects. This disorder was named after the French paediatrician **Antonin Bernard Jean Marfan** (1858–1942), who first described it in 1896.

marigold

A **marigold** is one of several annual herbaceous plants grown for their yellow or orange flower heads. The word marigold comes from a combination of the name of the **Virgin Mary**, the mother of Jesus, and the word *gold*. The name marigold was probably first applied to the plant now known as a pot marigold (*Calendula officinalis*), once used for healing wounds and as a flavouring for soups and stews.

Mariotte's law

In France and other countries on the continent of Europe, Boyle's law (qv) is known as **Mariotte's law**, after the French physicist **Edmé Mariotte** (1620–1684). Mariotte discovered the law independently of Boyle in 1676, 13 years after the publication of Boyle's law.

Marshall Plan

The **Marshall Plan** (officially known as the European Recovery Programme) was the programme of US economic aid to Europe after World War II. The Marshall Plan is named after the US general and statesman **George Catlett Marshall** (1880–1959), who originally proposed it when he was secretary of state (1947–1949). For this work, he was awarded the Nobel prize (qv) for peace in 1953. Earlier in his career, Marshall had been army chief of staff (1939–1945) and was responsible for organizing the expansion of American armed forces during World War II.

martin

A **martin** is a bird of the swallow family that has a square or slightly forked tail. Its name may come from the time

> St Martin is the patron saint of inn-keepers.

of the birds' migration, reckoned to be about the time of Martinmas, 11 November, the festival of **St Martin**, the fourth-century Bishop of Tours.

See also **St Luke's summer**.

martinet

A **martinet** is a strict disciplinarian. The word comes from the name of a French army officer during the reign of Louis XIV, **Jean Martinet**. Under Martinet's influence, the French army was transformed from an ill-disciplined body of men into an efficient military force by a rigorous system of drilling and training that even included punishing his soldiers with the cat-o'-nine tails. Thus Martinet's name became associated with harsh forms of discipline, and the term gradually entered non-military contexts.

Somewhat ironically, Martinet was 'accidentally' killed by his own forces. In the siege of Duisberg (1672), it is said that Martinet over-zealously entered the line of fire of his own rear ranks. But to those who had experienced the severity of Martinet's training methods, it seems quite possible that the event was not an accident.

Marxism

 Marxism is the theory of socialism of the German political philosophers **Karl Marx** (1818–1883) and Friedrich Engels (1820–1895).

Born in Prussia, Marx was educated at the universities of Bonn and Berlin. He edited the radical Cologne newspaper, the *Rheinische Zeitung* (1842–1843), but after its suppression he left Germany. At first he stayed in Paris, where he met Engels; later in Brussels the *Communist Manifesto* (1848) was written. Marx settled in London in 1849, where he spent the rest of his life. He assumed leadership of the International Working Men's Association (the First International) in 1864. His theories of the class struggle and the economics of capitalism were developed in *Das Kapital* (first volume, 1867; the remaining two volumes published posthumously).

> **Despite being one of the most famous economists of all time, Marx himself was constantly short of money.**

Marxism has come to stand for the theory that capitalism and the class struggle will give way to the dictatorship of the proletariat and then to the establishing of the classless society.

See also **Leninism**; **Maoism**, **Stalinism**; **Trotskyism**.

masochism

The word **masochism** is used to describe the mental disorder that causes a person to derive pleasure (especially sexual) from the experience of self-inflicted pain, humiliation, etc. The word derives from the name of the Austrian novelist **Leopold von Sacher-Masoch** (1836–1895), whose writings depicted this condition.

This form of obsession was reflected not only in the novels of Sacher-Masoch; it was also evident in his bizarre life – he was the self-appointed 'slave' of a number of mistresses and two wives in his lifetime. It was probably the German psychiatrist Richard von Krafft-Ebing (1840–1902) who coined the word 'masochism' after studying Sacher-Masoch's works.

Mason–Dixon line

The **Mason–Dixon line** (originally **Mason and Dixon's line**) was the name given to the boundary between the states of Maryland and Pennsylvania, set in 1763–1767. It is named after its English surveyors **Charles**

> Mason was not a surveyor by profession, but an astronomer working for the Greenwich observatory.

Mason (c. 1730–1787) and **Jeremiah Dixon** (died 1777). Before the American Civil War the line came to be regarded as the demarcation line between the North and South, the free states and the slave states.

Mata Hari

If a woman is described as a **Mata Hari**, she is seductive, treacherous and dangerous. **Mata Hari** (1876–1917), born Margaretha Geertruida Zelle, was a Dutch exotic dancer based in Paris, who spied for the German Secret Service during World War I. In 1917 she was arrested by the French authorities for spying, court-martialled, and sentenced to death by firing squad.

maudlin

The word **maudlin** is sometimes used to refer to someone who is tearfully sentimental or foolishly drunk. The word comes originally from the name **Mary Magdalene**, traditionally portrayed in paintings as a weeping penitent. The biblical text relates that Mary weeps when she discovers the empty tomb after the resurrection of Jesus (John 20:1–18).

See also **magdalen**.

Mauser

Mauser is the trademark used to describe a type of pistol. The word comes from the name of the German firearms inventors **Peter Paul von Mauser** (1838–1914) and his older brother **Wilhelm von Mauser** (1834–1882). The Mauser rifle (or pistol) was used by the Germany army for many years from 1871; modified versions were used in World

Wars I and II. The younger brother also invented the **Mauser magazine rifle** in 1897.

mausoleum

A **mausoleum**, a grand stately tomb, comes from the name of **King Mausolus**, ruler of Caria in ancient Greece. When he died in 353 BC, his widow, Artemisia, built a huge magnificent tomb at Halicarnassus in his honour. The monument was probably a raised temple with decorative statues and a pyramid-like roof; it was considered one of the seven wonders of the ancient world. It is believed that the monument was destroyed by earthquake in the Middle Ages.

maverick

A person who is independent and who does not wish to conform or be identified with a group is sometimes called a **maverick**. The word comes from the name of the American pioneer **Samuel Augustus Maverick** (1803–1870). Also known as a fighter for Texan independence and originally a lawyer, Maverick became a rancher when he gained a herd of cattle in settlement of a debt. He failed, however, to ensure that all his calves were branded, perhaps so that he could claim all unbranded calves as his own or so that neighbouring ranchers could put their own brands on them. In the course of time the word came to be used to refer not only to unbranded cattle but also to people who do not 'go with the herd', who do not give allegiance to a particular group, especially a political one.

Maxim gun

The **Maxim gun** is the name of the first fully automatic machine-gun – a water-cooled, single-barrelled weapon that used the recoil force of each shot to keep up the automatic firing. The machine-gun is named after the US-born British inventor Sir **Hiram Stevens Maxim** (1840–1916), who developed it in 1884.

Maxim also invented a kind of mousetrap and a fire sprinkler.

Maxim originally served as chief engineer for America's first electric company, the United States Electric Lighting Company. He later applied his engineering skills to inventing his machine-gun and other items.

maxwell

The **maxwell** is the unit of magnetic flux in the centimetre–gram–second system of measurement. The unit is named after the Scottish physicist **James Clerk Maxwell** (1831–1879).

Maxwell wrote his first scientific paper at the age of 15; he later became professor of physics at the University of Aberdeen and then London. In 1871 he became the first professor of experimental physics at Cambridge. Maxwell made significant advances in physics, notably in his unifying of electricity, magnetism and light into one set of equations (**Maxwell's equations**, published 1873 in his *Treatise on Electricity and Magnetism*), which form the basis of electrodynamics. Maxwell also made important contributions to the kinetic theory of gases and to the understanding of colour vision.

May

The fifth month of the year probably takes its name from the Roman goddess **Maia**, the goddess of spring and fertility, and daughter of Faunus and wife of Vulcan.

The Old English name for the month is said to have been of a more practical nature: *Thrimilce*, because in the longer days of spring, the cows could be milked three times between sunrise and sunset.

medusa

A **medusa** is the name given to a type of jellyfish and also to the free-swimming form in the life-cycle of a coelenterate animal. The word comes from the name **Medusa**, one of the hideously ugly Gorgons in Greek mythology. When the goddess Athena was incensed by Medusa's giving her favours to Poseidon, she changed Medusa's locks into serpents and made her face so hideous that everyone who looked at her was turned to stone. The name of the jellyfish comes from the resemblance of its tentacles to the serpent-like curls of the Gorgon.

Megan's law

Megan Nicole Kanka was a seven-year-old American girl who was brutally raped, tortured and strangled in 1991. Unknown to Megan's parents, her attacker was a twice-convicted paedophile who had set up home with two other paedophiles in a house directly opposite their family home in Hamilton Township, New Jersey. Megan's parents, in the belief that if they had known of the presence of convicted paedophiles in their neighbourhood, their daughter might still be alive, campaigned for the introduction of a new law giving parents the right to know when convicted paedophiles and other sex offenders are living in their community. In response to the overwhelming public support for this campaign, a new law, known as **Megan's law**, was introduced in New Jersey within 89 days of Megan's murder. Within two years this law was on the statute book of every state in the USA.

See also **Sarah's law**.

meitnerium

The artificially produced radioactive transuranic element known as **meitnerium** (formerly called unnilennium) is named in honour of the Austrian-born Swedish nuclear physicist **Lise Meitner** (1878–1968). Together with the German physicist Otto Hahn, Meitner discovered the chemical element protactinium in 1917 and, in collaboration with the German physicist Fritz Strassmann (1902–1980), they discovered nuclear fission in 1938.

See also **hahnium**.

Melba toast

Melba toast (thinly sliced toasted bread) and **peach Melba** (a dessert of peaches, ice-cream and raspberry sauce) owe their origin to the stage name of the Australian operatic soprano singer **Dame Nellie Melba** (1861–1931).

Born as Helen Porter Mitchell, and later adopting the name Melba (from Melbourne, near which she was born), the singer made her début in *Rigoletto* (Brussels, 1887) and went on to star in London, Paris and New York. It is said that Melba toast originated at the Savoy Hotel in London when Dame Nellie Melba ordered toast and was served with several pieces that were unusually thin and crisp and almost burnt; such toast was then named after her. Peach Melba is said to have been originally made by the French chef Auguste Escoffier (1846–1935) in her honour.

mendelevium

The artificially produced radioactive metallic chemical element known as **mendelevium** is named in honour of the Russian chemist **Dmitri Ivanovich Mendeleyev** (1834–1907). Mendeleyev was professor of organic chemistry at St Petersburg (1866–1890). After listening to a lecture on the subject of atomic weights by the Italian chemist Stanislao Cannizzaro (1826–1910), Mendeleyev became interested in a classification of the elements and in 1869 he devised the first version of the periodic table of the chemical elements.

Mendel's laws

Mendel's laws are the basic principles of heredity proposed by the Austrian botanist **Gregor Johann Mendel** (1822–1884). Mendel was a monk; however, because of his earlier scientific training and interest in botany he began to experiment with the hybrid breeding of pea plants in the monastery garden at Brno, Moravia. His conclusions were formulated in two principles – Mendel's laws – in 1865, but remained unrecognized until 1900, when they were rediscovered by Hugo de Vries and others. Mendel is now recognized as the founder of the science of genetics.

Ménière's disease

Ménière's disease is a disorder affecting the membranous labyrinth of the inner ear, which causes recurrent attacks of dizziness,

It is believed that Vincent Van Gogh and Jonathan Swift may have suffered from Ménière's disease.

buzzing in the ears and progressive deafness. It was named after
Prosper Ménière (1799–1862), a French physician specializing in
otorhinolaryngology, who published the first detailed description of this
disorder in 1861.

mentor

Mentor, the word for a wise and trusted adviser, comes from the name
of **Mentor**, Odysseus's loyal friend who was also tutor to his son, the
young Telemachus, in Homer's *Odyssey*. Mentor's identity is assumed by
Athene, the goddess of wisdom; she accompanies Telemachus in his
search for his father. The currency of the word in English is probably
due to the prominence of the character in *Les Aventures de Télémaque*
(1699) by the French theologian and writer François de Salignac de la
Mothe Fénelon (1651–1715).

Mephistophelean

A person may be described as being **Mephistophelean** if he or she is
diabolical or evil in a sinister, persuasive manner. The term comes from
the **Mephistopheles** of German legend – the contemptuous, merciless,
tempting evil spirit to whom Faust sold his soul. The origin of the word
Mephistopheles itself is uncertain; it is said to have been used by
magicians and alchemists in spells. The earliest form of the word is
Mephostophiles (*Faustbuch*, 1587), possibly meaning 'not loving the
light'.

Mercalli scale

 The **Mercalli scale**, a scale for expressing the intensity of earthquakes,
is named after the Italian vulcanologist and seismologist **Giuseppe
Mercalli** (1850–1914), who devised it in 1902. The scale ranges from I
to XII; a value of I can be felt by very few people, while earthquakes that
measure XII cause total destruction. Intensities II to III on the Mercalli
scale are approximately equivalent to magnitudes 3 to 4 on the Richter
scale, while intensities XI to XII approximate to magnitudes 8 to 9 on the
Richter.

See also **Richter scale**.

Mercator projection

Mercator (or **Mercator's**) **projection** is the form of map projection in which lines of latitude and longitude are straight lines that intersect at right angles and all lines of latitude are the same length as the equator. The projection is used for navigation charts but it has the disadvantage of distorting outlines and exaggerating sizes at increasing distances from the equator.

This form of map projection is named after the Flemish geographer **Gerardus Mercator** (original name Gerhard Kremer; 1512–1594) who devised it in 1568. Originally working in Louvain, Mercator had to flee to Protestant Germany in 1552 to escape charges of heresy.

See also **atlas**; **Peters projection**.

mesmerize

If you are **mesmerized** by something you are extremely fascinated, spellbound or even hypnotized by it. The word comes from the name of the Austrian physician and hypnotist **Franz Anton Mesmer** (1734–1815), who induced a hypnotic state in his patients. Born in Austria, Mesmer studied and later practised medicine in Vienna. He considered his medical success was due to his method (so-called 'animal magnetism') of stroking his patients with magnets.

In spite of the support of those he had treated, Mesmer was compelled by the Austrian authorities to leave Vienna, so he moved to Paris in 1778. Here, his healing technique became very fashionable. Wearing purple robes, he would wave his magic wand, and seek to treat individuals in a gathered group.

In 1784 Louis XVI appointed a scientific commission to investigate the practices; they concluded that Mesmer was a charlatan and an impostor. This led him to flee from Paris and he spent the rest of his life in obscurity in Switzerland. Mesmer believed that his success was due to the supernatural; today we would acknowledge that it was due to his hypnotic powers.

Messerschmitt

The **Messerschmitt** planes (particularly the Me-109 and the first mass-produced jet-fighter, the Me-262) of World War II are named after the German aircraft designer **Willy Messerschmitt** (1898–1978). Messerschmitt built his first aeroplane at the age of 18 and owned his own factory by the time he was 25. In 1927 he was appointed chief designer at the Bayerische Flugzeugwerke; in 1937 he received the Lilienthal prize for research into aviation.

After the war, Messerschmitt also designed cars and houses.

methuselah

A **methuselah** is a large bottle holding eight times the standard amount. Like many large bottles, it is named after a character from the Old Testament. According to Genesis, chapter 5, **Methuselah** was the son of Enoch and grandfather of Noah and lived to be 969 years old. The expression '**as old as Methuselah**', meaning very old, refers to the age of the patriarch.

See also **jeroboam**; **jorum**; **nebuchadnezzar**; **rehoboam**.

Micawber

Someone who is described as a **Micawber** or as being **Micawberish** is a person who does not make provision for the future, optimistically trusting that 'something is bound to turn up'. The name comes from the character **Wilkins Micawber** in the novel *David Copperfield* (published 1849–1850) by Charles Dickens. By the end of the story, Micawber, relieved of his debts and having emigrated to Australia, appears as a highly regarded colonial magistrate.

Michaelmas

Michaelmas is the feast of **St Michael the Archangel**, 29 September, and is one of the four quarter days when certain business payments become due. The autumnal celebration of St Michael is recalled in the naming of the **Michaelmas daisy**, an autumn-blooming aster, and **Michaelmas term**, another name for the autumn term at some universities.

> **St Michael is the patron saint of policemen, paratroopers, knights, grocers and pilgrims.**

See also **Hilary term**.

Mickey Finn

A **Mickey Finn** is slang for an alcoholic drink containing a drug to render someone unconscious. The expression is said to derive from a Chicago saloon-keeper at the end of the nineteenth century called **Mickey Finn**. He would add a knock-out drug to the drinks of his unsuspecting victims, and would rob them once they had passed out. It is possible that the original Mickey Finn was a laxative for horses.

Mickey Mouse

Something may be described as being **Mickey Mouse** if it is trivial or trite. The expression derives from the name of the simple-minded cartoon character **Mickey Mouse** created by the American film producer and animator Walt Disney (1901–1966).

> **Disney is said to have changed the mouse's name from Mortimer to Mickey after a chance meeting with the actor Mickey Roonie.**

Disney first drew Mickey Mouse in 1928; it seems that the character was based on his former pet mouse, Mortimer. Mickey Mouse made his debut in the first animated sound cartoon *Steamboat Willie* (November 1928), in which Disney used his own voice for Mickey's high-pitched speech. The mouse became an instant success, and by 1931 Mickey Mouse clubs had a million members throughout the USA.

Midas touch

Someone who has the **Midas touch** makes an easy financial success of all his or her business undertakings. The expression comes from **King Midas** of Phrygia in Greek legend. In gratitude to King Midas for his hospitality towards the satyr Silenus, the god Dionysus promised to fulfil any wish King Midas might make. The king told Dionysus that he wanted everything he touched to be turned to gold. Dionysus granted this – but on discovering that even his food and drink turned to gold, Midas asked that the gift be taken away. Dionysus then ordered King Midas to bathe in the River Pactolus and he was washed clean of his power.

mint

The word for the place where money is coined, a **mint**, comes from the Latin word for money, *moneta*. The Romans coined their money in the temple of the Roman goddess Juno, who was known by the title **Moneta**, 'the admonisher'; so it was that the mint and its product came to be known by this name.

Miranda warning

In 1963, **Ernesto Miranda** (1941–1976) was arrested on suspicion of stealing $8 in cash from a bank clerk in Phoenix, Arizona. He was never offered a lawyer, and under police questioning confessed not only to the theft, but also to kidnapping and raping an 18-year-old woman eleven days earlier. He was convicted and sentenced to 20 years in jail. An appeal was lodged, and in 1966 the United States Supreme Court granted Miranda a new trial at which his previous confession could not be admitted as evidence.

The case led to the establishment of new guidelines for American police to follow when making an arrest: the arresting officer must warn the arrested person of their legal right to remain silent and to consult with an attorney. This warning is known as a **Miranda warning**, and an officer issuing such a warning is said to **mirandize** the suspect.

Miranda died at the age of 34 after being stabbed in a bar-room fight. A suspect was arrested but, ironically, after being read the Miranda warning, he asserted his right to remain silent, and was never charged.

mithridatism

The word **mithridatism** is used to refer to an immunity to poison that is acquired by a gradual drinking of increasing doses. The expression comes from the name of the king of Pontus, **Mithridates VI**, called the Great (c. 132–63 BC), who allegedly produced this condition in himself.

King Mithridates engaged the Romans in many significant battles, but was eventually defeated by Pompey in 66 BC. During his whole lifetime he is said to have guarded himself from being poisoned by gradually drinking increasing amounts of poison, so rendering himself more and more immune to its effect. On his defeat by Pompey he decided to commit suicide only to discover that he had mithridatized himself too successfully. He was completely immune to poison and so ordered a mercenary to kill him with his sword.

Möbius strip

Möbius's mother was a descendant of Martin Luther.

A **Möbius strip** is a one-sided continuous surface that is made by twisting a strip of paper through 180° and joining the ends. It is named after the German mathematician **August Ferdinand Möbius** (1790–1868), who discovered it. The Möbius strip is significant because its unexpected properties are of interest in topology: if it is cut lengthways, it remains in one piece.

mogul

A **Mogul** was a member of the Muslim dynasty of rulers in India in the sixteenth to eighteenth centuries, and (with a small 'm') is an important or very rich person: for instance, 'a film mogul'. The founder of the dynasty was the Emperor Barbur (1483–1530). Both usages of the word have their origin in Persian *Mughul*, which in turn comes from Mongolian *Mongol*. The figurative sense probably comes from the Great Moguls, the first six rulers of the dynasty.

Mohammed

The idiomatic expression '**if the mountain will not come to Mohammed, Mohammed must go to the mountain**' means that if a person or set of circumstances will not change or be adapted to suit one's own wishes, then one must oneself change or adapt to suit them. The expression derives from the life of **Mohammed**, the prophet and founder of Islam (c. AD 570–632). It is said that when he brought his message of Islam to the Arabs, they demanded a miracle to prove his claims. Mohammed then ordered Mount Safa to come towards him. When it failed to do so, he explained that God had been merciful: if the mountain had moved, it would have fallen on them and destroyed them. Mohammed then proposed that instead he would go to the mountain, and give thanks to God for his mercy.

molly

The **molly** is a brightly coloured tropical fish that belongs to the genus *Mollienesia*, and is valued as an aquarium fish. The molly takes its name from the French statesman **Comte Nicolas-François Mollien** (1758–1850). Mollien served as financial adviser to Napoleon, although it seems his advice was often rejected. It is not clear why the fish is named after this French statesman; he was not even a collector of tropical fish.

Molotov cocktail

 The Soviet statesman **Vyacheslav Mikhailovich Molotov** (original surname Scriabin; 1890–1986) played a substantial role in the growth of the Soviet Union as a superpower. After the Bolshevik Revolution of October 1917, Molotov held a series of posts in the ranks of the Party, becoming (1921) a secretary to the Central Committee; in 1922 he was instrumental in promoting Stalin to general secretary. He was prime minister (1930–1941) and foreign minister (1939–1949; 1953–1956). He negotiated the Soviet-German non-aggression treaty (1939), and after the Germans invaded the Soviet Union he negotiated alliances with the Allies. He was also a prominent figure in the Cold War between the USA and the Soviet Union after World War II. Disagreements with Khrushchev led, however, to his dismissal from office in 1956 and in

1962 his expulsion from the Communist Party, although he was readmitted to the Party in 1984.

The crude petrol bomb known as the **Molotov cocktail** is named after the Russian statesman. It consists of a bottle filled with a flammable liquid, such as petrol, and stoppered with a saturated rag; the rag is ignited as the bottle is thrown. It seems that the device may have been used as early as 1934 but the term Molotov cocktail was not applied to the device until 1940, when the Finns used them against the tanks of the invading Russians.

Monroe doctrine

The US president **James Monroe** (1785–1831) is remembered for his proclamation to Congress on 2 December 1823 that has come

> **According to Thomas Jefferson, 'Monroe was so honest that if you turned his soul inside out there would not be a spot on it.'**

to be known as the **Monroe doctrine**. In this statement he warned the European nations against trying to interfere in or influence the affairs of the Americans; in return the USA would not intervene in Europe. The Monroe doctrine, largely the work of secretary of state John Quincy Adams, became a fundamental principle in the foreign policy of the USA.

Earlier, Monroe had fought and been wounded in the American Revolution; he had also served as minister to France (1794–1796) and Britain (1803–1807). His two terms in office (1817–1825) as president are known as the 'era of good feelings'; during this time Florida was acquired and five states were added to the Union.

Monrovia, the capital and main port of the African country of Liberia, is also named in honour of Monroe. The country was founded during Monroe's presidency, in 1822, as a settlement for freed American slaves.

Montagu's harrier

Montagu's harrier is a bird of the hawk family with narrow wings and a long tail. It is Britain's rarest bird of prey, and was on the verge of extinction in the middle of the twentieth century, although numbers have subsequently increased.

The bird is named after the English naturalist **Colonel George Montagu** (1753–1815). After a failed career in the

> **Montagu died of tetanus after cutting himself by stepping on a rusty nail.**

army and a disastrous marriage that led to the loss of his estates, Montagu turned his attention to ornithology. He published his *Ornithological Dictionary; or Alphabetical Synopsis of British Birds* in two volumes in 1802.

montbretia

 A **montbretia** is a plant of the iris family that bears showy orange or yellow flowers. The plant is named after the French botanist **A F E Coquebert de Montbret** (1780–1801).

Montessori method

The Italian physicist and educator **Maria Montessori** (1870–1952) is remembered for the development of an educational method that is named after her. In this method the creative potential of young children is developed; they are provided with different sensory materials in a prepared environment, and they progress at their own rate through free but guided play.

Born into a noble family, Montessori studied medicine at the University of Rome and became the first woman in Italy to receive a degree in medicine (1896). She then began to work with retarded children, later opening a school for children of normal intelligence in a slum area of Rome (1907). The success of her methods led to the founding of other schools in Europe and Asia. With some refinements, Montessori's ideas have had an important influence on the modern education of children.

Montezuma's revenge

 Montezuma's revenge is a jocular name for diarrhoea contracted by visitors to Mexico. **Montezuma II** (1466–1520), the emperor of Mexico

(c. 1502–1520), was the despotic last emperor of the Aztecs. During the Spanish conquest of Mexico, Montezuma

Montezuma inspired Neil Young's 1975 album *Zuma*.

was taken hostage and deposed by the Spanish under Hernando Cortés. He was killed in the ensuing Aztec uprising, either by his own people or by the Spanish. Today Montezuma allegedly takes his revenge on the hordes of invading tourists, in the form of 'travellers' diarrhoea'. In Spain, the equivalent of Montezuma's revenge is 'Spanish tummy'; in Egypt, 'Tutankhamen's curse'; in India, 'Delhi belly'.

Moog synthesizer

Moog is the trademark for a type of synthesizer. **Robert Arthur Moog** (born 1934) is an American physicist, engineer and electrician who designed the synthesizer that bears his name. Working with the composer H A Deutsch, Moog developed his device that could electronically reproduce the sounds of conventional musical instruments and also produce a variety of artificial tones. The Moog synthesizer was patented in 1965.

Moonie

Moonie is the name given to a member of the Unification Church founded by the Korean industrialist **Sun Myung**

Moon has been imprisoned six times in Korea and the US for offences as diverse as preaching Christianity, counterfeiting and tax evasion.

Moon (original name Yong Myung Moon; born 1920).

The religious group was established in 1954; its members believe that the 'Reverend' Moon has been given the responsibility, begun by Adam and Jesus, to unite the human race into a perfect family. The movement is also known for its indoctrination of potential recruits and its methods of fund raising.

Mormon

A **Mormon** is a member of the Church of Jesus Christ of Latter-Day Saints, founded in 1830 by Joseph Smith (1805–1844) in New York state. Smith claimed that led by visions he had, in 1927, discovered some gold plates which contained the *Book of Mormon*. This sacred book is named after its compiler, and, according to Mormon belief, was buried in the fifth century AD.

Smith published the book in 1830; Mormons see it as one of a series of scriptures that supplement the Bible. Following Smith's murder in Illinois, the movement was led by Brigham Young (1801–1877), and their headquarters were established at Salt Lake City, Utah, in 1847. The Mormons' practice of polygamy brought them into conflict with the Federal authorities until 1890 when it was disallowed.

mornay

Mornay sauce is a béchamel sauce flavoured with cheese, usually Parmesan and Swiss cheese; thus, broccoli mornay is broccoli served with a cheese-flavoured sauce. This sauce is probably named after **Philippe de Mornay**, Seigneur du Plessis-Marly (1549–1623), the French Huguenot leader during the wars of religion. Mornay was a prolific writer on the subject of Protestant theology and was called 'the Protestant pope'. In addition to mornay sauce, he is said to have invented béchamel sauce, sauce chasseur, sauce Lyonnaise and sauce Porto.

morphine

Morphine (or **morphia**) is an addictive narcotic drug used medicinally to alleviate pain and to induce sleep. The word is derived from the name **Morpheus**, the god of dreams in Greek mythology. He was the son of Sleep.

Morris chair

The **Morris chair**, an armchair that has an adjustable back and large loose cushions, is named after its designer, the English poet, artist and socialist writer **William Morris** (1834–1896). Morris founded a firm of designers and decorators in 1861 and he designed furniture, wallpaper and stained glass of a style different from that of the contemporary Victorian era. The work of William Morris and his Pre-Raphaelite associates led to the development of the Arts and Crafts movement in England.

Morris is also noted for his development of the private press, with his founding of the Kelmscott Press (1890) for his poetry and prose writings, and for his establishing of the Socialist League in England.

Morrison shelter

The **Morrison shelter** was an indoor air-raid shelter with a steel table-top and wired sides, used in World War II. It was named after the British statesman **Herbert Stanley Morrison** (1888–1965), later Baron Morrison of Lambeth. Morrison was home secretary and minister for home security in Churchill's war cabinet (1942–1945).

> **Morrison was Peter Mandelson's grandfather.**

See also **Anderson shelter**.

Morse code

Morse code is a telegraphic system of signalling in which letters and numbers are represented by dots and dashes. The code is named after its inventor, the American artist and inventor **Samuel Finley Breese Morse** (1791–1872).

Morse was originally an artist: he exhibited paintings at the Royal Academy in London and enjoyed a good reputation as a portrait painter. He founded and became the first president of the National Academy of Design in New York in 1826, and then was appointed professor of painting and sculpture at New York University.

Morse's interests gradually turned to electric telegraphy. His work was only very slowly recognized, but following financial backing from Congress, the first line, between Washington and Baltimore, was built

(1843–1844). The words 'What hath God wrought?' constituted the first communication in Morse code sent on 24 May 1844. Following a series of legal battles, Morse patented his system in 1854. Morse code was used as as an international standard for maritime communication until 1999 and is still in use today by many amateur radio operators.

Moses basket

A portable shallow wickerwork cradle for a baby is sometimes known as a **Moses basket**. This expression alludes to the papyrus cradle in which the infant **Moses** was hidden among the reeds by the River Nile (Exodus 2:3).

Mother Carey's chickens

Mother Carey's chickens are storm petrels – small sea-birds with dark plumage and paler underparts. It is not known who the original **Mother Carey** was; it is possible that the expression is a corruption of the Latin *Mater Cara* (Beloved Mother), a name for the Virgin Mary, considered to be the protector of sailors. An alternative suggestion is that the expression is an alteration of a nautical Spanish or Italian name.

Mother Hubbard

 A **Mother Hubbard** was a long loose dress with a yoke and long sleeves, worn unbelted by pregnant women, and with or without belt by working-class rural women, in the nineteenth century. **Mother Hubbard** was a character in a nursery rhyme popularized in *The Comic Adventures of Old Mother Hubbard and Her Dog* (1805) by the British writer Sarah Catherine Martin (1768–1826).

Mrs Grundy

A **Mrs Grundy** is a narrow-minded person noted for prudish conventionality in personal behaviour. The name comes from a character in the play *Speed the Plough* (1798) by the English dramatist Thomas Morton (c. 1764–1838). From the name **Mrs Grundy** the word **grundyism** is derived, referring to a disapproving or censorious, prudish attitude.

Mrs Mop

Mrs Mop is an informal expression for a lady who cleans a house or office. The name, often used in a facetious or derogatory way, derives from the character (**Mrs Mopp**) in the BBC radio programme *ITMA* broadcast during the years of World War II. Mrs Mopp was a Cockney charlady who first featured in the radio show on 10 October 1940. Her original question was, 'Can I do for you now, sir?' This was later shortened, by omitting the 'for', to the expression that has become a familiar catch-phrase, 'Can I do you now, sir?'

Müllerian mimicry

In zoology, **Müllerian mimicry** is a form of protective mimicry in which two or more distasteful or noxious species closely resemble each other in appearance, so that they are avoided equally by predators. This phenomenon was first described by the German–born Brazilian zoologist **Johann Friedrich Theodor** ('Fritz') **Müller** (1821–1897).

See also **Batesian mimicry**.

Münchhausen's syndrome

Münchhausen's syndrome is a mental disorder in which the patient feigns serious illness in order to obtain medical attention. This syndrome was named after **Baron Karl Friedrich Hieronymous von Münchhausen** (1720–1797), a German soldier. Münchhausen was the hero of *Baron Münchhausen's Narrative of His Marvellous Travels and Campaigns in Russia* (1785), a collection of exaggerated tales of adventure written in English by the German–born antiquary Rudolph Erich Raspe (1737–1794), and subsequently featured in similar tall tales by various other authors. His name has come to be associated with amusingly preposterous stories.

Münchhausen's syndrome by proxy is a variation on Münchhausen's syndrome in which the patient is usually a mother who claims her child is ill, sometimes even going so far as to cause the child to be ill, for example by administering poison to the child, again in order to obtain medical attention and sympathy.

Munro

Originally, a **Munro** was any one of the 277 Scottish mountains that are at least 3000 feet high. The Scottish mountaineer **Sir Hugh Thomas Munro** (1856–1919) published a list of these peaks in the Journal of the Scottish Mountaineering Club for 1891. In more recent years, the designation 'Munro' has been extended to apply to any mountain of that height in the British Isles. **Munro-baggers** are climbers who aim to climb every mountain that is designated a Munro. Unfortunately, Munro himself died without having climbed two of the mountains on his list. The first person to scale all of the Munros was the Reverend A E Robertson (1870–1958).

See also **Corbett**.

Murphy's law

'If anything can go wrong, it will' – this is the pithy wisdom of **Murphy's** (or **Sod's**) **law**. Other humorous rules of thumb that go under the name of Murphy's law include: 'Nothing is as easy as it looks,' and, 'Everything takes longer than you think it will.' It is not certain who the original **Murphy** was; quotations of the 'law' in print date back to the 1950s.

N

namby-pamby

Someone or something that is described as **namby-pamby** is thought of as being very sentimental in an insipid manner. The word was originally a nickname for the English poet **Ambrose Philips** (1674–1749). His verses about children (such as 'Dimply damsel, sweetly smiling' and 'Timely blossom, infant fair, Fondling of a happy pair') were mocked by writers such as Pope and Carey for their weak sentimentality. It was Henry Carey (c. 1687–1743) who is credited with the coining of the word namby-pamby: amby comes from the poet's first name and the alliterative p from his surname.

nap

Nap is a card game that is similar to whist in which the number of tricks that a player expects to win is declared. The longer version of the name of the card game is **napoleon**, which reveals the word's origin: the French Emperor **Napoleon Bonaparte** (1769–1821). It is, however, uncertain why the game is named after him.

The adjective **Napoleonic** is sometimes used with allusion to the Emperor's masterly tactics or the vastness of his ambitions.

Napierian

The mathematical functions known as logarithms, used in calculations of multiplication and division, were invented by the Scottish

> **Napier devised a primitive form of tank as a means of defence against the Spanish Armada.**

mathematician **John Napier** (1550–1647). He published his table of logarithms in 1614; these came to be known as **Napierian** or **natural logarithms**. A modified version of these mathematical functions (common logarithms) came into use later.

Napier also devised a simple calculating machine that consisted of a series of graduated rods known as **Napier's bones**.

narcissism

Extreme interest in or love for oneself is known as **narcissism**. This word comes from **Narcissus**, the beautiful young man in Greek mythology who, after spurning all offers of love, including that of the nymph Echo, was punished by falling in love with his own reflection in the waters of a fountain, thinking that it was a nymph. His attempts to approach the beautiful object were to no avail, however. He was driven to despair and pined away, finally being transformed into the flower that bears his name.

nebuchadnezzar

A **nebuchadnezzar** is a very large bottle holding the equivalent of 20 standard bottles. Like other large bottles, it is named after an Old Testament character, in this case **King Nebuchadnezzar II** of Babylon (died 562 BC).

Nebuchadnezzar extended the Babylonian Empire as far as the Mediterranean, gaining control of Syria and capturing Jerusalem. He is chiefly remembered for deporting the Jews into exile in Babylonia.

See also **jeroboam**; **jorum**; **methuselah**; **rehoboam**.

negus

A **negus** is a drink of wine (usually port or sherry), hot water, lemon juice, sugar and nutmeg. It is named after the English soldier and politician in the reign of Queen Anne, **Colonel Francis Negus** (died 1732), who is reputed to have invented it.

The Dictionary of National Biography records that on a certain occasion, Negus averted a fracas between Whigs and Tories 'by recommending the dilution of the wine with hot water and sugar. Attention was diverted from the point of issue to a discussion of the merits of wine and water, which ended in the compound being nicknamed "Negus".'

Nehru jacket

A **Nehru jacket** is a type of long narrow jacket with a stand-up collar. It was named after **Jawaharlal Nehru** (1889–1964), a leader in the movement for India's independence and the first prime minister of India (1947–1964), who often wore this style of jacket. Nehru's daughter, Indira Gandhi (1917–1984), herself went on to become prime minister of India (1966–1977 and 1980–1984). In the 1960s the Nehru jacket became a fashion item in the West. It was favoured by the Beatles and, perhaps most notably, by the American entertainer Sammy Davis, Jr., who owned more than 200 Nehru jackets.

nemesis

Nemesis means vengeance or something that is thought to be or to bring retribution. The word derives from **Nemesis**, the Greek mythological goddess of retribution. Nemesis personified the gods' resentment at, and just punishment of, human arrogance, pride and insolence. According to the early Greek poet Hesiod, Nemesis was a child of Night.

nestor

A **nestor** is a wise old man or a sage. **Nestor** was the king of Pylos in Greek legend. The *Iliad* describes him as being the oldest – he was about 70 – and most experienced of the Greek commanders in the Trojan War, who advised moderation to the quarrelling Greek leaders. He was well known for his wise advice and the narration of his deeds in earlier days, in spite of his wordiness.

newton

Newton, the metric unit of force, comes from the name of the British physicist and mathematician **Sir Isaac Newton** (1642–1727), one of the world's greatest scientists. Newton is particularly noted for his law of gravitation – said, as is well known, to have been inspired by the falling of an apple on his head – his laws of motion and his studies of calculus and the theory of light.

Newton was also a member of parliament (1689–1690), and master of the mint from 1699 to 1727, during which time he undertook a reform of the coinage. From 1703 he was president of the Royal Society and he was knighted in 1705. His last words are said to have been: 'I don't know what I may seem to the world. But as to myself I seem to have been only like a boy playing on the seashore and diverting myself in now and then finding a smoother pebble or prettier shell than ordinary, whilst the great ocean of truth lay all undiscovered before me.'

nicotine

 Nicotine, the chemical compound found in tobacco, comes from the name of the French diplomat **Jean Nicot** (1530–1600). Nicot was ambassador in Lisbon at the time that Portuguese explorers were bringing back seeds of tobacco from the newly discovered continent of America. In 1560, Nicot was given a plant from Florida, which he grew, sending tobacco seeds to the French nobility. When Nicot returned to France in 1561, he took a cargo load of tobacco with him. The powder quickly became so well known that the tobacco plant itself was named after Nicot: *Herba nicotiana*. It was in the early years of the nineteenth century that the liquid nicotine was isolated and named in Nicot's honour.

nightingale

 A **nightingale** was a flannel scarf with sleeves, formerly worn by hospital patients when sitting up in bed. It was named after the English nurse **Florence Nightingale** (1820–1910), who is known for her work during the Crimean War. She led a party of nurses to work in the military hospital at Scutari (1854), where she sought to improve the living conditions of the patients, who dubbed her 'the Lady with the Lamp'. After the war, Florence Nightingale devoted herself to raising the status of the nursing profession.

> **In 1907 Florence Nightingale became the first woman to receive the Order of Merit.**

Nimrod

The name **Nimrod** is sometimes used to describe a great, skilful hunter. Use of this word derives from the biblical **Nimrod**, the son of Cush, a warrior or hero of Babylon. Genesis 10:9 describes him as 'a mighty hunter before the Lord'.

Nimrod is credited with the founding of the cities of Ninevah and Calah (modern Nimrud) in Assyria.

Nissen hut

 A **Nissen hut** is a prefabricated military shelter that has a semicircular arched roof of corrugated iron sheeting and a cement floor. The hut was named after its inventor, the British mining engineer **Lieutenant Colonel Peter Norman Nissen** (1871–1930) and was used in both World Wars.

The American equivalent is the Quonset hut, which is not named after a person, but after Quonset Point, Rhode Island, where the huts were first made.

Nobel prize

The Swedish chemist, manufacturer and philanthropist **Alfred Bernhard Nobel** (1833–1896) is noted for his invention of dynamite (1866). A pacifist, Nobel believed that his explosives would be the foundation of a country's defence system and, acting as a deterrent towards belligerent countries, would bring about peace.

Nobel amassed a great fortune from the manufacture and sale of explosives and also from his exploitation of oil interests. His great wealth went towards the funding of the **Nobel prizes** – prizes awarded annually for outstanding contributions to the service of humanity in the fields of physics, chemistry, medicine, literature and peace. The first of these annual awards was given in 1901; in 1969 a prize for economics was added.

> **Marie Curie and Linus Pauling are the only people to win Nobel prizes in two different fields.**

The artificially produced element **nobelium**, discovered in 1957, is also named after Nobel.

nosey parker

A **nosey** (or **nosy**) **parker** is someone who pries very inquisitively into other people's affairs. It is said that the origin of the expression lies in the way of life of the Anglican churchman **Matthew Parker** (1504–1575).

Having moderate Protestant views, Parker was forced to flee to Germany during the reign of Queen Mary. Later, he was appointed Archbishop of Canterbury (1559–1575) and participated in the issue of the Thirty-nine Articles. He also directed the compilation of a new version of the Bible, the Bishops' Bible (published 1568), essentially a revision of the Great Bible.

Various sources point to different aspects of Parker's life in attributing the origin of the expression nosey parker to him; some note his over-long nose while others describe his intense curiosity about other people's affairs.

obsidian

Obsidian is a dark, glassy, volcanic rock that is formed by the fast cooling of molten lava. It has sharp edges and was originally used for weapons. The word obsidian is said to have come from a wrong manuscript reading of Latin *obsianus lapis*, stone of Obsius, a 'd' being incorrectly inserted in the spelling. According to Pliny the Elder in his *Natural History*, **Obsius** was the first person to discover the rock, in Ethiopia.

Ockham's razor

The philosophical principle known as **Ockham's** (or **Occam's**) **razor** is usually formulated as, 'Entities are not to be multiplied unnecessarily.' This means that an explanation should contain the simplest elements that are necessary, with as little reference as possible to unknown or assumed matters. This statement is attributed to the English philosopher and Franciscan **William of Ockham** (c. 1285–1349), but these actual words have not been found in his writings.

Ockham was a pupil of Duns Scotus (see **dunce**), but later became his rival. He is known for his nominalist views, holding that general (or universal) terms have no real existence that is independent from the individual things denoted by the terms. The expression Ockham's razor is therefore to be seen as an attack on the proposed existence of universals by the realists.

odyssey

An **odyssey** is a long quest or wandering that is full of adventures. The word comes from the *Odyssey*, the ancient Greek epic poem by Homer that describes the many adventures of the Greek king and hero **Odysseus** (Latin name, Ulysses) on his journey home from the Trojan War.

Oedipus complex

An **Oedipus complex** is the unconscious sexual attraction of a child (especially a boy) to the parent of the opposite sex, while having jealous, aggressive feelings towards the parent of the same sex.

The expression derives from **Oedipus**, the character in Greek mythology, who is the son of Laius and Jocasta, the king and queen of Thebes. When an oracle informed Laius that he was to perish at the hands of his son, he ordered his son to be destroyed, but Oedipus was rescued by a shepherd. Later, unaware of the identity of his parents, Oedipus killed his father, subsequently marrying his mother and having four children by her.

See also **Electra complex**.

oersted

The **oersted** is the unit of magnetic field strength in the centimetre–gram–second system of measurement. The unit honours the Danish physicist **Hans Christian Oersted** (1777–1851) who was a professor at Copenhagen University. Oersted discovered the magnetic effect of an electric current in 1819, thus founding the science of electromagnetism.

ohm

The **ohm**, the metric unit of electrical resistance, is named after the German physicist **Georg Simon Ohm** (1787–1854). In 1827 he discovered that the electric current that passes through a conductor is directly proportional to the potential difference between its ends; this formulation became known as **Ohm's law**.

After gaining a doctorate in physics, Ohm prepared to teach but failed to find sufficient financial support. It is said that following the publication of his first book – which included discussion of what is now known as Ohm's law – he sent copies to several of the ruling European monarchs. It was the king of Prussia who decided to give him financial backing. In 1841 he was awarded the Copley Medal of the British Royal Society, and

at the International Electrical Congress of 1893 it was decided to honour
Ohm by naming the unit of electrical resistance after him.

old Adam

See **Adam's apple**.

Old Bill

Old Bill, the slang expression for a policeman or the police, probably
comes from the name of a character in cartoons current at the time of
World War I. In the cartoons by the Indian-born British cartoonist and
author Charles Bruce Bairnsfather (1888–1959), **Old Bill** was the name
of a grousing old soldier with a large moustache. One particular cartoon
depicts two British infantrymen Bert and Bill with water up to their
knees in a shellhole. To Bert's complaint about the inconvenience of their
situation, Old Bill answers, 'If you know of a better 'ole, go to it.'
During World War II, Bairnsfather became an official war cartoonist.

Old Nick

There are several different theories of the origin of the expression **Old
Nick**, the informal or jocular name for the devil. Some suggest that
Nick, being the nickname for Nicholas, derives from the name of **St
Nicholas**, the fourth-century bishop of Asia Minor. The patron saint of
Russia, sailors and children, he is said to have brought gifts of gold to
three poor girls for their dowries. Those who support this view however
fail to show the link between the good-natured saint and the 'prince of
evil'.

Others propose that Nick refers to the Florentine statesman and
philosopher **Niccolò Machiavelli** (1469–1527). His supposed political
unscrupulousness is said to have been the origin of the satanic reference
to Old Nick. Still others point to non-eponymous sources, such as a
shortening of the German *nickel*, meaning goblin.

onanism

Onanism is used to refer to two sexual practices: coitus interruptus and masturbation. The word derives from the biblical character **Onan** who 'spilled his seed on the ground' (Genesis 38:9), though it seems that the biblical passage describes coitus interruptus rather than masturbation. When Onan's elder brother, Er, died, Judah commanded Onan to take his brother's wife, Tamar, under the custom of levirate law which said that if a married man died without a child, his brother was expected to take his wife. Onan, however, was not willing to follow this practice and did not fully consummate the union.

Orangeman

An **Orangeman** is a member of a society (the **Orange Order**) originally established in Ireland in 1795 to uphold the Protestant religion and defend the British monarch. The word Orangeman derives from the Protestant King William III of England (1650–1702), known as **William of Orange**. At the Battle of the Boyne, north of Dublin (July 1690), William defeated the Roman Catholic King James II. On 12 July, Protestants in Northern Ireland still celebrate the anniversary of this battle.

orrery

An **orrery** is a device that shows the relative positions and movements of planets, stars and other heavenly bodies round the sun. The first orrery was invented by the mathematician George Graham (1673–1751) in about the year 1700. Graham sent the device to an instrument maker, John Rowley, who built a copy of such an apparatus, presenting it to his patron, Charles Boyle, the 4th **Earl of Orrery** (1676–1731), and naming the device in his honour.

Orwellian

The adjective **Orwellian** is used to describe aspects of life that are thought to be typical of the writings of the English novelist **George Orwell** (real name, Eric Arthur Blair; 1903–1950). The adjective is most commonly used with reference to the nightmarish way of life that is

experienced in a totalitarian state –
for example, 'an Orwellian vision
of total uniformity' –
particularly as described in
Orwell's novel *Nineteen Eighty-Four*
(published 1949), in which life is controlled
by the ever-present Big Brother, the head of the Party.

> **Orwell said, 'If liberty means anything at all, it means the right to tell people what they do not want to hear.'**

Oscar

An **Oscar** is one of several gold statuettes awarded annually by the Academy of Motion Picture Arts and Sciences in the USA for outstanding achievements in the cinema.

The idea for the presentation of trophies came in 1927; the first were awarded in 1929; but they were not called Oscars until 1931, when, so the story goes, the Academy's librarian, Margaret Herrick, is alleged to have remarked that the statuettes reminded her of her Uncle Oscar. It is said that a newspaper reporter happened to be listening and he passed on the news to his readers that 'Employees of the Academy have affectionately dubbed their famous statuette "Oscar".' It seems that Herrick's uncle was **Oscar Pierce**, a wheat and fruit grower formerly of Texas, who later lived in California.

In Australia and New Zealand, 'Oscar' is also rhyming slang for 'cash', after the Australian actor **Oscar Asche** (1871–1936).

Otto engine

The German engineer **Nikolaus August Otto** (1832–1891) devised in 1876 the four-stroke petrol engine, the **Otto engine**, which represented the first practical internal-combustion engine. In Otto's engine, with the induction, compression, power and exhaust strokes, gas was used as a fuel. Subsequently, oil was used and the Otto engine became the source of power for motor cars. A variation of the Otto engine is the diesel (qv) engine.

ottoman

An **ottoman**, a heavily padded box used as a seat and usually without a back, originated in Turkey. The word ottoman comes from the French *ottomane*, which in turn comes via Arabic from the Turkish *Othman*. This was originally the name of the Turkish sultan **Osman I** (1259–1326) who founded the Ottoman Empire, which ruled in Europe, Asia and Africa from the fourteenth to the twentieth centuries.

out-herod Herod

The expression 'to **out-herod Herod**' means to exceed someone in a particular quality, especially wickedness or cruelty. The Herod referred to is **Herod the Great** (c. 73–4 BC), the ruler of Judaea who had all the baby boys of Bethlehem killed (Matthew 2:16). The source of the expression itself is *Hamlet* (Act 3, Scene 2): 'I would have such a fellow whipped for o'erdoing Termagant: it out-herods Herod: pray you, avoid it.'

P

paean

Nowadays, a **paean** is a piece of music or writing or a film that expresses praise, triumph, joy, etc. Originally, a paean was a hymn to Apollo, the god of healing and physician of the gods in Greek mythology. Apollo bore the title **Paion**. Songs or hymns were sung to Apollo to ask or give thanks for his healing favours. From this developed the modern sense of the word.

The herb or shrub known as **peony**, grown for its large, showy pink, red or white flowers, also comes from Paion: the plants were once widely used in medicine.

Paget's disease

Paget's disease is a name given to two separate diseases discovered by **Sir James Paget** (1814–1899), a British surgeon and professor of anatomy and surgery who, along with the German biologist Rudolf Virchow, is regarded as one of the founders of the science of pathology.

Paget's disease of the bone, also known as osteitis deformans, was discovered in 1877. This is a chronic disease affecting mainly middle-aged or elderly men in which there is softening and weakening of the bones, which causes the bones to be particularly susceptible to fracture.

Paget's disease of the nipple, which was discovered in 1874, is a form of breast cancer affecting the nipple and surrounding tissue, which produces itching and an eczema-like rash.

Palladian

The **Palladian** style of architecture is characterized by symmetry and free-standing classical columns in façades. The style is named after the Italian architect **Andrea Palladio** (1508–1580), who based his work on the architecture and principles of the first-century Roman architect

Vitruvius. Originally a stonemason, Palladio began his successful career as an architect by embarking on the remodelling of the basilica in his home town of Vicenza in 1549. He designed many villas, palaces and churches, especially in the vicinity of Vicenza and in Venice. His treatise *Four Books on Architecture* (1570) helped spread his ideas. It was the English architect Inigo Jones (1573–1652) who introduced Palladianism into England.

palladium

A **palladium**, something that gives protection, was originally the wooden statue of the Greek goddess **Pallas Athene** that was kept in the citadel of Troy. It was believed that the statue had been sent from heaven by Zeus and that the safety of the city of Troy depended on its protection. The word palladium later came to refer to anything, such as the constitution or the freedom of the press or religion, on which the safety of a country might be thought to depend.

pamphlet

The word for a **pamphlet**, an unbound printed publication with a paper cover, comes originally from a twelfth-century love poem, 'Pamphilus seu De Amore' (Pamphilus or On Love), **Pamphilus** being a masculine proper name. This short Latin love poem evidently became so popular that it came to be known simply as Pamphilet, later pamflet, and eventually pamphlet. The sense of a brief treatise on a matter of current interest was added in the sixteenth century.

pander

If you **pander** to someone's wishes, you do everything that he or she wants. This verb sense comes from the rarer noun form of the word, meaning a go-between in love affairs, a procurer and someone who exploits evil desires. The noun sense derives from the character **Pandarus**, who takes a role devised by the Italian Giovanni Boccaccio in his poem *Filostrato*, and who features in a number of romances, particularly Chaucer's *Troilus and Criseyde* and Shakespeare's *Troilus and Cressida*. Pandarus is the intermediary between the two lovers, procuring Cressida for Troilus.

The Pandarus of Greek legend is a Trojan archer who shot the Greek commander Menelaus with an arrow and was killed by Diomedes in the battle that followed.

Pandora's box

A **Pandora's box** is a source of great troubles; if it is opened, then difficulties that were previously unknown or under control are unleashed. The expression derives from the story in Greek mythology of **Pandora**, the first woman. Pandora was given a box into which all the powers that would eventually bring about the downfall of mankind had been put; the box was to be given to the man that Pandora married. There are several different conclusions to the story. According to one version, her husband Epimetheus opened the box against her advice, to release all the misfortunes that have beset the human race. Another version has Pandora herself opening the box out of curiosity and letting out all the ills that afflict mankind, leaving only hope inside.

> The name **Pandora means** literally 'all gifts'.

panic

Panic, the state of sudden overwhelming terror or fright, derives ultimately from **Pan**, the name of the Greek god of woods, shepherds and flocks. He is usually depicted as having a human body and the ears, horns and legs of a goat. Pan was, it seems, known for the mischievous trick he would play of suddenly springing out from the undergrowth to inspire panic in those walking by. The god was also considered the source of the weird noises that could be heard in the forests at night, filling lost wanderers with panic.

Pan is often depicted playing a musical instrument consisting of several reeds of different lengths fastened together, which he is said to have invented. This instrument is known as the syrinx or **Pan-pipes**.

pantaloon

The fourth-century Venetian physician and saint **San Pantaleone** is remembered for a number of words that do not seem compatible with the saint's mild personality. There was the stock character in the Italian *commedia dell'arte*, the lecherous old man known as **pantaloon**, who wore spectacles, slippers and tight breeches. In time, 'pantaloons' came to describe trousers; later the word was shortened to '**pants**', meaning in American English, trousers, and in British English, underpants.

paparazzi

The **paparazzi** are freelance photographers who pursue celebrities, often to a very intrusive extent, in order to take candid photographs, preferably of a newsworthy or scandalous nature, which they then sell on to newspapers or magazines for huge sums of money. The word 'paparazzi' comes from Italian, and is the plural form of the less commonly used 'paparazzo'. The Italian film

> **Fellini is said to have named the photographer Paparazzo after a hotel proprietor depicted in a 1901 travel book.**

director Federico Fellini (1920–1983) was responsible for popularizing the word 'paparazzi'. His film *La Dolce Vita* (1959), about Rome's café society, starred Marcello Mastroianni as a gossip columnist who worked with a photographer called **Paparazzo**. The Paparazzo character was based on Tazio Secchiaroli, one of a group of street photographers who exposed the secrets of film stars and other celebrities during the heyday of Rome's café society in the late 1950s. Secchiaroli was a consultant during the filming of *La Dolce Vita*.

Pap test

A **Pap test** (or **Pap smear**) is an examination for the early detection of cancer in which cells in a smear of bodily secretions, especially from the uterus or vagina, are examined. The test takes its name from the Greek-born American anatomist **George Nicholas Papanicolaou** (1883–1962), who devised it.

Pareto principle

Sometimes referred to as the 80:20 rule, the **Pareto principle** (or **law**) is seen, for example, in company sales: 80 per cent of the sales may come from 20 per cent of the customers. The expression derives from the name of the Italian economist and sociologist **Vilfredo Frederico Pareto** (1848–1923).

Pareto worked as director of Italian railways and superintendent of mines before being appointed professor of economics in 1892. His studies led him to analyse consumer demand and to formulate a law of the distribution of income within a society.

Pareto's law has since come to be formulated as the 80:20 rule and to apply to spheres outside economics and business; for example, one could speak of taking 80 per cent of the time to teach 20 per cent of the students.

Parkinson's disease

Parkinson's disease is a disease that is marked by a tremor of the limbs, weakness of the muscles and a peculiar gait. Also known as *paralysis agitans*, the disease is named after the British physician, **James Parkinson** (1755–1824), who first described it in 1817.

> Parkinson was a keen amateur palaeontologist.

Parkinson's law

The observation in office organization known as **Parkinson's law** states that, 'Work expands so as to fill the time available for its completion.' This was first formulated in the 1950s by the English historian and author **Cyril Northcote Parkinson** (1909–1993). In *Parkinson's Law* (published 1957), Parkinson also noted that, 'Subordinates multiply at a fixed rate regardless of the amount of work produced,' and that according to the law of triviality, 'The time spent on any item on the agenda will be in inverse proportion to the sum involved.'

Pascal's triangle

The French mathematician and philosopher **Blaise Pascal** (1623–1662) had an early interest in mathematics that led to his formulation of what has become known as **Pascal's triangle**, used in probability theory. He later made discoveries in fluid mechanics and also invented a hydraulic press and a calculating machine. Coming under Jansenist influence, he entered the convent at Port Royal in 1655. His best-known writings are *Lettres provinciales* (1656–1657), a defence of Jansenism, and *Pensées sur la religion* (1670), fragments of a defence of Christianity. Pascal is also remembered by having the **pascal**, the metric unit of pressure, and **Pascal**, the high-level computer programming language, named in his honour.

pasquinade

In former times, a **pasquinade** was a poem, song or story satirizing a particular person that was displayed in a public place, usually anonymously. The word 'pasquinade' comes from the Italian *pasquinata*, which in turn comes from **Pasquino**, the name of a shop owner in Rome in the fifteenth century. Outside Pasquino's shop, near the Piazza Navona, there was an old statue on which satirical poems were often posted. Most of these were believed to have been written by Pasquino himself, who was known as a wit. On the other side of the city there was another old statue called Marforio, on which replies to these pasquinades were often displayed.

pasteurize

When milk or another drink or a food is **pasteurized**, bacteria in it are destroyed by a special heating process. The word pasteurize derives from the name of the French chemist and bacteriologist **Louis Pasteur** (1822–1895).

> As a student, Pasteur wanted to give up science to be an artist, but his father forced him to continue with his studies.

The son of a tanner, Pasteur studied chemistry, but was graded as only a mediocre student. He became a teacher and lecturer, and in 1854 was

appointed dean of the faculty of science at Lille University. Pasteur first
developed the process now known as pasteurization on wine and beer.
He found that certain micro-organisms caused wine to ferment very
quickly and that the fermentation could be prevented if the wine was
subjected to heat and then cooled rapidly.

Pasteur also devised methods of immunization (**pasteurism** or
Pasteur treatment) against anthrax and rabies.

Paul Jones

The dance known as the **Paul Jones**, in which couples change their
partners, is probably named after the American naval commander **John
Paul Jones** (original name John Paul; 1747–1792).

Born in Scotland, Jones went to America where he was commissioned
into the American navy and was involved in several naval exploits
against the British in the American War of Independence. In 1779,
commanding the ship the *Bon Homme Richard*, Jones defeated the British
frigate *Serapis* in a long battle. Refusing to surrender, even though his
ship was on the verge of sinking, Jones is said to have uttered to the
British captain Richard Pearson, 'I have not yet begun to fight.'

After the War of Independence, Jones served in the navies of Russia and
France. The dance was probably named after Paul Jones in honour of his
exploits.

Paul Pry

A **Paul Pry**, someone who is inquisitive and interfering, comes from the
character of that name in the farce *Paul Pry* (published 1825) by the
English dramatist John Poole (c. 1786–1872). Brewer describes the figure
Paul Pry as 'an idle, meddlesome fellow, who has no occupation of his
own, and is always interfering with other folk's business.' He constantly
enters with the apology, 'I hope I don't intrude.'

pavlova

 The Russian ballerina **Anna Pavlova** (1885–1931) is remembered for her
popularizing of ballet throughout the world. At the age of 21 she was

the prima ballerina at the Russian Imperial Ballet and later she joined Diaghilev's Ballet Russe for a short time. From 1914, Pavlova began to tour throughout the world with her own company, and she is particularly remembered for her roles in *Giselle* and *The Dying Swan*. To celebrate her ballet performances in Australia and New Zealand, chefs in these countries popularized **pavlova** – a meringue cake topped with cream and fruit.

Pavlovian

The Russian physiologist **Ivan Petrovich Pavlov** (1849–1936) is remembered for his studies of digestion and conditioned reflexes. In his experiments with dogs Pavlov showed that a reflex response could be evoked by a stimulus that was different from the one that usually produced it. He found that dogs produced saliva in response to the sight of food accompanied by a bell. Eventually they would learn to associate the bell with the appearance of food and would produce saliva in response to hearing the bell alone. The adjective **Pavlovian** has therefore come to refer to something that is predictable or is evoked automatically as a response to a stimulus (a **Pavlovian reaction**).

Pavlov later applied his theories to cover other aspects of human and animal behaviour, such as learning. Although he persistently criticized the communist regime, the authorities continued to fund his work, and his studies have influenced the behaviourist school of psychology.

peach Melba

See **Melba toast**.

pecksniffian

The character **Seth Pecksniff** in the novel *Martin Chuzzlewit* by Charles Dickens (published 1843–1844) has given his name to the adjective **pecksniffian**. In the story, Pecksniff is a

> **Dickens describes Pecksniff's character as 'full of promise but of no performance'.**

smooth-talking hypocritical figure who gives an appearance of kindness and benevolence but is in reality mean, selfish and treacherous.

peeping Tom

A **peeping Tom**, a voyeur or a man who takes pleasure in secretly looking at women undressing, derives from the name of a legendary English tailor. The traditional story relates how Leofric, the eleventh-century Lord of Coventry, imposed crippling taxes on his people. Leofric's wife, Lady Godiva, pleaded with him to ease the tax burden on the citizens. Eventually he said he would on condition that Lady Godiva rode naked through the streets. Lady Godiva agreed and, having asked the citizens to keep the shutters on their windows closed, she rode naked through the streets on a white horse. Everyone respected her request except for the tailor, **Tom**, who peeped – only to be struck blind for his brazenness.

peony

See **paean**.

Père David's deer

The rare Chinese deer, **Père David's deer**, is named in honour of the French missionary and explorer of China **Père Armand David** (1826–1900). Père David also has a species of buddleia (qv) named after him.

Pershing missile

A **Pershing missile** is a US Army ballistic missile that is capable of carrying a nuclear or conventional warhead.

The Pershing missile was named in honour of the American general **John Joseph Pershing** (1860–1948), known as 'Black Jack'. General Pershing served in the Spanish-American War (1898), in the Philippines (1899–1903), and in Mexico (1916). In 1917 he commanded the American Expeditionary Forces in Europe during World War I. After the

> Pershing acquired the nickname 'Black Jack' at West Point military academy on account of his strict discipline.

war, he was Chief of Staff (1921–1924). He won a Pulitzer Prize for his book *My Experiences in the World War* (1931).

Perthes' disease

 Perthes' disease, also known as **Legg–Calvé–Perthes disease**, is a disorder that causes gradual weakening of the upper end of the thigh bone, where it joins the pelvis. Either or both hip joints may be affected. The cause may be vascular disturbance resulting from trauma, or there may be a predisposing genetic defect of the cartilage. This disorder mainly affects white Caucasian children aged three to twelve. **Arthur Thornton Legg** (1874–1939), an American orthopaedic surgeon, published the first description of Legg–Calvé–Perthes in 1910. That same year, **Jacques Calvé** (1875–1954), a French surgeon, and **Georg Clemens Perthes** (1869–1927), a German surgeon, independently published their descriptions of it. Perthes, who was a pioneer in radiotherapy, used deep X-ray therapy for the first time in 1903.

Pestalozzi

The emphasis of the Swiss educationalist **Johann Heinrich Pestalozzi** (1746–1827) on observation in learning has had a profound influence on primary education. Born in Zurich into a wealthy family, Pestalozzi studied the writings of Rousseau and later attempted to establish schools for poor children. In spite of the apparent failure of the schools, his writings, including his book *Wie Gertrud ihre Kinder lehrt* (1801), have affected later educational developments. **Pestalozzi International Children's Villages** have also been established, for example in Sedlescombe, East Sussex.

Peter Pan

A **Peter Pan** is a man who never seems to grow up or who is unwilling to give up boyish or immature ways. The name is taken from the character in the play *Peter Pan, or The Boy Who Would Not Grow Up* by the Scottish dramatist and novelist Sir James Matthew Barrie (1860–1937). The play, an immediate success when first performed at the Duke of York's Theatre in London, was developed from fantasy stories Barrie had created for the young sons of friends. Barrie became famous because of his writings, especially *Peter Pan*, and was made a baronet (1913) and awarded the Order of Merit (1922) and several honorary degrees. From 1930 he was chancellor of Edinburgh University.

See also **Wendy house**.

Peter principle

'In a hierarchy, every employee tends to rise to the level of his incompetence.' This humorous semi–scientific statement is known as the **Peter principle**, after the Canadian educator **Dr Laurence J Peter** (1919–1990) who with Raymond Hull (1919–1985) wrote the book *The Peter Principle – Why Things Always Go Wrong*, published in 1969.

petersham

 Petersham, a tough, corded ribbon used, for example, in belts and hatbands takes its name from the English army officer Charles Stanhope, **Viscount Petersham**, 4th Earl of Harrington (1780–1851).

Viscount Petersham, it seems, was something of a dandy; he designed and popularized a kind of overcoat made of a heavy woollen cloth. The coat cloth and then the ribbon came to be known by his name.

> Petersham is also said to have invented an original mixture of snuff.

Peter's pence

 Peter's pence was originally an annual tax of one penny formerly levied on all English householders for the maintenance of the Pope. Dating from the ninth century, it was abolished by King Henry VIII in 1534; it is now a voluntary contribution made by Roman Catholics to the Pope. The phrase derives from the tradition that the apostle **Peter** was the first Pope.

Peters projection

The **Peters projection** is a form of map projection that provides a more accurate representation of the relative size of land masses than the Mercator projection (qv) does. A square inch anywhere on this type of map represents an equal number of square miles. The Peters projection was named after **Dr Arno Peters** (1916–2002), the German historian and cartographer who created it in 1974.

Petrarchan sonnet

The **Petrarchan sonnet**, also called the Italian sonnet, originated in thirteenth-century Italy and was associated with the Italian poet **Petrarch** (Italian name, Francesco Petrarca; 1304–1374). The 14-line poem is divided into two parts: the first eight lines rhyme *abbaabba* and the remaining six lines rhyme *cdecde*.

Born the son of a notary in Florence, Petrarch spent most of his life in Provence. He travelled throughout Europe and is particularly noted for *Canzoniere*, a series of love poems addressed to Laura, and also his humanist and spiritual writings. In 1341 he was crowned poet laureate in Rome.

See also **Shakespearean**.

Petri dish

A **Petri dish** is a shallow transparent dish with an overlapping cover, used in bacteriological laboratories for producing cultures of microorganisms. It was named after the German bacteriologist **Julius Richard Petri** (1852–1922), who worked as an assistant to the renowned bacteriologist Robert Koch. The monument to Koch in Berlin depicts him holding a Petri dish.

Phaedra complex

A **Phaedra complex** is the problematic relationship that may sometimes arise between a new stepparent and the son or daughter of the new husband or wife.

philippic

The expression derives from **Phaedra**, the character in Greek mythology, who married Theseus, the King of Athens, and then fell in love with her stepson Hippolytus. When he rejected her amorous advances, Phaedra hanged herself, leaving a suicide note accusing Hippolytus of rape. Theseus refused to believe his son was innocent and banished him.

philippic

Philippic, meaning bitter and biting denunciation, derives from the name of the speeches in defence of Athenian liberty by the Athenian orator and statesman Demosthenes

> **Although he was a great ruler in his own right, Philip is now better known as the father of Alexander the Great.**

(384–322 BC) against **King Philip II of Macedon** (382–336 BC). In the three orations, known as the *Philippics* ('speeches relating to Philip'; 351, 344, 341 BC), Demosthenes attacked Philip's ambitions to make Athens part of his kingdom, and attempted to arouse the citizens against their cruel ruler. Philip, however, defeated Athens at the Battle of Chaeronea in 338, thus ending the self-government of the Greek city states and making his conquests of Greece complete. Philip was, however, assassinated two years later.

Later, Cicero's eloquent speeches against Mark Antony were referred to as philippics, and now philippic refers to passionate speech against anyone.

Phillips screwdriver

Phillips screwdriver is a trademark for a screwdriver with a cross-shaped tip, which fits into a slot of corresponding shape in the head of a **Phillips screw** (also a trademark) in order to turn it. Both the screwdriver and the screw were invented in the 1930s by **Henry F Phillips** (1890–1958), an American businessman.

Pickwickian

The adjective **Pickwickian** is used in allusion to the character **Mr**

Pickwick in the novel *Pickwick Papers* by Charles Dickens (first published 1836–1837). In particular, Pickwickian is used to mean kind and generous in a simple manner and, also, to describe a word or expression that is not used in its ordinary or literal sense, from the scene in the opening chapter in which Mr Pickwick and Mr Blotton appear to insult each other, whereas in reality they respected each other greatly.

Pilates

Pilates is an exercise regime that involves small controlled movements, sometimes using specially designed equipment involving resistance against tensioned springs, in order to develop specific muscle groups. It was devised by the German-born sportsman **Joseph Humbertus Pilates** (1880–1967) early in the twentieth century, originally to help athletes improve strength and technique. Nowadays Pilates is practised by lay people who want to improve their fitness and suppleness as well as their figure. It is also particularly helpful in treating sports injuries as well as conditions such as arthritis, whiplash and back problems.

pinchbeck

Pinchbeck, was originally an alloy of copper and zinc – five parts copper and one part zinc – used to imitate gold in cheap jewellery. The word derives from the name of the English watchmaker **Christopher Pinchbeck** (c. 1670–1732). Pinchbeck used the alloy in the manufacture of watches and jewellery. Later, the word came to be used for anything counterfeit or shoddy, probably partly because the 'pinch' in the name has associations with cheapness.

> **Pinchbeck also designed astronomical clocks and candle snuffers.**

Plantin

The style of type known as **Plantin** derives its name from its designer **Christophe Plantin** (c. 1520– 1589), a French printer. Plantin ran printing houses in Antwerp, Leyden and Paris and produced famous Bibles and editions of the Greek and Latin classics.

platonic

A **platonic** relationship is a close relationship between a man and a woman that does not involve sex. Such platonic love – spiritual or intellectual in contrast to physical – was first described by the Greek philosopher **Plato** (c. 427–347 BC), in his *Symposium*, originally with reference to the pure love of Socrates towards young men.

> The name 'Plato' is a nickname meaning 'broad-shouldered'. His real name was Aristocles.

Born into a wealthy Athenian family, Plato was known as a poet and athlete before becoming a follower of Socrates. Following Socrates' death, Plato travelled widely before returning to Athens to found his Academy in about 385 BC, teaching philosophy, mathematics and government. Many of his writings survive, in which ethical and philosophical matters are discussed.

Plimsoll line

The **Plimsoll line** is a set of markings on the side of a ship that show the various levels that the ship may safely be loaded to. The pattern of lines is named in honour of the English leader of shipping reform **Samuel Plimsoll** (1824–1898).

Originally the manager of a brewery, then a coal dealer, Plimsoll was elected MP for Derby in 1868. He called the overloaded ships of his day coffin-ships and determined to make maritime transport safer. His book *Our Seamen* was published in 1872 and, following his insistent efforts, a bill providing for rigorous inspection of ships became law in 1876. The Plimsoll line was adopted in that same year to mark the limit to which a ship may be loaded.

Plimsoll is also honoured in the light rubber-soled canvas shoe that bears his name, since the top edge of the rubber was thought to resemble a Plimsoll line.

poinciana

Poinciana is a prickly tropical tree of the pea family that has showy orange or red flowers with long crimson pods, which are sometimes used for fuel in the West Indies. The pods are sometimes called 'woman's tongue' because of the rattling noise that they make in the wind. The poinciana, which has repeatedly been voted one of the five most beautiful trees in the world, was named after **Monsieur de Poinci**, a seventeenth-century governor of the French West Indies.

poinsettia

The traditional Christmas evergreen plant known as a **poinsettia** takes its name from the American diplomat **Joel Roberts Poinsett** (1779–1851). Born in Charleston, South Carolina, Poinsett was educated in Europe. He left his medical and legal studies, however, preferring to travel. During the course of his wanderings he is said to have met several political leaders including Napoleon, Metternich and the Tsar of Russia. When Poinsett returned to the United States, he was sent by President Madison to be consul to South America, where, however, he supported the Chilean revolutionaries.

Following several years' service as a congressman, he was appointed as American minister to Mexico (1825). He is said to have sent back to the United States specimens of the fiery plant now named after him, although it seems that it had already been introduced into the country. Because Poinsett was a well-known public figure at that time, the plant was named in his honour.

Poinsett later became secretary of war in the cabinet of Van Buren and a Unionist leader in the Civil War.

Pollyanna

A person who is constantly optimistic is sometimes described as a **Pollyanna**. The name was originally that of the heroine in the novel *Pollyanna* (published in 1913) by the American writer Eleanor Porter (1868–1920).

Pollyanna is an eleven-year-old orphan who is sent to her very strait-laced Aunt Polly – who only takes her in as it is her duty. When she was younger, to cope with the very poor life they lived as a missionary family, her father taught Pollyanna the 'glad game' – always to look for something to be glad about in whatever unhappy circumstances one finds oneself. The result is that she is always a happy, smiling child.

Pollyanna passes on the 'glad game' to every needy person she meets in the village of Beldingsville with some quite startling results. A Pollyanna is therefore someone who can find something good in even the blackest circumstances.

pompadour

The word **pompadour** was used originally for a woman's hairstyle that was fashionable in the early eighteenth century, in which the hair was raised back, usually over a pad, into loose rolls round the face. A similar later style, in which the hair is combed straight up from the forehead, came to be worn by men and women. The name of the hairstyle derives from the **Marquise de Pompadour**, the title of Jeanne Antoinette Poisson (1721–1764), mistress

> **Mme de Pompadour served as patron to scholars such as Voltaire and Diderot.**

of Louis XV of France. From 1745 until her death, Mme de Pompadour exerted great influence on political matters. She was to a great extent responsible for the French defeats in the Seven Years' War (1756–1763).

The French court was renowned for its wasteful extravagance at that time, and after being reproved for such excesses, Mme de Pompadour is said to have replied with the now famous words, 'Après nous le déluge' – literally, 'After us the flood.'

Prader–Willi syndrome

Prader–Willi syndrome is a rare congenital disorder characterized by short stature, mental handicap, and obsessive eating leading to obesity and sometimes to diabetes mellitus in later childhood. This disorder is named after **Andrea Prader** (1919–2001) and **Heinrich Willi** (1900–1971), the Swiss paediatricians who first described it in 1956.

praline

 A **praline**, a confection of nuts – usually almonds – and sugar, is named after César de Choiseul, **Count Plessis-Praslin** (1598–1675). Count Plessis-Praslin was a French field marshal, and it seems that it was his chef who first concocted the confection. Later, the count served as minister of state under Louis XIV. Originally known as a praslin, in time its spelling became praline.

Pre-Raphaelite

 A **Pre-Raphaelite** is the term used for a member of a particular artistic group known as the Pre-Raphaelite Brotherhood (PRB), a group of artists, including Dante Gabriel Rossetti, John Everett Millais and William Holman Hunt, founded in 1848. This group aimed to emulate the earlier Italian schools, in reaction to the contemporary taste for the Italian painter **Raphael** (original name Raffaello Santi; 1483–1520). The Pre-Raphaelite Brotherhood sought to oppose what they saw as the superficial conventionalism of much painting at that time by returning to a faithfulness to nature. Their works depict moral or religious scenes, and are marked by fine detail and vivid colours.

Prince Albert

 A **Prince Albert** is a man's long double-breasted frock coat. It is named after **Prince Albert Edward**, later King Edward VII of England (1841–1910). He is said to have worn the formal coat at afternoon social functions and so established it as a fashionable garment.

There is also a piercing of the penis called a Prince Albert. This is said to be named after Albert Edward's father **Prince Albert** (1819–1861), Prince Consort of Queen Victoria. He is alleged to have worn a ring attached to his penis, which was strapped to his thigh, in order to create a smooth line in the tight trousers fashionable in that period.

See also **albert**, **King Edward potato**.

Procrustean

Procrustes was a robber in Greek mythology who forced his victims to lie on a bed. If they were too long, he would lop off their limbs; if they were too short, he would stretch their bodies to the necessary length until they fitted the bed. The word *prokroustes* literally means 'the stretcher', and the adjective **Procrustean** has come to describe something designed to enforce or produce conformity to a particular teaching by violent or arbitrary methods. Similarly, a **Procrustean bed** (or a **bed of Procrustes**) has come to refer to a predetermined system or standard to which a person or thing is forced to conform exactly.

Promethean

The adjective **Promethean** is used to describe something that is exceptionally creative or original. The word derives from **Prometheus**, a demigod in Greek mythology who is known for his bold, skilful acts: he made mankind out of clay, stole fire from Olympus and gave it to man and taught man many arts and sciences. Zeus punished him by chaining him to a rock in the Caucasus mountains where during the day an eagle fed on his liver only for it to grow again each night. Eventually Prometheus was freed from this torture by Hercules.

> Mary Shelley's *Frankenstein* is subtitled *The Modern Prometheus.*

protean

Proteus was the sea-god of Greek mythology who tended the flocks of Poseidon. He was noted for his ability to take on different shapes at will. The adjective **protean**, deriving from his name, has therefore come to mean 'variable or diverse' or 'capable of assuming different shapes, sizes or roles', as in 'a protean personality'.

Proteus is also remembered in the **protea**, a South African shrub or small tree with large cone-shaped flower heads.

Przewalski's horse

Przewalski's horse is a wild horse with an erect dark-coloured mane, a stocky body, short legs and a

> A herd of Przewalski's horses is said to have caused Genghis Khan to fall off his horse in 1226.

short neck. It was discovered in 1879 in the Altai Mountains of West Mongolia by the Russian explorer **General Nikolai Mikhailovich Przewalski** (1839–1888). Przewalski's horse is the only true wild horse; sadly, it no longer exists in the wild, with only a small number surviving in captivity.

puckish

A **puckish** grin or a puckish sense of humour is a mischievous or impish one. **Puck**, also known as Robin Goodfellow, was a mischievous sprite in Celtic mythology and English folklore. He caused mayhem for the young lovers in William Shakespeare's *A Midsummer Night's Dream* (1595).

Pulitzer prize

The **Pulitzer prizes** are prizes awarded annually for outstanding achievements in journalism, literature and music. The awards take their name from the Hungarian-born US newspaper publisher **Joseph Pulitzer** (1847–1911). Persuaded to emigrate in 1864, Pulitzer served for a year in the Union army before settling in St Louis, where he set up the *Post-Dispatch* newspaper in 1878. He later moved to New York where he founded the *World* (1883). The prizes were established by Pulitzer's will, in which he provided a fund to Columbia University for the setting up and endowment of a school of journalism. The prizes have been awarded since 1917; since 1943 a prize for musical composition has also been presented.

Pullman

A **Pullman**, the luxurious railway passenger coach, is named after the American inventor **George Mortimer Pullman** (1831–1897). Originally a cabinet-maker, Pullman began improving railway coach accommodation in the 1850s and, with his colleague Ben Field, built the first sleeping car, the *Pioneer*, in 1864. This cost $20,000 and had chandeliers, walnut woodwork, painted ceilings, a heavy-pile carpet and folding upper berths for the sleeping accommodation.

It was the assassination of President Lincoln in 1865 that brought the *Pioneer* – and Pullman – to fame. Every area brought out its finest railway transport and so the *Pioneer* was brought into service to form part of the presidential funeral train. Bridges were raised and platforms narrowed to accommodate the *Pioneer*; it proved so popular that other railway companies wanted similar carriages. Pullman then formed a company, the Pullman Palace Car Company, to manufacture sleeping and dining cars, the profits from which made him a multi-millionaire.

Next, Pullman had a model town built in Chicago, but he was discredited when the courts found that the rents he was charging were much higher than those for the houses in the surrounding area.

Towards the end of his life Pullman suffered a further blow – the railway workers' strike and riots of 1893–1894 in which at least twelve people died. His name is, however, still remembered for the special trains that provide comfortable and luxurious accommodation.

Pyrrhic victory

A **Pyrrhic victory** is a victory won at such a great cost that it amounts to no victory at all. It is named after **Pyrrhus**, king of Epirus (312–272 BC), who won several victories against Rome, particularly that of Asculum (279 BC) in which he lost very many of his men. After this battle he is said to have uttered, 'One more such victory and we are undone!'

See also **Cadmean victory**.

Pythagoras's theorem

Pythagoras's theorem states that in a right-angled triangle the square on the hypotenuse is equal to the sum of the squares on the other two sides. The theory is named after the sixth-century-BC Greek philosopher and mathematician **Pythagoras**, whose work had a significant effect on the development of mathematics, music and astronomy. It seems, however, that the ancient Egyptian surveyors, and

President Garfield published a simple proof of Pythagoras's theorem in 1876.

also the Babylonians at least a hundred years before Pythagoras, were already familiar with such triangles, but it was Pythagoras or one of his followers who developed the actual theorem that has been named after him.

python

The large non-venomous snake that winds itself around its prey and then crushes it by constriction is known as a **python**. The word derives from the name of the monstrous serpent **Python** of Greek mythology. This dragon arose from the mud after the flood that Deucalion survived and guarded Delphi. It was after killing Python that Apollo set up his oracle at Delphi.

Q

quassia

Quassia is used to refer to the genus of tropical trees and shrubs that have a bitter bark and wood, and also the bitter drug obtained from this bark and wood. The drug was formerly used as a tonic and vermifuge and is now used as an insecticide. The name honours an eighteenth-century Surinam slave, **Graman Quassi**, who in about 1730 discovered the medicinal value of the tree.

Queen Anne is dead

'**Queen Anne is dead**' is a saying used as a reply to mean, 'Your news is stale; everyone knows this.' Born in 1665, **Queen Anne** was queen of England and Scotland (known as Great Britain from 1707) and Ireland (1702–1714). The last of the Stuart monarchs, she died in 1714; her death led to the coming of the Hanoverians.

The expression 'Queen Anne is dead' is first recorded in a ballad of 1722, eight years after her death. Obviously everyone knew of the monarch's passing; to tell stale news needed to be met with such a slighting rejoinder.

> **Queen Anne had 17 children and outlived them all.**

Queen Anne is the term used to describe a style of furniture popular in the eighteenth century, marked by plain curves, walnut veneer and cabriole-legged chairs, and also a style of early-eighteenth-century architecture marked by plain red brickwork in a restrained classical form.

Queensberry rules

The **Queensberry rules**, representing the basis of modern boxing, were written under the sponsorship of John Sholto Douglas, the 8th **Marquess of Queensberry** (1844–1900), and were published in 1867. The Queensberry rules established the use of padded gloves – up to that time fighting had been with bare fists – rounds of three minutes and limitations on the kinds of blows permitted.

The expression 'Queensberry rules' in also sometimes used to stand for fair play or proper behaviour in sport in general – or elsewhere.

> **Queensberry is also known for his legal battle with Oscar Wilde, which led to Wilde's imprisonment.**

quisling

A **quisling** is a traitor who collaborates with an invading enemy. The word derives from **Vidkun Abraham Quisling** (1887–1945), the Norwegian politician who collaborated with the Germans in World War II.

Having served as a military attaché in Russia and France, Major Quisling worked for the League of Nations, entering politics as a zealous anti-communist in 1929. A defence minister in the Norwegian government (1931–1933), Quisling resigned to form his right-wing National Unity Party in 1933, which met with little success, however.

When Hitler invaded Norway in April 1940, Quisling became 'puppet' prime minister, and later minister president. Under his rule, a thousand Jews were sent to concentration camps. He lived in a reinforced 46-room villa on an island near Oslo; he was so paranoid that all the food he ate had to be previously sampled by others.

When the Germans surrendered in Norway on 15 May 1945, Quisling was arrested. He was found guilty of war crimes and was shot by a firing squad on 24 October 1945.

Quixotic

Someone who is carried away by the impractical pursuit of romantic ideals and who has extravagant notions of chivalry is sometimes referred to as **quixotic**. The word comes from the name of **Don Quixote**, hero of the novel *Don Quixote de la Mancha* (published in two parts 1605, 1615) by the Spanish novelist Miguel de Cervantes Saavedra (1547–1616). The novel tells how Don Quixote, infatuated with stories of chivalry, feels himself called to roam the world in pursuit of noble adventures.

The expression 'tilt at windmills', to attack an imaginary enemy in the belief that it is real, comes from part 1, chapter 8, of the romance. Don Quixote travels through the countryside attacking windmills in the belief that they are giants.

R

Rabelaisian

Rabelaisian is sometimes used to describe coarse humour or, less commonly, fantastic extravagance or sharp satire. These features are considered characteristics of the works of the French writer **François Rabelais** (1483–1553).

A Franciscan and then a Benedictine monk, Rabelais left the monastery to become a physician. Renowned for his fine scholarship and satirical wit, he wrote many works, of which the most famous are *Pantagruel* (1532) and *Gargantua* (1534) – the source of the word gargantuan (qv).

Rachmanism

The unscrupulous exploitation of tenants by a landlord known as **Rachmanism** takes its name from **Peter (Perec) Rachman** (1920–1962), a Polish-born British landlord, who indulged in such a practice.

Under the 1957 Rent Act, rents in Britain were kept at an artificially low level compared with the market value of property as long as the property remained in the hands of the tenant. This led to unscrupulous practices by some landlords who harassed tenants in order to evict them. The property could then be sold or relet at an exorbitantly high rent.

Rachman was one such landlord who bought cheaply rented houses in London in the 1950s and early 1960s and used blackmail, intimidation and physical violence to evict the tenants. He then let the properties out at very high rates to prostitutes, etc, or sold them to businesses, making a great profit.

Rafflesia

The genus of parasitic Asian herbs known as **Rafflesia** is named after the British colonial administrator **Sir Thomas Stamford Raffles**

(1781–1826) who discovered it. After a renowned administrative career in Penang and Java, Raffles acquired Singapore for the East India Company in 1819. The famous Raffles Hotel in Singapore is named after him.

The species *Rafflesia arnoldi* has the largest bloom in the world, measuring up to three feet in diameter and weighing up to 15 pounds. This mottled orange-brown and white flower – also known as stinking-corpse lily – grows on the roots of vines in south-east Asia. Only the bloom of the plant can be seen above the ground. Its growing fungus below the ground smells of rotting meat and attracts carrion flies that act as pollinators.

raglan

A **raglan**, a loose-fitting coat that has sleeves (**raglan sleeves**) that extend to the collar without shoulder seams, is named after the British field marshal Fitzroy James Henry Somerset,

> When Raglan's arm was amputated, he is alleged to have said, 'I say, bring back my arm – the ring my wife gave me is on the finger!'

1st **Baron Raglan** (1788–1855). Raglan served in the Napoleonic Wars, and was wounded at the Battle of Waterloo, causing him to have his arm amputated. He later became secretary to the Duke of Wellington (then commander-in-chief of the British forces) and field marshal. Despite his success at the Battle of Inkerman in the Crimean War, his tactics at the Battle of Balaclava were heavily criticized. It was during the Crimean War that Raglan became known for wearing his raglan overcoat.

See also **cardigan**.

raise Cain

The expression 'to **raise Cain**' – to behave in a wild, noisy manner; to cause a loud disturbance; to protest angrily – derives from the biblical **Cain**, the eldest son of Adam and Eve, the brother of Abel and the first murderer in the Bible (Genesis 4:3–12). It seems that in earlier times,

Cain was a euphemism for the devil, religious people preferring 'raise Cain' to 'raise the devil'.

Two expressions derive from the judgement of God on Cain after he killed Abel. The **'curse of Cain'**, the fate of someone who is forced to lead a fugitive life, wandering restlessly from place to place, derives from the punishment mentioned in Genesis 4:11–12: 'And now art thou cursed from the earth ... a fugitive and a vagabond shalt thou be in the earth.' The **'mark of Cain'** is a stain of a crime on one's reputation, with reference to the protective mark God gave him to prevent him from being killed himself, mentioned in Genesis 4:15: 'And the Lord set a mark upon Cain, lest any finding him should kill him.'

Ramboesque

Ramboesque behaviour is extremely aggressive and lawless. **John Rambo** is the principal character, played by Sylvester Stallone, in the enormously successful series of Hollywood action films *First Blood* (1982), *Rambo: First Blood Part II* (1985) and *Rambo III* (1988), about a disgruntled former Green Beret, a Vietnam War veteran, who sets himself against the forces of law and order to right perceived wrongs in an increasingly violent manner.

Rastafarian

 Haile Selassie (1892–1975) became Emperor of Ethiopia in 1930. His title **Ras Tafari** (*Ras* meaning 'Lord' and *Tafari*, a family name) was adopted by Black West Indians, who venerated Haile Selassie as God, and wanted deliverance for the Black race and the founding of a homeland in Ethiopia. **Rastafarian** beliefs were developed by the Jamaican founder of the Back to Africa Movement, Marcus Garvey (1887–1940).

Haile Selassie lived in exile in England from 1936 to 1941 during the Italian occupation of Ethiopia. He was finally deposed in a military rising in 1974.

Raynaud's disease

 Raynaud's disease is a peripheral vascular disorder that mainly affects women. In affected people, cool temperatures cause recurrent spasms of the blood vessels in the fingers or toes, causing them to turn white, then blue, and then red, and also causing numbness or pain. This disorder is named after **A G Maurice Raynaud** (1834–1881), the French physician who first described it in 1862.

Reaganomics

Reaganomics is the name that was given to the free-market economic programme followed by the administration of the US president **Ronald Reagan** from 1980, which involved cuts in taxes, reduced spending on social services, and increased defence spending, along with deregulation of domestic markets. Ronald Wilson Reagan (born 1911) was the 40th president of the United States (1981–1989). Before turning to politics, he

> Reagan said, 'I can tell a lot about a fellow's character by the way he eats jelly beans.'

was a Hollywood film actor, his greatest role being in *King's Row* (1941). He was governor of California (1967–1975) before defeating Jimmy Carter in the 1980 presidential election.

Réaumur scale

The **Réaumur scale** is a scale of temperature in which the freezing-point of water is 0° and the boiling-point of water 80°. It is named after the French scientist, **Réne Antoine Ferchault de Réaumur** (1683–1757) who devised it. A naturalist as well as a physicist, Réaumur studied the chemical processes of animal digestion and also developed a method of tinning iron that was used in French industry.

rehoboam

A **rehoboam** is a wine bottle holding the equivalent of six standard bottles, named after **Rehoboam**, a son of Solomon, last king of the united Israel and first king of Judah, whose name means 'may the people expand'.

See also **jeroboam**; **jorum**; **methuselah**; **nebuchadnezzar**.

Rett's syndrome

Rett's syndrome is a complex neurological disorder that affects mainly girls, becoming evident during the second year. Features of Rett's syndrome include dyspraxia, autism, dementia and hand–wringing. **Andreas Rett** (1924–1997), an Austrian paediatrician, first described this syndrome in 1966.

Reye's syndrome

Reye's syndrome is a rare, and often fatal, metabolic disease of children that affects the brain, liver and kidneys. It is named after **Ralph Douglas Kenneth Reye** (1912–1978), the Australian paediatrician and pathologist who first described it in an article published in 1963.

rhesus monkey

A **rhesus monkey**, *Macaca mulatta*, is a south Asian monkey that is widely used in medical research. It seems that the description rhesus was chosen arbitrarily in honour of **Rhesus**, king of Thrace, in Greek mythology. The Greek hero Odysseus and King Diomedes killed Rhesus and twelve of his men, carrying off his splendid horses, because an oracle had said that if Rhesus' horses had tasted Trojan pasture and drunk of the River Scamander, Troy would not fall.

The **rhesus factor** (or Rh factor) in blood is called after the rhesus monkeys in which it was first discovered. The Rh factor is a blood protein that is present in the red cells of most people, those who do have it being classified as Rh–positive and those who do not as Rh–negative. It can cause strong reactions in the blood during pregnancy or blood transfusions.

Rhodes scholarship

A **Rhodes scholarship** is one of 72 scholarships that are awarded annually on

Famous people who have been Rhodes scholars include ex-president Bill Clinton, psychologist Edward de Bono and singer Kris Kristofferson.

merit to American and Commonwealth students to enable them to study at Oxford University in England. These scholarships were founded by **Cecil John Rhodes** (1853–1902), a British statesman and financier in South Africa. After making a fortune in diamond mining, Rhodes became prime minister of the Cape Colony (1890–1896) and helped to develop **Rhodesia** after 1889.

Richard Roe

See **John Doe and Richard Roe**.

Richter scale

 The **Richter scale**, a scale for expressing the magnitude of earthquakes, is named after the American seismologist **Charles Richter** (1900–1985). Richter devised the scale in 1935 in association with the German Beno Gutenberg (1889–1960), thus it is sometimes called the Gutenberg-Richter scale. The logarithmic scale ranges from 0 to 10; a value of 2 can just be sensed as a tremor, while earthquakes that measure values greater than 6 cause damage to buildings. The strongest earthquake so far recorded measured 8.6 on the Richter scale.

See also **Mercalli scale**.

Rip van Winkle

Someone who has outdated views and is completely out of touch with contemporary ideas is sometimes referred to as a **Rip van Winkle**. The description comes from the character in the story *Rip Van Winkle* (published in 1819) by the American author Washington Irving (1783–1859). In the story, **Rip van Winkle** falls asleep for 20 years and wakes to find his home in ruins and the world utterly different.

Washington Irving used to write using the pseudonym Dietrich Knickerbocker: see **knickerbockers**.

ritzy

The adjective **ritzy** is used in informal English to mean smart, especially in a showy manner. This usage derives from Ritz hotels, a chain of luxury hotels established by the Swiss hotelier **César Ritz** (1850–1918).

The original Ritz hotels in Paris (founded 1898) and London (1906) were known for their elegance and luxury. The 1920s saw the growth of 'Plazas and Astorias and Ritzes all over the hinterland' (H L Mencken), and also the development of the word ritzy in association with ostentatious smartness. The word **ritz** also featured in the song by Irving Berlin 'Putting on the Ritz', sung by Fred Astaire.

Roland for an Oliver

Roland and **Oliver** were two of the legendary twelve peers or paladins who attended Charlemagne, king of the Franks (c. AD 742–814). Roland, Charlemagne's nephew, once fought Oliver in a duel that lasted several days. The knights were so evenly matched, each man answering the other's blows in kind, that the duel was declared a draw and the two knights became ardent friends. The expression '**a Roland for an Oliver**' thus came to mean an effective retaliation or tit for tat.

Both knights were slain at Roncesvalles in north-east Spain in 778. The early-twelfth-century French epic poem *Chanson de Roland* describes the heroic stand of the knights at this battle.

Rolfing

Rolfing is a massage technique developed by **Dr Ida P Rolf** (1897–1979), an American biochemist and physiotherapist. This technique is aimed at correcting the vertical alignment of the body by vigorous manipulation of the muscle and connective tissue, thereby releasing muscular tension and improving both physical and mental wellbeing.

Rolls-Royce

Rolls-Royce, the trademark for a type of luxurious car of outstanding quality, is also applied to something that is considered to be the foremost of its kind. The car is named after its designers, **Charles Stewart Rolls** (1877–1910) and **Sir Frederick Henry Royce** (1836–1933).

Royce originally established an engineering business in Manchester in 1884, where he manufactured electric dynamos and cranes. In 1904 he began to build cars and so impressed Rolls that they formed a partnership, the Rolls–Royce Company, in 1906. Royce was the engineer, while Rolls promoted the cars.

The partnership ended abruptly when Rolls was killed in a flying accident in 1910. Royce was forced, because of poor health, to move to the South of France, where he designed some of their most famous cars and also the aero-engine that was developed into the Merlin engine that was used in Spitfires in World War II.

Romeo

A romantic lover is sometimes known as a **Romeo**, after the hero in William Shakespeare's tragedy *Romeo and Juliet* (published in 1594). The two most important families of Verona, the Montagues and the Capulets, were great rivals; **Romeo**, son of Lord Montague, fell in love with Capulet's daughter, Juliet. Shakespeare based his play on Arthur Brooke's poem *The Tragicall Historye of Romeus and Juliet* (1562).

See also **juliet cap**.

röntgen

 A **röntgen** (or **roentgen**), the former unit of dose of ionizing radiation, is named after the German physicist **Wilhelm Konrad Röntgen** (1845–1923). Röntgen was awarded the first Nobel prize (qv) for physics in 1901 for the outstanding achievement of the discovery of X-rays (formerly known as **roentgen rays**). While professor of physics at Würzburg University, Bavaria, Röntgen accidentally discovered the mysterious rays when he was undertaking research into the luminescence of cathode rays in 1895. Because the phenomenon of X-rays was unknown to him, he borrowed the symbol X from algebra to describe them. The discovery that X-rays pass through matter was quickly appreciated by the medical world and they soon became used in medical diagnosis.

Rorschach test

The **Rorschach test** is a psychological test in which the interpretation by a subject of a series of inkblots reveals aspects

> **The artist Roy Lichtenstein said, 'Paintings are like Rorschach ink blots. They are what you want them to be.'**

of the subject's personality. The test is named after the Swiss psychiatrist **Hermann Rorschach** (1884–1922), who devised it in 1921.

Roscius

Quintus Roscius Gallus (c. 126–62 BC), was a famous Roman actor. A friend of Cicero, he became regarded as the most distinguished Roman comic actor. The name **Roscius** is thus sometimes applied to an outstanding actor; and a **Roscian** performance is one that displays great theatrical mastery.

Rubik's cube

Rubik's cube is a puzzle consisting of a cube, each face of which is divided into nine small coloured squares that can rotate around a central square. The aim of the puzzle is to rotate the squares on the cube so that the whole of each face shows one colour only. The total number of positions that can be reached on the Rubik's cube is 43,252,003,274,489,856,000.

Rubik's cube is named after its inventor, the Hungarian designer, sculptor and architect **Ernö Rubik** (born 1944). Originally intended to help Rubik's students understand three-dimensional design, it first became generally known to mathematicians at a Mathematical Congress at Helsinki in 1978. In the following few years it quickly became a craze throughout the world.

Rudbeckia

The **Rudbeckia** genus of flowers has showy flowers with yellow rays and dark-brown to black conical centres. Also called cone-flowers, several of the plants of the genus, particularly *Rudbeckia hirta*, are known as black-eyed Susan. The name derives from the Swedish botanist **Olof Rudbeck**

> **Olof Rudbeck senior wrote a book in which he argued that Sweden had been the site of Plato's Atlantis.**

(1630–1702) – also noted for his discovery of the lymphatic system – and his son, also **Olof Rudbeck** (1660–1740).

rutherford

The **rutherford**, a unit of radioactivity, honours the British physicist **Ernest Rutherford**, 1st Baron Rutherford (1871–1937).

Born in New Zealand, Rutherford was educated at Christchurch and later Cambridge. He is known for his pioneering research into the nature of radioactivity – initially in Montreal, then in Manchester and Cambridge, where he was director of the Cavendish Laboratory. Most well known for his discovery of the

> **When someone commented, 'You are a lucky man, Rutherford, always on the crest of a wave', he retorted, 'Well I made the wave, didn't I?'**

atomic nucleus in 1911, he was awarded the Nobel prize (qv) for chemistry in 1908, the Order of Merit in 1925 and made a baron in 1931.

S

Sabin vaccine

The **Sabin vaccine** is an orally administered vaccine against polio. It replaced the Salk vaccine (qv) in the 1960s as it provided greater immunity from polio and for a longer period. The Sabin vaccine is named after the Polish-born American microbiologist **Albert Bruce Sabin** (1906–1993), who developed it in 1955.

sadism

Sadism – the pleasure derived from inflicting pain on others – is named after the French soldier and writer **Count Donatien Alphonse François de Sade**, known as **Marquis de Sade** (1740–1814). De Sade's writings depict sexual perversion. His most famous writings, including *Les 120 Journées de Sodome* (1785) and *Justine* (1791), were composed during the 1780s and 1790s while he spent many years imprisoned for sexual offences. The final years of de Sade's life were spent in a mental asylum in Charenton.

St Anthony's fire

St Anthony's fire is a name given to two diseases – ergotism and erysipelas – that cause reddening or blistering of the skin. They were probably associated with **St Anthony** in the sixteenth century because it was believed that praying to him led to healing.

> **St Anthony is the patron saint of swineherds.**

St Anthony of Egypt (c. AD 251–356) was known as a hermit and also as the founder of Christian monasticism. At the age of about 18, he gave up all his possessions and some years later withdrew to the desert, there to be tempted by demons disguised as wild animals. He emerged in about AD 305 to organize his followers into a monastic community.

St Bernard dog

The Italian churchman **St Bernard of Menthon** (923–1008) founded hospices on two alpine passes, which came to be named after him, the Great St Bernard Pass between Italy and Switzerland and the Little St Bernard Pass between Italy and France. The monks of the hospice at the Great St Bernard Pass used to keep a breed of large working dog that was trained to track down travellers lost in blizzards and the breed came to be named after the founder of the hospice.

The breed is the heaviest breed of domestic dog in the world, the heaviest recorded example weighing 22 stone 2 pounds (140.6 kg).

St Elmo's fire

The expression **St Elmo's fire** refers to the luminous discharge sometimes seen in stormy weather at points that project into the atmosphere, such as a church spire or the mast of a ship. Known technically as corposant, the luminous appearance derives from small electrical discharges.

St Elmo's fire is probably so called because it was associated with **St Elmo**, an

> **St Erasmus is said to have been killed by having has intestines wound out using a windlass.**

Italian alteration of the name St Erasmus (died AD 303), the Italian bishop and patron saint of Mediterranean sailors. According to one legend, in reward for being saved from drowning by a sailor, Erasmus is said to have promised that a light would be displayed to indicate an impending storm.

St John's wort

St John's wort, also known as *Hypericum perforatum*, is a herb or shrub with bright yellow flowers. It was named after **St John the Baptist**, either because the leaves have red spots which allegedly appeared when he was beheaded or because the plant blooms from June to August and was traditionally gathered on 24 June, which is St John's Day, as a protection against evil spirits. St John's wort has been used since ancient times, and is still used today, as a natural remedy for anxiety and mild depression.

St Leger

The **St Leger** horse race is a flat race for three-year-old colts run annually in September on the Town Moor, Doncaster, South Yorkshire. Founded in 1776, it is named after a leading local sportsman of that time, **Anthony Saint Leger** (died 1786) of Park Hill, Doncaster.

St Luke's summer

St Luke's summer and **St Martin's summer** both refer to periods of exceptionally warm weather in the autumn. The summery weather is associated with the saints because of the dates of their feast-days, St Luke's Day being 18 October and St Martin's Day 11 November.

St Luke, traditionally regarded as the author of the third Gospel and also the Acts of the Apostles, was the Gentile doctor who accompanied Paul on his missionary journeys. **St Martin** (c. 315–397) was Bishop of Tours. Born into a non-believing family, it is said that he became a Christian after dividing his cloak into two to give half to a beggar.

See also **martin**.

St Vitus' dance

St Vitus' dance is the non-technical name for Sydenham's chorea (qv), the disease of the central nervous system marked by involuntary jerky movements. The disease is named after **St Vitus**, a child who was martyred with his nurse and tutor during the persecution of Christians by the Roman Emperor Diocletian in about 303. The description of the disease as St Vitus' dance arose in the seventeenth century, when sufferers prayed to St Vitus for healing, dancing around a statue of him.

salchow

A **salchow** is a standard jump in figure skating, in which the skater takes off from the rear inside edge of one skate, turns a full revolution in the air, and lands on the rear outside edge of the other skate. The salchow is named after the Swedish skater **Ulrich Salchow** (1877–1949), who first executed the single salchow in 1909. Between 1898 and 1913, Salchow won ten World Championship titles and nine European Championship titles.

Salk vaccine

The American microbiologist **Jonas Edward Salk** (1914–1995) developed the first successful vaccine against polio, which came to be named after him and was used initially in 1954. The **Salk vaccine** was widely used but by the 1960s it was replaced by the Sabin vaccine (qv), which provided greater immunity from polio and for a longer period.

> **Salk was named as one of *Time Magazine*'s 100 Most Important People of the 20th Century.**

Sally Lunn

A **Sally Lunn**, a slightly sweetened tea-cake, is said to have been named after a late-eighteenth-century English baker. It seems that **Sally Lunn** used to advertise her wares by shouting out her name in the city of Bath. A resourceful local baker named Dalmer developed mass production of the buns and also wrote a song to express their delights; so their fame spread.

salmonella

Salmonella is the name of the rod-shaped bacteria that cause diseases, including food poisoning (**salmonellosis**), in humans. The genus of bacteria has nothing to do with the fish but is named after the American veterinary surgeon **Daniel Elmer Salmon** (1850–1914), who first identified it. Many cases of salmonellosis are thought to have been caused by inadequate thawing of frozen poultry before cooking.

Samaritans

See **Good Samaritan**.

samarskite

Samarskite, the velvet-black mineral discovered in Russia in 1857, is named after a Russian mine official **Colonel M von Samarski**. When, in 1879, the French chemist Lecoq de Boisbaudrian discovered a new lanthanide element spectroscopically, he named the element **samarium** after samarskite, since it contained this mineral. Thus a little-known mine official is remembered by having a chemical element named in his honour.

Sam Browne belt

A **Sam Browne belt** is the military officer's leather belt supported by a light strap that passes over the right shoulder and designed originally as a belt for supporting a sword or pistol. The belt is named after the British army officer **Sir Samuel J Browne** (1824–1901) who designed it.

Born in India, Browne had a distinguished military career. His decisive role in the Indian Mutiny (1857–1859) earned him the Victoria Cross, and in 1888 he was promoted to general.

A version of the belt is worn by cyclists, etc, to increase their visibility.

Samson

A man of great strength is sometimes known as a **Samson**, with reference to the biblical judge of Israel. **Samson**'s outstanding feats of strength included the tearing of a lion apart with his bare hands, catching three hundred foxes and then tying them tail to tail in pairs, and striking down a thousand men with the jawbone of a donkey.

When the treacherous Delilah (qv) eventually discovered that the secret of his strength lay in his hair, she had it all shaved off so that his strength left him and the Philistines seized him, gouging out his eyes. However, as his hair grew back his strength returned and Samson's final act was to take revenge on the Philistines at the temple of Dagon. Calling upon God, he braced himself against the two central pillars that supported the temple, in which about three thousand people had assembled to bait him. Pushing with all his strength, he brought down the whole edifice, killing himself but at the moment of his death killing more Philistines than during his life.

sandwich

Sandwich is one of the most famous eponyms in the English language. The name of the snack consisting of two slices of buttered bread with a filling between them derives from the English diplomat John Montagu, 4th **Earl of Sandwich** (1718–1792).

The earl was addicted to gambling, some of his gambling sessions lasting as long as two days non-stop. He was so compulsive a gambler that, rather than leave the gaming table to take food and so interrupt the game, he would order his valet to bring him food. Invariably, he would be brought slices of cold beef between two slices of bread. Within a few years the snack became generally known as a sandwich, although it had of course been eaten before this time.

The Earl of Sandwich was also notorious for his part in the prosecution of his former friend John Wilkes, and the inadequacy of the English navy during the American War of Independence is attributed to the corruption that was rife while he was first lord of the Admiralty.

> **Captain Cook honoured the Earl of Sandwich by naming what is now Hawaii the Sandwich Islands.**

Sanforized

Sanforized is the trademark used for the process of pre-shrinking a fabric before it is made into articles, such as clothes. In the process, the fibres are compressed mechanically. The word derives from the name **Sanford Lockwood Cluett** (1874–1968), the American director of engineering and research of a firm of shirt and collar manufacturers, Cluett, Peabody and Co, of Troy, New York.

Sapphism

Sapphism is another, more literary, word for lesbianism, or female homosexuality. It was so called after **Sappho** (c. 632–556 BC), the renowned Greek lyric poet who, it is believed, may have been homosexual. Sappho was born on the island of Lesbos, or Lésvos, which is the source of the word 'lesbian'. Such fragments of her poems as remain indicate that she was devoted to a group of girls that she taught, composing bridal odes for them when they left to get married. This, combined with the homosexual themes in her poems, led later commentators to accuse Sappho of 'immorality and vice'.

Sappho invented the **Sapphic** verse form, based on a four-line stanza in which the first three lines are each eleven syllables long and the fourth is five syllables long.

Sarah's law

Sarah Payne was an eight-year-old English girl who was abducted and murdered in Sussex in July 1999. After Sarah's death, her parents campaigned for the introduction of a new law known as **Sarah's law**, based on Megan's law (qv) in the USA, which would give parents the right to know when convicted sex offenders move into their community. The British Government has so far refused to introduce such a law, on the grounds that it would be difficult to police, there would be a risk of vigilante attacks, and it might force sex offenders underground, which could be even more dangerous for potential victims. However, in 2000 the Government did announce new powers for police and probation services, which it claims will provide greater protection than Megan's law.

sarrusophone

The **sarrusophone** is a woodwind instrument made of brass with a double reed, like an oboe. It was named in honour of **Pierre-Auguste Sarrus** (1813–1876), the French bandmaster who invented it in 1856.

The sarrusophone was originally invented to replace oboes and bassoons in military bands. Sarrus had a long military career (1836–1867), for most of this time as a bandmaster.

Saturday

Saturday, the seventh day of the week, derives its name from the Roman god of agriculture **Saturn**. The Old English name *Sæternes dæg* was a translation of the Latin *Saturni dies*, day of Saturn.

savarin

A **savarin** is a ring-shaped cake made with yeast, containing nuts and fruit, and flavoured with rum or a liqueur. It was named in honour of **Jean Anthelme Brillat-Savarin** (1755–1826), the French politician and gourmet, who was one of the first serious writers on the subject of gastronomy. Brillat-Savarin was mayor of Belley in the Bresse region of France but, following the French Revolution, he was forced to flee the country. He lived in the USA until he was allowed to return to France in 1796, where he became a judge in the Supreme Court of Appeal.

saxophone

The **saxophone**, the keyed woodwind instrument with a brass body and a single-reed mouthpiece, is named after its inventor, the Belgian musical-instrument maker **Adolphe Sax** (1814–1894). It seems that it was while working in the musical-instrument workshop of his

> **Sax also patented instruments called the saxtromba, sax-tuba and sax-horn.**

father Charles Joseph Sax (1791–1865) in the early 1840s that Adolphe invented several instruments, the most famous of which was to become known as the saxophone.

The instrument was first shown to the public in 1844, and enjoyed a great deal of success. Composers such as Berlioz and Bizet wrote music for the instrument and today the saxophone is most commonly used for jazz and dance music.

Schick test

 The **Schick test** is a test to determine susceptibility to diphtheria, made by injecting the skin with a dilute diphtheria toxin, which will cause a red inflamed area to develop within two or three days in susceptible individuals. This test is named after **Béla Schick** (1877–1967), the Hungarian–born American paediatrician who devised it in 1913. Within five years of its introduction, the Schick test had virtually eliminated the deadly childhood disease. Schick also made important studies on scarlet fever, tuberculosis, allergies and nutrition for infants.

Scrooge

A miserly person is sometimes called a **Scrooge**, after the character **Ebenezer Scrooge** in the story *A Christmas Carol* (published in 1843) by Charles Dickens. On Christmas Eve, Scrooge is visited by the ghost of his

Alastair Sim, Albert Finney, Henry Winkler and Michael Caine have all played the character of Scrooge in films.

former business partner Marley. He sees visions of the past, present and future, including one depicting his own death unless he quickly changes his ways, which he then proceeds to do.

Scylla and Charybdis

The expression '**between Scylla and Charybdis**' is used to refer to a situation in which one is faced with two equally dangerous alternatives: avoiding one danger immediately exposes one to the other. The expression originally referred to the narrow sea passage, the Straits of Messina, between Italy and Sicily. In Greek mythology, the female sea monster **Scylla** was believed to live there in a cave off the Italian coast. On the Sicilian side lived **Charybdis**, the monster in the whirlpool. Thus, sailors who tried to avoid one danger were exposed to the other.

seaborgium

 The artificially produced radioactive transuranic element known as **seaborgium** (formerly called unnilhexium and rutherfordium) is named in honour of the American nuclear chemist **Glenn Theodore Seaborg** (1912–1999) – the first time a new element had been named after a living person. Between 1940 and 1958, Seaborg, along with colleagues, produced nine of the transuranic elements (plutonium to nobelium). Seaborg and his colleague Edwin McMillan (1907–1991) were jointly awarded the Nobel prize (qv) for chemistry in 1951.

Semitic

A **Semitic** person, or a **Semite**, is a member of any of the peoples, supposedly descended from Noah's son **Shem** from the Old Testament, who speak a Semitic language, ie any of a family of languages including Hebrew, Arabic and Aramaic. This group of peoples includes the Arabs and the Jews.

Sometimes 'Semitic' is used to mean, specifically, 'Jewish'; **anti-Semitic** means 'hostile to or prejudiced against Jews'.

See also **Hamitic**.

sequoia

 The most massive tree in the world, the giant sequoia, is named after the American Indian **Sequoya** (c. 1770–1843). The name **sequoia**, referring in fact to either of two giant Californian coniferous trees, the big tree (giant sequoia) or the redwood, was chosen by the Hungarian botanist Stephen Ladislaus Endlicher in 1847.

Sequoya – who believed himself to be the son of a white trader and so adopted the name George Guess – was sure that the power of the white man lay in his possession of a written language. He therefore set about writing down his own language. Over a period of twelve years, Sequoya established a writing system of 86 characters that represented all the sounds in the Cherokee language. Thousands of Cherokees quickly mastered the writing system and soon a weekly Cherokee newspaper was published and a constitution written in the Cherokee language.

See also **washingtonia**.

shaddock

The **shaddock** is a large yellow citrus fruit, grown widely in southeast Asia, that has a thick yellow rind and bitter pulp resembling the grapefruit in flavour. It is named after **Captain Shaddock**, an English ship's commander who introduced it to the West Indies in 1696. This fruit is sometimes called a pomelo.

Shakespearean

The adjective **Shakespearean** (or **Shakespearian**) is used in reference to **William Shakespeare** (1564–1616) or his writings, particularly when considered to show great vision and power. The name of the famous English dramatist and poet is also remembered in the **Shakespearean sonnet**, a 14-line poem in the form *abab cdcd efef gg*. Also known as the English sonnet, it is a variant of the Petrarchan sonnet (qv).

Shavian

The adjective **Shavian** describes the life, works or ideas of the Irish dramatist and socialist **George Bernard Shaw** (1856–1950). GBS, as he was known, disliked the adjective Shawian, so coined Shavius as the Latin form of Shaw, then derived the adjective Shavian from it. **Shavian wit** is sometimes used to describe the particular style of humour of Shaw's plays.

> **Shaw is the only person to have won a Nobel prize and an Oscar.**

Sheraton

The English furniture-maker **Thomas Sheraton** (1751–1806) is remembered for a style of furniture named in his honour. The style is known for its elegance, straight lines and inlaid decoration.

Sheraton is particularly famous for his writings, especially *The Cabinet-Maker and Upholsterer's Drawing Book* (published in four volumes, 1791–1794) and *The Cabinet Dictionary* (1802). He taught drawing, but there is no record that he ever owned a workshop where he undertook furniture design.

shrapnel

The explosive device known as a **shrapnel shell**, the projectile that contains bullets or fragments of metal and a charge that is exploded before impact, takes its name from the English artillery officer **Henry Shrapnel** (1761–1842) who invented it.

Shrapnel spent many years developing this deadly weapon, which was originally known as the spherical-case shot; it was eventually adopted in about 1803. It was first used in action against the Dutch in Surinam (Dutch Guiana) and was important in the defeat of Napoleon at Waterloo in 1815.

Shrapnel gained promotion for his efforts – he was finally a general – but he received scant financial reward for all his work.

Shylock

A pitiless and extortionate moneylender is sometimes referred to as a **Shylock**. The name was originally that of the ruthless usurer in William Shakespeare's *Merchant of Venice*. The expression 'have [get, etc] one's pound of flesh' also derives from the play. **Shylock** agreed to lend the merchant Antonio money against the security of a pound of Antonio's flesh, but as the debt could not be repaid when due, Shylock demanded his pound of flesh.

shyster

A **shyster** is a person who is unscrupulous in the pursuit of his or her profession; the word is used chiefly in American English to describe a lawyer or a politician. The word possibly derives from the name **Scheuster**, a mid-nineteenth-century lawyer who on several occasions was admonished in a New York court for pettifoggery. Other authorities suggest the ultimate origin as the German *Scheisse* meaning excrement.

sideburns

Sideburns are the strips of hair that grow down the sides of a man's face reaching from the hairline to below the ears. The word comes from **Ambrose Everett Burnside** (1824–1881).

After a short time as a tailor's apprentice and a brief period of military service, Burnside set up in business to manufacture a breech-loading rifle that he had invented. The business failed, however.

Later, he became a general, fighting for the Union in the American Civil War, and was renowned for the defeats under his command at Fredericksburg (1862) and Petersburg (1864). Despite these failures, Burnside remained popular and was elected governor of Rhode Island (1866–1869) and a US senator from 1875.

The general is notably remembered for his shaving habits: he sported so-called burnsides, full side whiskers joining the moustache. With the passage of time, the side whiskers became shorter and the two parts of the word mysteriously changed places to give sideburns.

siemens

 Siemens, the metric unit of electrical conductance, is named after the German electrical engineer **Ernst Werner von Siemens** (1816–1892). A pioneer in telegraphy, Siemens is known for his work in laying a government telegraph line from Berlin to Frankfurt. With his three brothers, Friedrich Siemens (1826–1904), Sir William Siemens (Karl Wilhelm Siemens; 1828–1883) – who invented the open-hearth process of making steel – and Karl Siemens (1829–1906), he created the immense Siemens industrial empire.

> **The siemens unit was formerly known as a *mho* – a word formed by reversing the letters of another eponymous word, ohm.**

silhouette

A **silhouette**, the outline of a dark shape set on a light background, takes its name from the French politician **Étienne de Silhouette** (1709–1767), but the precise reason for this is uncertain.

As controller of finances (1759), Silhouette had to restore the French economy after the Seven Years' War. He therefore instituted a series of stringent tax revisions, which made him unpopular. His measures were seen as niggardly and the phrase *à la silhouette* meaning 'on the cheap' became current. The sense of parsimony was then applied to the partial shadow portraits that were fashionable at that time.

Other sources suggest that the brevity of Silhouette's period of office as controller-general – he was forced to resign after only nine months – is the origin of the incompleteness of the portraits.

Still others claim that Silhouette's hobby was in fact making such outlines and he is said to have displayed many examples of this art form in his château.

silly-billy

The term **silly-billy** is sometimes used in informal English – particularly by or to children – to describe someone who is foolish or silly. The expression, deriving from Billy, the nickname for William, may well have first been applied to **King William IV** of England, formerly Duke of Clarence (1765–1837). He was known as silly Billy, from, it seems, his carefree attitude towards his royal responsibilities. The nickname was also given to the nobleman **William Frederick**, Duke of Gloucester (1776–1834).

simony

Simony, the practice of buying or selling of church or spiritual benefits or offices, derives from **Simon Magus**, a first-century-AD sorcerer. After becoming a Christian, Simon tried to buy the gift of spiritual power from the Apostles, but was strongly rebuked by Peter (Acts 8:9–24).

smithsonite

Smithsonite, the whitish mineral that is an important ore of zinc, takes its name from the English chemist **James Smithson** (original name James Lewes Macie; 1765–1829).

Smithson left a bequest that an institution named after him should be set up in Washington DC, 'for the increase and diffusion of knowledge among men'. The American Congress spent many years discussing whether to accept the bequest and finally agreed to do so. The **Smithsonian Institution** was founded in 1846, and today conducts scientific research and maintains several art galleries and museums.

Socratic

The Greek philosopher **Socrates** (c. 470–399 BC) wrote no philosophical works himself, his beliefs only being known through the works of his pupils, Plato and Xenophon. His supposed method of reasoning (**Socratic method**) involved questions and answers designed to evoke truths that he considered every rational person knew, even if only implicitly.

> Socrates said, 'The unexamined life is not worth living.'

The expression **Socratic irony** derives from his pretended ignorance in arguments, so leading the person answering his questions to be easily defeated by his skilful interrogation.

In 399 BC Socrates was condemned to death by the Athenian government for impiety and corruption of youth. He was forced to commit suicide by drinking hemlock.

Sod's law

See **Murphy's law**.

Solomon

Solomon, the tenth-century-BC king of Israel and son of David and Bathsheba, was noted for his great wisdom and wealth. His wisdom has become proverbial, being evoked in expressions such as '**need the**

wisdom of Solomon' and '**as wise as Solomon**', and was demonstrated when two women came to him each claiming that a particular baby was her own. Solomon's suggestion that the baby be divided in two revealed the true mother: the one who would rather hand the baby over to her rival than see the baby killed (1 Kings 3:16–28).

Solomon's seal is the name given to any of the genus *Polygonatum* of the lily family that have greenish-white flowers, long smooth leaves, and a fleshy white underground stem. The underground stem is marked with prominent leaf scars, which are said to resemble seals – hence the name. Solomon's seal is also the name of a mystic symbol, the Star of David, that is traditionally associated with Solomon.

> **According to one tradition, the descendants of Solomon and the Queen of Sheba became the royal family of Ethiopia.**

soubise

Soubise, a white or brown sauce containing a purée of onions, takes its name from the French nobleman Charles de Rohan, **Prince de Soubise** (1715–1787). It seems that the sauce was probably named in the prince's honour by his chef Marin. The Prince de Soubise was a renowned military leader and general and became marshal of France in 1758 through the influence of Madame de Pompadour.

sousaphone

A **sousaphone**, the large tuba that encircles the player with a forward-facing bell, is named after its inventor, the American bandmaster and composer **John Philip Sousa** (1854–1932).

Known as 'the march king', Sousa was appointed leader of the US Marine Corps band in 1880, and twelve years later formed his own Sousa Band, which toured the world, gaining him great fame.

> **Sousa's *Liberty Bell March* was used as the theme for *Monty Python's Flying Circus*.**

Sousa composed over a hundred popular marches, including 'The Stars and Stripes Forever', 'The Washington Post' and 'Liberty Bell'.

Spartacist

In 73 BC a Thracian gladiator named **Spartacus** successfully led a slave revolt against Rome. Two years later he and his followers were defeated by the Roman politician Marcus Licinius Crassus.

During World War I the German socialists Karl Liebknecht and Rosa Luxemburg formed a radical socialist group known as the Spartacus League (which developed into the German Communist Party), Karl Liebknecht adopting the name Spartacus. Members of the group were called **Spartacists**. Both leaders were murdered following the unsuccessful communist revolt of 1919.

Stanley Kubrick's 1960 film *Spartacus* won Oscars for best cinematography, sets and costumes, and best supporting actor (Peter Ustinov).

spencer

A **spencer** – a short, waist-length, close-fitting jacket, which was fashionable in the late eighteenth and early nineteenth centuries – takes its name from the English politician **George John Spencer**, 2nd Earl of Spencer (1758–1834). According to one account, the earl won a bet that he could set a new fashion simply by appearing in the streets wearing a new kind of garment.

While lord of the admiralty under the prime ministership of William Pitt the Younger, Earl Spencer chose Nelson to command the Fleet in the Mediterranean – which led to the British victory in the Battle of the Nile (August 1798).

Spenserian

The English poet **Edmund Spenser** (c. 1552–1599) is noted for his moral allegory *The Faerie Queen* (1590; 1596). It consists of nine-line stanzas that have come to be known as **Spenserian stanzas**: eight lines in iambic pentameter followed by an iambic line of six feet, rhyming *ababbcbcc*. Spenser also developed a form of sonnet with the rhyming scheme *abab bcbc cdcd ee*, which came to be known as the **Spenserian sonnet**.

spinet

The **spinet**, a type of small harpsichord with one manual, may take its name from the sixteenth-century Italian musical instrument maker **Giovanni Spinetti**. It is said that Spinetti invented this instrument at the beginning of the sixteenth century. Alternatively, the word spinet may possibly derive from Italian *spina*, a thorn, with reference to the thorn-like quills used in plucking the strings of the instrument.

Spode

The British potter **Josiah Spode** (1754–1827) was famous for a type of porcelain that came to bear his name.

His father, also Josiah Spode (1733–1797), had started his own works at Stoke-on-Trent in 1770. The son succeeded his father in 1797, developing porcelain (1800), by introducing bones into the paste as well as feldspar, and stone china tableware in about 1805.

spoonerism

The English clergyman and educationist **Reverend William Archibald Spooner** (1844–1930) was, it seems, renowned for slips of the tongue in which the initial sounds of words were accidentally transposed, often with a comical effect. Some examples of such '**spoonerisms**', as they came to be called, attributed to the clergyman include: 'a half-warmed fish' instead of 'a half-formed wish'; 'kinkering congs' instead of 'conquering kings'; 'a well-boiled icicle' instead of 'a well-oiled bicycle'; reference to God as 'a shoving leopard' instead of 'a loving

> Spooner was an albino whose poor eyesight may have contributed to errors when reading.

shepherd'; and to Queen Victoria as 'our queer old dean' instead of 'our dear old queen'.

Stableford

Stableford is a name given to a points-scoring system in golf in which points are awarded according to the number of strokes taken to complete each hole. This system is named after **Frank B Stableford** (1870–1959), the English doctor and amateur golfer who devised it. The first competition using this system took place on 30 September 1898 at the Glamorganshire Golf Club in Wales.

Stakhanovite

A **Stakhanovite** was an industrial worker in the former USSR who was offered special incentives for producing an output that is greater than the norm. The word Stakhanovite, a member of the movement known as Stakhanovism, derives from the Russian coal-miner **Alexei Grigorievich Stakhanov** (1906–1977). In 1935 Stakhanov reorganized his coal-mining team, so greatly increasing the production.

Stalinism

Stalinism describes the form of communism developed by the Soviet leader **Joseph Stalin** (original name Josef Vissarionovich Dzhugashvili; 1879–1953). A variant of Marxism-Leninism, Stalinism is marked by a policy of establishing socialism in one country, strict bureaucracy, extensive use of terror, and devotion to Russian nationalism.

Succeeding Lenin as head of the Communist Party, Stalin (his name means 'steel') created a totalitarian state in the USSR. He introduced rapid collectivization of industry and agriculture. Notorious for his ruthless dictatorship, Stalin crushed all opposition, particularly in the purges of the 1930s. By the outbreak of World War II Stalin was in complete control of the country. By the time of his death the Soviet Union had been transformed into a world power.

> **Stalin originally trained for the priesthood, but was expelled from his theological seminary.**

After his death, Khrushchev denounced Stalin and a process of de-Stalinization followed. Stalin's body was transferred from Lenin's mausoleum and the names of all places honouring him were changed.

See also **Leninism**; **Marxism**; **Trotskyism**.

Stanislavski method

 The **Stanislavski method** is a naturalistic approach to acting developed by the Russian theatre director and actor **Konstantin Sergeyevich Stanislavski** (original name, Konstantin Sergeyevich Alekseyev; 1863–1938). Along with Vladimir Ivanovich Nemirovich-Danchenko, Stanislavski co-founded the Moscow Art Theatre in 1897. His theories, which were later developed into Method acting, have had a profound influence on modern acting and directing. According to the Stanislavski method, the actor takes a psychological approach, basing his or her portrayal on the character's inner motivation. Stanislavski encouraged actors to recall their own emotions and past experiences and to use them in their expression of their characters' emotions, thereby achieving a more powerful and realistic performance.

Stanley knife

Stanley knife is a trademark for a knife with a short, very sharp, retractable blade that can be replaced when it becomes blunt. Stanley knives are used for cutting carpets and other DIY purposes. The Stanley knife was named after **Frederick T Stanley**, an American businessman who founded a factory producing handles, bolts and hinges in 1843. The retractable-blade knife was introduced in the 1940s and is manufactured at Stanley's steelworks in Sheffield, England.

Sten gun

 The **Sten gun**, the light 9-millimetre sub-machine-gun used in World War II, was named using the initials of the surnames of its inventors: **Major R V Shepherd**, a twentieth-century English army officer, and **H J Turpin**, a civil servant, plus the 'en' of England (or Enfield, London).

stent

 A **stent** is a medical device, such as a slender rod or catheter, inserted temporarily inside a blood vessel or other tubular structure, to keep it open. It can also be used of a device used to provide support to or maintain pressure on a body part in order to aid healing, especially in the case of a skin graft. This device is probably named after the English dentist **Charles R Stent** (1845–1901). Stent came from a family of dentists, including his father Charles T Stent (1807–1885) and his brother Arthur H Stent (1859–1900), who used a special apparatus to support poorly aligned teeth.

stentorian

If someone speaks in **stentorian** tones, he or she is speaking extremely loudly. The adjective derives from the name of **Stentor**, a herald in Greek mythology who died when he lost a shouting contest with Hermes, herald of the gods.

> **According to Homer, Stentor had a voice as loud as the voices of 50 men.**

Stetson

 Stetson is trademark for a type of wide-brimmed, high-crowned, felt hat. It is named after the American hat-maker **John Bauerson Stetson** (1830–1906) who designed it.

When Stetson travelled in the western USA at the time of the Civil War, it occurred to him that hats suitable for the needs of the cowboys were not being manufactured. When he returned to Philadelphia in 1865, therefore, he started to mass-produce a wide-brimmed hat that became popular with cowboys and was known as a stetson or a John B.

Stevenson screen

 The **Stevenson screen** is a standard piece of meteorological equipment used to ensure that observers at weather stations around the world make accurate measurements of local conditions. The screen is a white-painted wooden box resembling a beehive, with louvred sides and a door, which allow free movement of air. It also has a double-layered roof with an intervening air space to provide insulation, and it is built on stilts at a height of

> **Stevenson was the father of the novelist Robert Louis Stevenson.**

1.2 metres above the ground. The Stevenson screen is used to store wet and dry bulb thermometers used to record humidity and air temperature. It was invented in the 1870s by **Thomas Stevenson** (1818–1887), a Scottish lighthouse engineer.

Stokes–Adams syndrome

Stokes–Adams syndrome, also called Adams–Stokes syndrome, is a condition in which there is dizziness, fainting and convulsions caused by complete heart block with a very slow pulse rate. This syndrome was named after the Irish physicians **William Stokes** (1804–1878) and **Robert Adams** (1791–1875), who discovered it.

stonewall

If you **stonewall**, then you act in an obstructive or defensive manner. The expression gained currency as a result of the nickname of the US Confederate general in the American Civil War, Thomas Jonathan Jackson, known as **Stonewall Jackson** (1824–1863). In the first Battle of Bull Run (1861), he and his forces were described as 'standing like a stone wall' against the Federal troops.

From Jackson's name derives 'stonewalling', the act of obstructing something with stubborn resistance. The word is found particularly in cricket, to describe cautious defensive batting, and also in discussion, where a speaker talks for a long time expressly to stop other people from voicing their opinion.

Stradivarius

A **Stradivarius**, or **Stradivari**, is a violin, cello or viola made by **Antonio Stradivari** (c. 1644–1737) of Cremona, Italy, or by a member of his family. Stradivari served as an apprentice to Nicola Amati and worked in his workshop for a while. The most celebrated of all violin-makers, Stradivari developed the proportions of the modern violin. There are over 600 instruments made by Stradivari still in existence.

See also **Amati**.

stroganoff

 Beef stroganoff is a dish consisting of strips of beef cooked with onions, mushrooms and paprika, with soured cream swirled in. This dish was named after the Russian diplomat, **Count Pavel Aleksandrovich Stroganov** (1772–1817). The Stroganov family was a rich merchant family who loved the arts and fine cuisine. They lived in the Stroganov Palace in St Petersburg, which is now a museum. Beef stroganoff was a creation of the Palace kitchen.

sucre

 The **sucre** is the basic monetary unit of Ecuador, which is divided into 100 centavos. This is named after the Venezuelan revolutionary and statesman **Antonio José de Sucre** (1795–1830). As Simon Bolivar's chief lieutenant, Sucre fought for independence from Spain in Peru, Bolivia, Ecuador and Colombia. He later became the first president of Bolivia (1826–1828).

See also **bolivar**.

Svengali

A **Svengali** is a man who exerts a powerful, controlling, and often sinister, influence on someone, especially a young woman. **Svengali** is a character in *Trilby* (1894), a novel by the English artist and writer George du Maurier (1834–1896), grandfather of the novelist Daphne du Maurier. In *Trilby*, the heroine Trilby O'Ferrall is hypnotized by the evil musical genius Svengali. Under his influence she becomes a famous singer but, when he dies suddenly, she loses her voice and dies too.

See also **trilby**.

Swedenborgian

The Swedish scientist and theologian **Emanuel Swedenborg** (original surname Svedberg; 1688–1772) is known for his system of teachings showing the importance of the spiritual structure of the universe.

Originally a mining engineer and mineralogist, Swedenborg became more spiritually orientated in about 1743, claiming to have mystical visions. His works include *Arcana Coelestia* (1756) and *Divine Love and Wisdom* (1763). The religious group known as the New Jerusalem Church, also known as the New Church or **Swedenborgians**, was established after his death in 1787.

sweet Fanny Adams

Sweet Fanny Adams now means 'nothing at all': 'What's been happening while I've been away?' – 'Sweet Fanny Adams.' It is sometimes shortened to 'sweet FA'.

The expression comes originally from **Fanny Adams**, a girl who was murdered in Alton, Hampshire in 1867. Her body was found in the River Wey, cut into pieces.

Fanny's name became popularized by sailors talking about a distasteful meal of tinned mutton – it is said that a sailor found a button in a tin of mutton and with gruesome humour called the tin's contents Fanny Adams. From this slang usage, the meaning of the word developed to refer to something of little value and then to the current meaning.

Swiftian

Swiftian is sometimes used to mean satirical in a keen and bitter way: 'The appointment of a mathematician to lead the enquiry into the teaching of English language shows an undeniable Swiftian logic.' The adjective clearly derives from the name of the Anglo-Irish clergyman, poet and satirist

Swift left his entire estate to be used in setting up a psychiatric hospital in Dublin, noting ironically that 'No nation wanted it so much.'

Jonathan Swift (1667–1745), whose numerous writings included *A Tale of a Tub* (1704), a satire 'on corruptions in religion and learning', and the famous *Gulliver's Travels* (1726), a satire on the human condition, particularly the politics of that period.

sword of Damocles

In classical legend, the courtier **Damocles** declared enviously that the tyrant of Syracuse, Dionysius the Elder (405–367 BC), was the happiest of men. Flattered by this remark but wanting to teach Damocles a lesson, Dionysius invited Damocles to a banquet, where he could see the ruler's happiness. Damocles accepted the invitation, and sat down to a sumptuous feast, but above him was a sword, suspended by a single hair. Damocles was so troubled that he could not enjoy the banquet.

The moral was that fears and threats of danger constantly prevent those that have power from fully enjoying that power. The expression '**sword of Damocles**' has thus come to refer to impending disaster.

Sydenham's chorea

Sydenham's chorea is a neurological disorder, formerly known as St Vitus' dance (qv), that affects mainly children and often occurs following a bout of rheumatic fever. It is characterized by involuntary movements of the limbs and face. This disorder was named after **Thomas Sydenham** (1624–1689), the English physician who first described it.

Sydenham is often called the founder of epidemiology and clinical medicine or, less formally, 'the English Hippocrates'. In addition to the chorea that bears his name, Sydenham was first to describe scarlet fever, and arthritis due to gout. He also introduced the use of opium for medical purposes and was one of the first to prescribe iron for anaemia.

syphilis

The venereal disease **syphilis** derives from the name of a character in a poem published in 1530 with the title *Syphilis, sive Morbus Gallicus*

(Syphilis, or the French Disease) by the Italian physician and poet Girolamo Fracastro (1483–1553).

In the poem, **Syphilis**, the hero of the book and a shepherd, angers the sun god to such an extent that he is struck down by this disease. Fracastro probably coined the name Syphilis from the Greek *suphilos*, 'lover of pigs' or 'swineherd'.

T

Tammany Hall

Tammany Hall is the headquarters of the Tammany Society, the central organization of the Democratic Party in New York City. Originally founded in 1789, it was notorious for its political corruption in the nineteenth and early twentieth centuries.

The society is named after **Tammanend** (also known as Tammenund or Tammany), a seventeenth-century Delaware Indian chief, who, it seems, may have negotiated with William Penn over the transfer of land that eventually became the state of Pennsylvania.

tam o' shanter

Tam o' shanter, the brimless cap of Scottish origin that usually has a pom-pom on the top, is named after the hero of the poem *Tam o' Shanter* (published 1791), by the Scottish poet Robert Burns (1759–1796). Often shortened to tam or tammy, it is possibly the only item of male headgear that takes its name from a poem.

tantalize

Tantalize, to tease someone by offering something desirable to view and then withholding it, derives from Greek mythology. **Tantalus**, the mythical king of Phrygia, was punished for offences against the gods. In Hades he was condemned to stand in water that receded whenever he tried to drink it and under branches of fruit that moved away whenever he tried to grasp them.

tarte tatin

Tarte tatin is an upside-down apple tart consisting of apple slices in caramelized sugar, covered with pastry and baked. The tart is then flipped over before serving. Like many great culinary delights, this recipe was created as the result of a blunder. In the late nineteenth century, two sisters called **Stéphanie and Caroline Tatin** ran a hotel catering to city-dwellers and hunters in Lamotte-Beuvron, in the Loire region of France. In their haste to prepare dinner for a group of returning hunters one day, they accidentally omitted the pastry in an apple tart before putting it in the oven. When they realized their mistake and opened the oven, they found that the apples had caramelized. Improvising, the sisters topped the tart with a pastry crust and, when it was baked, they served it upside down, and *voilà!* a delicious new dessert was created.

Tartuffe

Tartuffe is the name of the principal character in the 1664 satirical play *Tartuffe* by the great French dramatist Molière (pseudonym of Jean-Baptiste Poquelin; 1622–1673). This character is a religious hypocrite, and his name is used to refer to any religious hypocrite, or to a person who pretends to excellence or to any positive quality that he or she does not in fact possess.

Tasmanian devil

The ferocious marsupial known as the **Tasmanian devil** ultimately owes its name to the Dutch navigator **Abel Janszoon Tasman** (1603–1659).

Appointed by the Dutch colonial administrator Anthony van Diemen (1593–1645), Tasman explored the south Pacific Ocean for trading purposes (1642–1644). Tasman sighted an island south of mainland Australia, originally calling it Van Diemen's Land after his patron. The island was known as this until 1856, when its name was changed to **Tasmania**. The island is home to a number of distinctive species, including the Tasmanian devil.

tawdry

The queen of Northumbria, **St Audrey** (Ethelrida; died 679), was patron saint of Ely. In olden times a fair was held annually on 17 October in her honour. The fair was noted for its good-quality jewellery and fine silk scarves, which in time came to be known as St Audrey's laces. Later, however, the fine scarves were replaced by cheap, gaudy imitations and so the word **tawdry** developed, a shortening and alteration of (Sain)t Audrey('s laces), a term that is now applied to anything that is cheap and showy.

Some versions of the story add that St Audrey died of a tumour in her throat, which she considered a punishment for wearing showy jewel necklaces as a child.

Tay–Sachs disease

 Tay–Sachs disease is a hereditary disease in which there is an accumulation of lipids in the brain and the nerves, resulting in progressive mental impairment and loss of sight. This disease typically affects people of Eastern European Jewish ancestry. It was named after the British physician **Warren Tay** (1843–1927) and the American neurologist **Bernard Sachs** (1858–1944). Tay first described this condition in 1881, while Sachs published a more comprehensive description in 1887, quite independently of Tay.

teddy bear

The **teddy bear**, the soft stuffed toy bear, takes its name from the US president **Theodore Roosevelt** (1858–1919), who was nicknamed Teddy. Well known as a hunter of bears, it is said that on one occasion Roosevelt spared the life of a brown bear cub while on a hunting expedition. The story was later depicted in a cartoon in the *Washington Post* by the cartoonist Clifford K Berryman, and stuffed toy bears became known as teddy bears.

> Teddy Roosevelt's motto was 'Speak softly and carry a big stick.'

The president's association with teddies remained. He presented several bears to the Bronx Zoo, and when, in 1911, he received an honorary degree at Cambridge University, a large teddy bear was lowered from the ceiling onto his head while he stood on the platform.

Teddy boy

Teddy boys, young men in the Britain of the 1950s, wore tightly fitting trousers and long jackets reminiscent of fashions during the reign of **King Edward VII** (1841–1910; reign 1901–1910), Teddy being the nickname for Edward.

Associated with early rock-and-roll music, the Teddy boys were known for their unruly or violent behaviour.

See also **King Edward potato**; **Prince Albert**.

tesla

Tesla, the metric unit of magnetic flux density, is named after the Croatian-born American electrician and inventor **Nikola Tesla** (1857–1943). Tesla is known for his work on the distribution of alternating electrical current and many inventions including a transformer, a dynamo and a generator.

Thatcherism

Thatcherism is the term used to describe the policies of the Conservative government of the UK under the prime ministership of **Margaret Thatcher**, later Baroness Thatcher of Kesteven, from 1979–1990.

Born in Grantham in 1925, Margaret Hilda Thatcher studied chemistry at Oxford University. After studying and practising law, she was elected MP for Finchley in 1959. She served as secretary of state for education and science (1970–1974) and became leader of the Conservative Party in 1975 and prime minister in 1979.

> **As a young research chemist, Margaret Thatcher helped develop a method of making ice cream cheaper to produce by doubling the amount of air in it.**

As prime minister, she led a firm government that adopted a monetarist economic policy, seeking generally to reduce public expenditure, and policies of privatizing nationalized services and industries.

theremin

The **theremin** is an electronic musical instrument played by moving the hands through electromagnetic fields created by two antennae to vary pitch and volume. It is named after **Lev Theremin** (1896–1993), the Russian scientist who invented it. The theremin is probably best known for producing the high–pitched wailing sound featured on the Beach Boys' 1966 recording 'Good Vibrations'.

thespian

The late-sixth-century-BC Greek poet **Thespis** is traditionally thought to have been the founder of Greek tragic drama. Up to that time performances had been given only by a chorus; he is said to have introduced an actor who represented a historical or legendary figure. Thespis is also said to have toured the country with his plays. From his name comes **thespian**, used as a word for an actor and as an adjective to refer to drama.

Thursday

The name of the fifth day of the week comes from the Old English *Thursdaeg*, the day of **Thor**, the Norse god of thunder. Thor is said to have made thunder with a chariot that was pulled by he-goats across the sky. Armed with a massive hammer, he was considered the strongest and bravest of the Norse gods.

Also named after Thor is **thorium**, a radioactive metallic element that resembles aluminium. It is used to strengthen alloys, in electronic equipment, and as a source of nuclear power. Thorium was discovered in 1828 by Jons Jakob Berzelius (1779–1848).

Tiffany glass

Tiffany glass, also called favrile, is a type of coloured iridescent glassware developed at the turn of the twentieth century by **Louis Comfort Tiffany** (1848–1933), the American glassmaker, designer and interior decorator. One of the USA's foremost exponents of Art Nouveau, L C Tiffany is best known for his leaded–glass lamps and decorative stained–glass panels. His father was Charles Lewis Tiffany (1812–1902), the founder of Tiffany & Co., the famous jewellery store in New York City, immortalized in Truman Capote's novella *Breakfast at Tiffany's* (1958) and in the 1961 film starring Audrey Hepburn.

titan

The **Titans** were twelve primeval gigantic gods and goddesses in Greek mythology, the children of Uranus (sky or heaven) and Gaea (earth). There were six Titans (Oceanus, Coeus, Crius, Hyperion, Japetus and Cronus) and six Titanesses (Thea, Rhea, Themis, Mnemosyne, Phoebe and Tethys).

The Greeks believed that the Titans once ruled over the earth in a golden age. The youngest of the twelve, Cronus, became their leader when he overthrew his father Uranus. Later, Cronus was himself overthrown by his son, Zeus.

The noun **titan** and the adjective **titanic** have come to describe a person or thing that is extremely large or strong. The *Titanic* was, of course, the luxury passenger ship that struck an iceberg near Newfoundland on its maiden voyage on the night of 14–15 April 1912, with the loss of 1513 lives.

titchy

Someone or something that is described as **titchy** is very small. The word derives from **Little Tich**, the stage name of the English actor Harry Relph (1867–1928). The word Tich may derive from the Tichborne case, a legal case of the 1870s, in which a certain podgy Arthur Orton, to whom Harry Relph is said to have borne a strong facial resemblance, was found to have impersonated a Roger Charles Tichborne (1829–1854), the heir to a vast fortune, who was presumed lost at sea. Eventually Orton was discredited and imprisoned (1874–1884).

Titian

 The adjective **Titian** is sometimes used to describe bright golden-auburn hair. The word derives from the Italian painter **Titian** (original name

Tiziano Vecellio; c. 1487–1576). A renowned artist of the Venetian school, Titian is noted for his mythological and religious works, frescoes and portraits. In many of his works, Titian depicted a model with hair of a reddish-brown hue that came to be named after him.

Tom Collins

 A **Tom Collins** – the tall iced drink consisting of gin, lime (or lemon) juice, sugar and soda water – is said to have been named after a bartender, but his exact identity is unclear. A possible candidate is the nineteenth-century bartender at Limmer's public house in London.

tommy

 Tommy, a representative British soldier, especially a private, is the shortened form of the name **Thomas Atkins**. Use of the name Thomas Atkins dates back to the early nineteenth century: it first appeared on sample army enlistment forms in 1815.

Tommy gun

 The name of the lightweight sub-machine-gun known as a **Tommy gun** comes from a different source than tommy (qv). It was invented by the American army general **John Taliaferro Thompson** (1860–1940), the American navy commander John N Blish and others towards the end of World War I. First manufactured in 1921, the Tommy gun was popularized by the Chicago gangsters of the Prohibition era (1920–1933).

> While in the US army, Thompson devised tests to assess the effectiveness of ammunition by firing at human corpses and live cattle.

Tom Thumb

A **Tom Thumb**, a person of restricted growth, derives from the tiny hero of nursery tales. **General Tom Thumb** was the stage name of the American person of restricted growth, Charles Sherwood Stratton

(1838–1883), who was exhibited by P T Barnum in his circuses. He was 3ft 4in (102 cm) tall.

tontine

 Tontine, a financial scheme that provides life annuities to a group of subscribers, is named after the Italian banker **Lorenzo Tonti** (1635–1690), who devised the scheme and introduced it to France in 1653. Under the scheme, a number of people subscribe to the tontine. When one of the subscribers dies, his share is divided among the remaining members, until the last surviving member takes the whole income. The scheme was used by governments to raise money, particularly in the seventeenth and eighteenth centuries.

Tony

 Tony, the medallion awarded annually for 'distinguished achievement' in the American theatre, is named after the American actress **Antoinette Perry** (1888–1946), known familiarly as Tony. Making her début in 1905, Perry became a successful actress and producer and was appointed to the chair of the American Theatre Council.

Tourette's syndrome

 Tourette's syndrome is a relatively rare psychoneurological disorder, which is characterized by multiple tics. In mild cases, the tics might include blinking and sniffing; in severe cases, they can include uncontrollable bursts of swearing and obscenities, and even barking. This syndrome takes

There have been suggestions that Mozart and Dr Johnson may have been affected by Tourette's syndrome.

its name from the French physician **Georges Gilles de la Tourette** (1857–1904), who described it in 1884.

Tradescantia

 The genus of flowering plants known as **Tradescantia**, which have striped leaves and are usually grown as house plants, includes the

popular varieties known as wandering Jew and spiderwort. The genus is
named after the English traveller and gardener **John Tradescant** (c.
1570–1638), who was gardener to Charles I. John Tradescant travelled
widely with his son, also John Tradescant (1608–1662), and introduced
into Britain many vegetables, fruits, trees and flowers, including figs,
runner beans, oranges, lupins and the lilac. He established his own
nursery in Lambeth in London.

trilby

Trilby, the soft felt hat with an indented crown, derives from the
dramatized version of *Trilby*, the novel (published in 1894) by the
English artist and writer George du Maurier (1834–1896). In the original
stage version of the novel (1895), the heroine, **Trilby O'Ferrall**, wore
such a hat.

Trotskyism

Trotsky wrote, 'Old age is the most unexpected of all things that happen to a man.'

Trotskyism is the theory of communism propounded by Russian
revolutionary **Leon Trotsky** (original name Lev Davidovich Bronstein;
1879–1940). Trotsky called for permanent worldwide revolution, in
contrast to Stalin's insistence on the establishing of socialism in one
country in isolation.

A leader with Lenin of the October Revolution (1917), Trotsky was
commissar of foreign affairs and war (1917–1924) and built up the Red
Army. On Lenin's death, he was ousted by Stalin, and was expelled from
the Communist Party in 1927. Banished from the Soviet Union, he
eventually settled in Mexico, where he was assassinated, probably by
Soviet agents.

See also **Leninism**; **Marxism**; **Stalinism**.

trudgen

The **trudgen** (or **trudgen stroke**) is a type of swimming stroke that
uses a double overarm action and a scissors kick. It is named after the

English swimmer **John Arthur Trudgen** (1852–1902), who introduced it to Britain in the 1870s after observing its use while travelling in South America.

Trudgen was inducted into the International Swimming Hall of Fame in 1974.

tsar

Tsar (or **czar**), used as a title of the rulers of Russia from 1547 to 1917 or to describe someone who exercises authority, derives ultimately from the Latin use of the name Caesar to mean emperor.

The title **kaiser**, adopted by the emperor of the Holy Roman Empire and also the emperors of Germany and Austria, similarly derives from Caesar.

Opinions are divided, however, as to which Roman statesman is the source of this usage. Some propose (**Gaius**) **Julius Caesar** (100–44 BC); others, more plausibly, suggest his adopted son, Augustus, known as **Gaius Julius Caesar Octavianus** (63 BC–AD 14), the first to be proclaimed Emperor of Rome (*see also* **August**).

Tuesday

The name of the third day of the week comes from the Old English *Tiwesdaeg*, the day of **Tiw** (or Tyr), the Anglo-Saxon god of war and the sky. Latin writers, beginning with Tacitus, identified Tiw with Mars, the Roman god of war – hence the Latin name for **Tuesday**, *dies Martis*, day of Mars.

Tupperware

Tupperware is a trademark for a range of airtight plastic containers for storing and transporting food. It was named after its American inventor and manufacturer, **Earl Silas Tupper** (1907–1983). In the 1940s Tupper developed a method for purifying black polyethylene slag into a flexible, non-porous, non-greasy, translucent substance. He also developed an airtight watertight lid, known as the **Tupper seal**. These two inventions led to the development of Tupperware. The new product

was marketed in an innovative way, being sold not in shops but by
agents hosting **Tupperware parties** in their own homes. In 1958 Earl
Tupper sold his company to Rexall.

Turing machine

The **Turing machine** is a mathematical model of a hypothetical
universal computing machine. It could read from a tape a series of ones
and zeroes describing the steps required to solve a particular problem and
perform these steps in sequence, resulting in the correct answer. This
concept was instrumental in the early development of computer theory.
The Turing machine was named after its inventor, **Alan Mathison
Turing** (1912–1954), an English mathematician and a pioneer in the
development of computer logic. During World War II, Turing used his
mathematical skills to work as a code-breaker for the British
Government, helping to decipher the code of German Enigma machines.

Turing is also known for the
Turing test. This is a test
for intelligence in a
computer by which a
computer is considered intelligent if a
human being is unable to distinguish it from another human being from
the replies to questions that are put to both.

> **Turing's life story is the
> subject of the play and film
> *Breaking the Code*.**

Tweedledum and Tweedledee

Tweedledum and Tweedledee – two individuals or groups that can
scarcely be distinguished – was a description first applied to the
musicians George Frederick Handel (1685–1759) and Giovanni Bononcini
(1670–1747), when a rivalry arose between them. The probable first
occurrence is in an epigram by John Byrom (1692–1763):

> *Some say compared to Bononcini*
> *That mynheer Handel's but a ninny;*
> *Others aver that he to Handel*
> *Is scarcely fit to hold a candle.*
> *Strange that such high dispute should be*
> *'Twixt Tweedledum and Tweedledee.*

Tweedledum and Tweedledee

The names were popularized by the fat twin characters in *Through the Looking Glass* (published in 1872) by the English writer Lewis Carroll (1832–1898).

U

Uncle Tom

Uncle Tom is a derogatory term for a Black person who wants to co-operate with and win the favour of Whites. The name was originally that of the Black slave in the abolitionist novel *Uncle Tom's Cabin* (published in 1852) by the American author Harriet Beecher Stowe (1811–1896). The novel aroused strong anti-slavery feelings; and Abraham Lincoln is alleged to have said that the novel helped to start the Civil War.

Uzi

The **Uzi** is a type of compact sub-machine gun that is easy to load and is accurate even when fired automatically. This weapon was named after **Uziel Gal** (1923–2002), the Israeli Army officer who designed it after the 1948 Arab–Israeli War. The Uzi was introduced in 1952 and is used throughout the world by police and special forces.

V

valentine

A **valentine** – a card sent anonymously to one's sweetheart on 14 February – derives from either of two third-century-AD Christian martyrs. One **St Valentine** was a Roman priest who was martyred for assisting persecuted believers. He is said to have been martyred on the Flaminian Way, the road from Rome to Ariminum (Rimini) in about 270. The other **St Valentine** was a bishop of Terni, martyred in Rome at about the same time.

The connection between the feast of St Valentine (14 February) and courtship is not associated with either saint, however. The traditions linked with St Valentine go back to the Roman feast of Lupercalia (15 February) and the popular belief that 14 February is the date that birds select their mates.

Van Allen belts

The **Van Allen belts**, two regions of electrically charged particles surrounding the earth in the outer atmosphere, are named after the American physicist **James Alfred Van Allen** (born 1914). It was during the International Geophysical Year of 1958 that, as the Carver Professor of Physics at Iowa University, Van Allen inferred the existence of two belts of radiation. By examining the readings recorded by the *Explorer* satellites, he explained the existence of two belts of radiation, one at 1000–5000 km (620–3100 miles) and the other at 15,000–25,000 km (9300–15,500 miles) above the equator.

Van de Graaff generator

A **Van de Graaff generator** is a machine for creating very high voltage electricity. It uses a belt that moves continuously at high speed to accumulate charge on the surface of a large hollow metal globe. Van de Graaff generators can create voltages as high as 15 million volts.

The device is named after the American physicist **Robert J Van de Graaff** (1901–1967). Van de Graaff constructed the first

> Van de Graaff was inspired to take up physics by hearing Marie Curie's lectures at the Sorbonne in Paris.

working model of the generator in 1929. Later, he adapted it for use as a particle accelerator, and it became a major research tool in atomic and nuclear physics.

vandyke

The Flemish painter **Sir Anthony Van Dyck** (or **Vandyke**; 1599–1641) was court painter to King Charles I. His portraits are noted for their depiction of subjects wearing a trim pointed beard (**vandyke beard**) and a wide collar with deeply indented points forming a border (**vandyke collar**). **Vandyke brown** is the dark brown colour that the artist liked to use.

Born one of twelve children to a rich silk merchant, Van Dyck was by the age of 19 an assistant to Rubens. In 1620 he first came to England and worked for King James I. After travels round Europe, he returned to England in 1632 to be court painter to Charles I, who conferred on him a knighthood.

venereal

The word **venereal** is most often used in the expression **venereal disease**, a disease spread by sexual intercourse, for example gonorrhoea or syphilis. The word venereal derives from Latin *venus* meaning sexual love, from **Venus**, the Italian goddess. Originally the goddess of gardens and fertility, Venus became identified with the Greek Aphrodite as goddess of love: *see also* **aphrodisiac**.

Venus occurs in many compounds, particularly in the names of flowers and plants, such as **Venus flytrap** (*Dionaea muscipula*), and even the small creature **Venus's flower basket**, a deep-sea sponge of the genus *Euplectella*.

Venn diagram

A diagram in which circles
and other shapes are drawn to
overlap at certain points to represent
mathematical and logical relationships is known as a **Venn diagram**.
The name honours the English mathematician and logician **John Venn**
(1834–1923), who devised the system.

> **Venn also built a
> successful machine for
> bowling cricket balls.**

Venus

See **venereal**.

vernier

A **vernier** is a small additional scale that is attached to a measuring
instrument to allow measurements to be taken that are finer than those
on the main scale. The scale is named after the French mathematician
Pierre Vernier (1580–1637), who described it in a treatise that he
wrote in 1631. The scale was in fact a development of the *nonius*,
invented by, and named after, the Portuguese mathematician Pedro
Nuñez (1492–1577).

A **vernier rocket** (or **vernier engine**) is an alternative term for a
rocket thruster, the small engine or gas nozzle that makes fine
adjustments to the speed, altitude or direction of a space vehicle or
missile.

Very light

The **Very light** is a coloured or white flare used as a signal. It is fired
from a special pistol, a **Very pistol**. The light and pistol are named after
the American naval officer **Edward W Very** (1847–1910), who
invented them in 1877.

vesta

The kind of short match known as a **vesta** is named after the Roman
goddess **Vesta**. Vesta was the goddess of the hearth, who was venerated
by every Roman household. The **Vestal virgins** were the virgin

priestesses who kept the sacred fire at the altar in the Temple of Vesta constantly aflame.

Victorian

The adjective **Victorian** is sometimes used to refer to the moral standards or behaviour popularly associated with the reign of **Queen Victoria** (1819–1901; reign, 1837–1901). Some examples of the use of the word are: 'She rebelled against her strait-laced Victorian upbringing'; 'traditional Victorian values'; 'the solid Victorian virtues of self-help and hard work'. The qualities regarded as typically Victorian are thus seen to emphasize 'good' morals, often to the point of prudery, and strict discipline. The divergence between moral standards and practices during Queen Victoria's reign is reflected in the word's further associations of narrow-mindedness and hypocrisy.

Queen Victoria instituted the **Victoria Cross** (VC) in 1856, the highest military decoration capable of being awarded to members of the armed forces of Britain and the Commonwealth for bravery in battle. The queen also gave her name to numerous places, including the **Victoria Falls**, **Victoria** state and **Lake Victoria**.

Queen Victoria is further honoured in the word **victoria** itself which is used variously to refer to a light, four-wheeled carriage with a folding hood, a kind of water-lily and a large sweet variety of plum (**victoria plum**).

See also **Georgian**.

volcano

 A **volcano**, an opening in the earth's crust out of which molten matter issues in an eruption, derives from **Vulcan** the Roman god of fire and metalworking. As Ernest Weekley comments, 'There was ... for the ancient world, only one volcano ... Etna ... in the bowels of which Vulcan and the Cyclopes forged the thunderbolts of Jupiter' (*Words and Names*).

To **vulcanize** – to treat natural rubber chemically, in order to increase its elasticity, hardness, etc – also derives from the god Vulcan.

volt

 Volt, the metric unit of (electric) potential, is named after the Italian physicist **Count Alessandro Volta** (1745–1827). Volta is particularly noted for his invention (1800) of what was the first real battery (the **voltaic cell** or **pile**), and the electrophorus (1775) a device that accumulates electric charge. Widely praised for his experiments, he received numerous awards and medals from many countries; Napoleon conferred a countship on him in 1801.

vulcanize

See **volcano**.

W

Wagnerian

The adjective **Wagnerian**, used to mean grandiose or intense in a dramatic manner, derives from the music of the German composer **Wilhelm Richard Wagner**

> **Wagner was Hitler's favourite composer.**

(1813–1883). Particularly noted for his origination of the music drama, Wagner's operatic cycle *Der Ring des Nibelungen* was first produced in 1876.

Walter Mitty

The expression **Walter Mitty** is used to refer to an ordinary person who indulges in extravagant day-dreaming and fantasies in an attempt to escape from reality. The description derives from the hero of the short story *The Secret Life of Walter Mitty* by the American humorist and cartoonist James Grover Thurber (1894–1961).

Wankel engine

The **Wankel engine**, a type of internal-combustion engine that has a triangular-shaped rotating piston with slightly curved convex sides, is named after its inventor, the German engineer, **Felix Wankel** (1902–1988).

> **Wankel gained his engineering skills in private study and through correspondence courses.**

Wankel became interested in rotary engines in 1924 and developed the engine before and during World War II. Cars powered by the Wankel engine were produced by the early 1960s but the engine's inherent design problems have never been fully overcome.

washingtonia

Washingtonia, another name for the sequoia (qv), is named after the American statesman and first president of the United States, **George Washington** (1732–1799; president 1789–1797).

Born into a rich Virginian family, Washington was a surveyor before serving in the French Indian War (1754–1763). He became a strong opponent of British government policy in the Continental Congresses and when the American War of Independence broke out, he was appointed commander-in-chief of the American forces. Having gained the final victory over Cornwallis at Yorktown in 1781, Washington became president of the Constitutional Convention in 1787.

The popular story that the young George Washington virtuously admitted to his father that he had felled the cherry tree is probably an invention. He is alleged to have said, 'Father, I cannot tell a lie. I did it.' The story seems to have originated in the biography of Washington by the American clergyman Mason Locke Weems, first published in the fifth edition of the book (1806).

Washington is the most frequently used place name in the USA. The capital of the USA, **Washington** state, **Lake Washington**, **Mount Washington** and other places all honour the first president. In Britain, **Washington** (new town) in Tyne and Wear was the home of George Washington's forebears before they moved to Sulgrave, Northamptonshire.

Wassermann test

The **Wassermann test** (or **reaction**), a test for detecting syphilis, is named after the German bacteriologist **August von Wassermann** (1866–1925), who invented it. An assistant to Robert Koch at his Institute for Infectious Diseases in Berlin, Wassermann later became director of the department of experimental therapy and serum research. In 1906, he developed a test for syphilis, which, using the 'complement-fixation' technique, indicates the presence or absence in the blood of a specific antibody. Wassermann is also noted for his development of a diagnostic test for tuberculosis.

watt

Watt, the metric unit of power, is named after the Scottish engineer and inventor **James Watt** (1736–1819). Watt is particularly famous for his development of the steam engine.

> **Watt and Boulton were the first people to coin the term 'horsepower'.**

Born at Greenock, Scotland, Watt worked at Glasgow University. While repairing a model of the Newcomen steam engine (1765), Watt realized that it would be more efficient if it were fitted with a separate condenser. Thus Watt's steam engine, developed in 1769, soon replaced the Newcomen model. From 1774–1775 he worked in partnership with the businessman and engineer Matthew Boulton (1728–1809) to manufacture steam engines.

Watt's other inventions included a centrifugal governor and a manuscript-copying machine.

Watteau back

A **Watteau back** (or **Watteau dress**) has broad back pleats that fall from the neckline to the hem without a girdle. A **Watteau hat** is one that has a shallow crown and a wide brim that is turned up at the back to hold decorative flowers. Both features are named after the French painter **Antoine Watteau** (1684–1721), in imitation of characteristics of his art.

Originally training as a painter of scenery for the theatre, Watteau later had the opportunity of studying Rubens' work, which proved to be highly influential in the development of his style. He became famous in England and France for his scenes of gallantry (*fêtes galantes*).

Wedgwood

Wedgwood is a trademark used to describe a kind of ceramic ware made originally by the English potter **Josiah Wedgwood** (1730–1795). Wedgwood pottery is known for its classical ornamentation in white relief particularly on a blue (**Wedgwood blue**) background.

Born at Burslem, Staffordshire, Wedgwood was handicapped as a child when his right leg had to be amputated, but he nevertheless experimented with clays and firing and worked in the family's small pottery shop. He eventually founded a firm in Staffordshire which produced a wide range of ceramic ware that was to become famous throughout the world. He collaborated with the sculptor John Flaxman (1755–1826) and built a factory (and a village for his workers) at Etruria in Staffordshire.

Wednesday

 The fourth day of the week comes from the Old English *Wodnesdaeg*, Woden's day. Known also as Odin, **Woden** was the god of wisdom, culture and war. He was also the god of the heroes who died in battle and were brought to Valhalla by his personal attendants, the Valkyries. His yearning for wisdom was so great that he surrendered his right eye so that he could drink from Mimir's fountain of knowledge.

Weil's disease

 Weil's disease is a severe, often fatal, infectious disease that is caused by spirochaete bacteria transmitted to humans by animals, particularly in rat urine. It is characterized by jaundice, fever, muscle pain and kidney failure. Weil's disease is named after **H Adolf Weil** (1848–1916), the German physician who published a description of it in 1886. Weil also isolated norleucine in 1913.

wellington boot

 The **wellington boot** was originally a leather boot which covered the front of the knee and was cut away at the back. Nowadays the wellington is a waterproof rubber boot, without fastenings, that reaches to the knee. The boot is, of course, named after the British soldier and statesman Arthur Wellesley, 1st **Duke of Wellington** (known as the Iron Duke; 1769–1852). Wellington is known for his victory against the French in the Peninsular

> **Wellington is said to have originated the phrases 'Publish and be damned' and 'If you believe that, you'll believe anything.'**

War (1814) and, with Blücher, for the final defeat of Napoleon at Waterloo (1815). He served as prime minister (1828–1830) but his opposition to parliamentary reform led to his resignation. He was commander-in-chief of the British army (1827–1828; 1842–1852).

Apart from the boots named in his honour – he is said to have worn the boots during his military and political careers – the capital of New Zealand is named after the Duke, as is the **wellingtonia**, the giant Californian coniferous tree, known also as the 'big tree'.

Wendy house

A **Wendy house** is a small model house that children can play in. It is named after the house built for **Wendy Darling**, the girl in the play *Peter Pan, or The Boy Who Would Not Grow Up* by the Scottish dramatist and novelist Sir James Matthew Barrie (1860–1937).

See also **Peter Pan**.

Wesleyan

 John Wesley (1703–1791) was the English preacher who founded Methodism, the word being used to describe his followers, especially in the branch of Methodism known as **Wesleyan Methodism**.

Born the fifteenth son of a rector in Epworth (now in North Lincolnshire), Wesley was ordained in 1735. After a conversion experience in 1738, he determined to devote the rest of his life to evangelistic work. From 1742 he travelled throughout Britain, and is said to have preached over 40,000 sermons and travelled 250,000 miles before he died.

His brother Charles Wesley (1707–1788) is known for his composition of several thousand hymns, including 'Jesus, lover of my soul'; 'Love divine, all loves excelling'; and 'And can it be that I should gain'.

Williams pear

 The **Williams pear** is a widely grown variety of dessert pear with yellow skin and sweet juicy flesh, which is eaten fresh or tinned.

Originally discovered in 1765 by an English schoolmaster named Stair, the Williams Pear was originally referred to as Stair's Pear. A Middlesex nurseryman named **Williams** later acquired the variety and distributed it more widely in Britain, the pear becoming known as the Williams Pear. Its full name is William's Bon Chrétien. In North America, the Williams pear is known as the Bartlett.

See also **Bartlett pear**.

Winchester rifle

Winchester rifle is the trademark of a type of repeating rifle with a tubular magazine below the barrel. The name derives from its American manufacturer **Oliver Fisher Winchester** (1810–1880). The Winchester was first made in 1866 at his factory in New Haven, Connecticut. The Winchester became well known as a cowboy rifle in the Wild West period of American history.

Winchester's original line of business was the manufacture of men's shirts; his special competence lay in the adaptation of the inventions of others. In fact, the Winchester rifle was a development of the Henry rifle, a repeating rifle invented by Benjamin Tyler Henry (1821–1898).

Windsor knot

A **Windsor knot** is a wide triangular knot in a tie, produced by making extra turns when tying it. It was so called in the mid twentieth century after the **Duke of Windsor**, who wore his tie in this fashion and was purported to have invented it, though he later denied this. Duke of Windsor was the title granted to Edward VIII (1894–1972), King of Great Britain and Ireland in 1936, after he had abdicated in order to marry the American divorcee Wallis Simpson (1896–1986) in 1937.

wisteria

Wisteria, the genus of twining climbing plants with purple flowers in hanging clusters, is named after the American anatomist **Caspar Wistar** (1761–1818).

The son of a well-known glass-maker, Wistar was a Philadelphian Quaker who was professor of anatomy at the University of Pennsylvania. He wrote America's first textbook on anatomy. It was, it seems, an error by Thomas Nuttal, the curator of the botanical garden in Harvard in 1818, that resulted in the misspelling of Wistar's surname in the designating of the plant as *wisteria* rather than *wistaria*.

X

Xanthippe

Socrates' wife, **Xanthippe**, was notorious for being bad-tempered and nagging; so an ill-tempered or irritable woman or wife is sometimes referred to in the same way. Shakespeare refers to her in *The Taming of the Shrew* (Act 1, Scene 2):

> *Be she as foul as was Florentius' love,*
> *As old as Sibyl, and as curst and shrewd*
> *As Socrates' Xanthippe, or a worse,*
> *She moves me not.*

> **Antisthenes described Xanthippe as 'one of the most difficult women of times past, present or future'.**

Xanthippe's nagging is discussed in different ways by various authors. Some see it as the cause of Socrates' delight in outdoor discussions, while others argue that Socrates was such an unconventional husband that living with him must have taken up all his wife's patience.

Y

Yale lock

Yale, the trademark for a type of cylinder lock, is named after the American locksmith **Linus Yale** (1821–1868) who invented it. Yale invented numerous other kinds of locks between the 1840s and the 1860s, but it is for the lock which has a revolving barrel that he is particularly remembered. Yale set up a company, the Yale Lock Manufacturing Company, to produce locks at Stamford, Connecticut in 1868.

Yankee

Yankee – someone from the USA in British English in a derogatory sense, and someone from the northern USA (particularly New England) in American English – probably comes from a Dutch name. Yankee may well originally have been **Jan Kass**, a derogatory nickname for a Hollander, meaning 'John Cheese'.

After the Dutch settled in New York, they applied the term to the neighbouring English settlers in north Connecticut. By the time of the American War of Independence, the term was used by the British to describe any colonist. (The song 'Yankee Doodle' originally mocked the poorly clad colonial forces, but the colonial troops changed the song's lyrics and used it as a marching song.)

In the American Civil War, the South used Yankee as a derisive term for a Union soldier, and by the outbreak of World War I, all American soldiers were known as Yankees (or Yanks) by the rest of the world. From that time on, Yankee and Yank have been used to describe an American.

yarborough

 A **yarborough** is a hand in bridge or whist in which none of the cards is higher than nine. The word comes from Charles Anderson Worsley, 2nd **Earl of Yarborough** (died 1897). An enthusiastic card-game player, Lord Yarborough is said to have bet 1000 to 1 against the dealing of such a hand. In fact, the true mathematical odds have been calculated as 1827 to 1 against.

Zamboni

Zamboni is a trademark for a machine that is used to clean, resurface and smooth the ice that has been churned up by the actions of skaters in ice rinks and sports arenas. Watching the machine make its circuit of the ice is a regular feature of the intervals in ice hockey games. Indeed, during a dull game, watching the Zamboni smooth the ice may be the most memorable feature of the evening's entertainment.

The machine is named after **Frank J Zamboni** (1901–1988), a former mechanic and ice salesman who bought a skating rink in Paramount, California in 1940. Zamboni was frustrated at the amount of time it took to scrape, spray, clean and refreeze the surface of his ice rink. Drawing on his earlier experience in the motor and dairy industries, he designed his first machine for resurfacing ice in 1949.

zapata moustache

A **zapata moustache** is a large moustache that droops down on either side of the mouth – a style that became very popular among hippies in the late 1960s and early 1970s. It is so called because this style of moustache was favoured by **Emiliano Zapata** (1879–1919), the Mexican revolutionary and champion of agrarian reform. Zapata fought in guerrilla warfare both during and after the Mexican Revolution (1911–17). Zapata and Pancho Villa led revolts against General V Huerta and Venustiano Carranza.

Zeppelin

A **Zeppelin** is an airship, and in particular a large rigid cylindrical airship built in Germany in the early twentieth century. It takes its name from the German general and aeronautical pioneer **Count Ferdinand von Zeppelin** (1838–1917). Zeppelin served in the American Civil War and the Franco-Prussian War. On retiring from the army in 1891, he developed his earlier interest in airships and by 1900 had built the first rigid airship. Between 1910 and 1914 Zeppelins were widely used in Germany to carry passengers. During World War I, the Germans used these airships to bomb Britain, the first raid being over Great Yarmouth in 1915. From that time onwards, the story of airships was generally one of disaster – notably the British R101 disaster (1930) and the German Hindenburg (1937) – but in more recent times, airships are again being used, using non-flammable gas.

zinnia

Zinnia, a genus of annual or perennial plants of the family Compositae native to tropical America, is named after the German botanist and anatomist **Johann Gottfried Zinn** (1727–1759). A professor of medicine, Zinn published in 1753 what is reported to have been the first book to describe the anatomy of the eye.

Zoroastrianism

The pre-Islamic Persian religion of **Zoroastrianism** was founded in the sixth century BC by the prophet **Zoroaster** (in Avestan, Zarathustra). Zoroaster (c. 660–583 BC) received at the age of about 30 a vision of Ahura Mazda who inspired him to teach a new religion proclaiming that he was the god of light.

Zoroastrianism recognizes two principles, good and evil, which are personified by Ahura Mazda (god of light, wisdom) and Ahriman (or Angra Mainyu; prince of darkness; the destroyer). Life is considered as a struggle between these two spirits, which will be won by the eventual triumph of good over evil.

The scriptures of Zoroastrianism are the Avesta. Written in Old Iranian, its five books contain prayers, hymns and songs (Gathas), and teaching on ritual, worship and law. Zoroastrianism survives in India amongst the Parsees and in Iran.

Zwinglian

Zwinglian is used to describe the teachings of the Swiss theologian **Ulrich Zwingli** (1484–1531), especially his understanding of the holy communion. In contrast to Luther, Zwingli had a purely symbolic interpretation of the eucharist.

Ordained as priest in 1506, Zwingli became a preacher in Zurich in 1519, strongly criticizing Roman Catholic teachings. His New Testament lectures marked the beginning of the Swiss Reformation. His conflict with Luther was seen at the Colloquy of Marburg (1529), which failed to bring about a union between the two men and a united Protestantism became impossible. The Reformation divided Switzerland and in the civil war that followed, Zwingli, serving as a chaplain, was killed.

Thematic Index

 Art and Architecture

baroque

churrigueresque

Claude Lorraine
 glass

Fabergé eggs

Georgian

Jacobean

Lalique glass

Palladian

Pre-Raphaelite

Spode

Tiffany glass

Titian

vandyke

Wedgwood

 Botany

Aaron's beard

aubrietia

banksia

begonia

bignonia

bougainvillaea

buddleia

camellia

cattleya

cinchona

dahlia

deutzia

Dioscorea

Douglas fir

eschscholtzia

euphorbia

filbert

flora

forsythia

freesia

fuchsia

gardenia

gentian

gerbera

godetia

hyacinth

iris

Jacob's ladder

Judas tree (*see
 under* **Judas**)

Leylandii

lobelia

macadamia

magnolia

marigold

Michaelmas daisy
 (*see under*
 Michaelmas)

montbretia

peony (*see under*
 paean)

poinciana

poinsettia

protea (*see under*
 protean)

quassia

Rafflesia

Rudbeckia

St John's wort

sequoia

Solomon's seal (*see
 under* **Solomon**)

Tradescantia

Venus flytrap (*see
 under* **venereal**)

victoria (*see under*
 Victorian)

washingtonia

wellingtonia (*see
 under* **wellington
 boot**)

wisteria

zinnia

Clothes

 Entertainment

 Food and Drink

carpaccio

Cattley guava (*see under* **cattleya**)

cereal

chaptalize

charlotte

chateaubriand

clementine

Cox's orange pippin

Delia

demijohn

Earl Grey

eggs Benedict

epicure

frangipane

gallize

garibaldi

graham flour

Granny Smith

greengage

grog

Hay diet

jeroboam

John Barleycorn

jorum

King Edward potato

kir

lamington

loganberry

Lucullan

lush

McIntosh red

madeleine

Melba toast

methuselah

Mickey Finn

mornay

nebuchadnezzar

negus

pavlova

peach Melba (*see under* **Melba toast**)

praline

rehoboam

Sally Lunn

sandwich

savarin

shaddock

soubise

stroganoff

tarte tatin

Tom Collins

Tupperware

victoria plum (*see under* **Victorian**)

Williams pear

Language and Literature

alexandrine

atlas

Baedeker

Baskerville

Bic

Biro

blurb

Bodoni

Booker Prize

bowdlerize

Bradshaw

Braille

clerihew

comstockery

Crockford

Cyrillic

Debrett

Dewey Decimal System

Esperanto

euphuism

Garamond

Georgian

Gilbertian

Gill

Gongorism

grangerize

Grimm's law

King James Bible

malapropism

pamphlet

pasquinade

Petrarchan sonnet

Lamaze
lazaret
listeria
Lou Gehrig's disease
Marfan syndrome
Ménière's disease
mithridatism
Montezuma's revenge
morphine
Münchhausen's syndrome
Oedipus complex
Paget's disease

Pap test
Parkinson's disease
pasteurism (*see under* **pasteurize**)
Perthes' disease
Phaedra complex
Prader-Willi syndrome
Raynaud's disease
Rett's syndrome
Reye's syndrome
Rolfing
Rorschach test
Sabin vaccine
St Anthony's fire

St Vitus' dance
Salk vaccine
salmonella
Schick test
stent
Stokes–Adams syndrome
Sydenham's chorea
syphilis
Tay-Sachs disease
Tourette's syndrome
venereal
Wassermann test
Weil's disease

Money

balboa
bolivar
colón
cordoba

Dow–Jones average
Gresham's law
Keynesianism
Midas touch

mint
Peter's pence
sucre
tontine

Music

Amati
calypso
Dolby
Gregorian chant
Hammond organ
Köchel number

Moog synthesizer
paean
Pan-pipes (*see under* **panic**)
sarrusophone
saxophone

sousaphone
spinet
Stradivarius
theremin
Wagnerian

Thematic Index

 Politics

Blairism	Hansard	Monroe doctrine
cabal	jim crow	Reaganomics
Downing Street	Leninism	Spartacist
Fabian	McCarthyism	Stalinism
Gallup poll	Machiavellian	Tammany Hall
Gaullism	Maoism	Thatcherism
gerrymander	Marxism	Trotskyism

 Religion

Abraham's bosom	Franciscan	Old Nick
Amish	Gideon	Rastafarian
Bahai	Huguenot	simony
Buddhism	Jansenism	Swedenborgian
Calvinism	Jesuit	Wesleyan
Christian	Lutheran	Zoroastrianism
Druse	Manichaeanism	Zwinglian
Erastianism	Moonie	
euhemerism	Mormon	

 Science (see also **Botany**; **Medicine**)

Achilles tendon (see under **Achilles' heel**)	arachnid	Beaufort scale
	Archimedes' principle	becquerel
Ada	Avogadro's constant	Bernoulli effect
Adam's apple		Bessemer process
Aldis lamp	Baily's beads	bohrium
algorithm	Bakelite	Boolean algebra
ammonia	Barr body	boson
ampere	Bartholin's glands	Boyle's law
ångström	Batesian mimicry	Broca's area
Appleton layer	baud	Brownian

Sport

 ## Time

 ## Transport

War